Erich Neumann

The Theory

Jungian, Developmental,
Relational & Metapsychological

Lidar Shany, Ph.D.

CHIRON PUBLICATIONS • ASHEVILLE, NORTH CAROLINA

www.ChironPublications.com

Interior and cover design by Danijela Mijailovic
Printed primarily in the United States of America.

From *Depth Psychology and a New Ethic* by Erich Neumann. Copyright © 1969 by Hodder & Stoughton Ltd. and the C. G. Jung Foundation for Analytical Psychology. Reprinted by arrangement with The Permissions Company, LLC on behalf of Shambhala Publications Inc., Boulder, Colorado, shambhala.com.

From *The Child* by Erich Neumann. Copyright © 1973 by the C. G. Jung Foundation for Analytical Psychology, Inc. Reprinted by arrangement with The Permissions Company, LLC on behalf of Shambhala Publications Inc., Boulder, Colorado, shambhala.com.

Used with permission of Princeton University Press, from *Analytical Psychology in Exile: The Correspondence of C. G. Jung and Erich Neumann* by C. G. Jung and Erich Neumann, 2015, permission conveyed through Copyright Clearance Center, Inc.

ISBN 978-1-68503-547-1 paperback
ISBN 978-1-68503-548-8 hardcover
ISBN 978-1-68503-549-5 electronic
ISBN 978-1-68503-550-1 limited edition paperback
ISBN 978-1-68503-551-8 limited edition hardcover

Library of Congress Cataloging-in-Publication Data

Names: Shany, Lidar, author.
Title: Erich Neumann : the theory : Jungian, developmental, relational & metapsychological / Lidar Shany.
Description: Asheville, North Carolina : Chiron Publications, [2025] |
Includes bibliographical references. | Summary: "This book traces the developmental, relational, metapsychological theory that emerges from Erich Neumann's writings, while considering the influences of his life circumstances and relationship with Jung. It revisions, reevaluates, and consolidates the emerging theory, in the hope of reviving interest in Neumann's writings, and indicate his importance as a Jungian theoretician. This manuscript shows that Neumann's theory effectively supplements Jung's original writings, and is relevant to both theory and therapeutic practice. It presents Neumann's formulations of psychological development from birth to the advanced stages of individuation process as a synthesis of his various writings. The books The Origins and History of Consciousness, The Great Mother, Jacob and Esau, Depth Psychology and a New Ethic, and The Child are at the center of focus, supported and amplified by some of Neumann's metapsychological Eranos articles"-- Provided by publisher.
Identifiers: LCCN 2025003622 (print) | LCCN 2025003623 (ebook) | ISBN 9781685035471 (paperback) | ISBN 9781685035488 (hardcover) | ISBN 9781685035501 (limited edition paperback) | ISBN 9781685035518 (limited edition hardcover) | ISBN 9781685035495 (ebook)
Subjects: LCSH: Neumann, Erich. | Jungian psychology. | Spiritualism. | Individuation (Psychology) | Psychology--Philosophy. | Psychologists--Germany--Biography. | LCGFT: Biographies. https://id.loc.gov/authorities/genreForms/gf2014026049
Classification: LCC BF109.N48 S53 2025 (print) | LCC BF109.N48 (ebook) | DDC 150.19/54--dc23/eng/20250404
LC record available at https://lccn.loc.gov/2025003622
LC ebook record available at https://lccn.loc.gov/2025003623

To Nir Dana Eyar Alon and Shlomi

Acknowledgments

This book is the satisfying, rewarding, and meaningful outcome of a long journey, beginning in 2013, and evolving traveling between three continents. I could never have overcome the countless obstacles had I not been fortunate to receive the help of dear people to whom I am thankful.

I would like to thank my professors, Dr. Susan Rowland, who was the first scholar inspiration who believed in me as a writer, and Dr. Lionel Corbett, for his kind and loving mentorship. I also thank Dr. Martin Liebscher, who has been a wellspring of treasures for my research. His dedicated research on the details of the historical time and events surrounding Neumann's career paved the way and enabled mine and others' work.

Dear Erel Shalit was a bridge between my worlds at Pacifica and in Israel. His work signified the possibility of understanding and communicating the depth and breadth of Neumann's ideas, and his untimely death is a great loss. His role in inspiring my research is significant, and I cherish his memory in gratitude.

Far away from Pacifica, in Tel Aviv, is Debora Kutzinski, whom I thank for the hours spent in her study. Sitting beside her, the window to the left and the library in front, I held the English version and she the German one. These hours with Debora were the womb of this book, and I hold those hours, and her, warmly in my heart.

To Brian Feldman, Batia Brosh, David Weiler, and Rivka Lahav, all experienced Jungian analysts, each an expert of his or her domain, my heartfelt thanks and appreciation for your help and willingness to discuss aspects of my dissertation research and to add your perspective and insights. You all were of great help. Thank you.

To Moshe Alon, thank you for believing in me and imagining beyond what I could imagine. Thank you for so generously granting me with the insights and experience of your lifelong work. Thank you for your willingness to read pages and pages in English, for being genuinely interested and involved, exited with me, and for being such good and close friend.

To the most important five people in my life, my family, my husband and four children. You are my home, my ground, my earth. Alon, Eyar, Dana, and Nir, you are the essence of my life, the air I breathe, and much more important than any idea in my head. Shlomi, you are my lifelong partner, and gave me the greatest gift a woman in the second half of life could wish for, you understood that I need to find and fulfill my Self, and you give me wings. I fly. I love you.

Table of Contents

Part II

Early Life Developmental Relational Theory

Personal Disclosure

I was led to Neumann's work by destiny. It is only retrospectively that the dots can be connected and traced back to where the path was first taken. Twenty-seven years ago, I became a mother; my firstborn was followed by three siblings, and motherhood became the essence of my life, defining my identity, my passion, my success, and my creativity. Alongside the actual activity of rearing children, mothering my children was a process of psychological growth, enabling me to be at one with my archetypal role as Mother. Being a researcher by nature, and a doubtful first-time mother with my firstborn, I found refuge in Donald Winnicott's writings, which described the "good-enough mother" that I felt I could be and was, with my baby. Reading his descriptions, I was amazed at how he could understand and so accurately describe my inner lived experience as a mother. Most importantly, I felt affirmation for doing well by knowing that what I experienced, including the doubts, was exactly as it "should" be. Nonetheless, 30 years ago, I did not know what an archetype was; I just felt the heart and rhythm of the *participation mystique* experience with my first offspring.

During the next fifteen years, I gave birth to three more babies and was actively mothering my four children, breast feeding each one of them for about a year and immersing myself in the maternal uroboric unity with each newborn I delivered. Gradually I recognized that my archetypal capacity for motherhood—my tendency, ability, and passion to mother (as a verb), bears meaning that goes beyond being a mother to my children. Reading Jung and becoming familiar with the term *archetype*, I eventually realized that I am called by the Motherhood that is rooted in a psychic place much deeper and much older than my physical womb.

Upon enrolling at Pacifica Graduate Institute in the summer of 2013, I was aiming for a PhD and naturally for a dissertation that would make use of my experience as a mother. Through my studies, my interest and intuitive understanding of the relational theories of Winnicott and others was revived, and I chose motherhood as the focus of my research and was planning to use Neumann's *Great Mother* as a primary source. Destiny took charge, and Neumann's theory became the subject of inquiry and research. Looking backwards, I can now connect the dots.

Upon first encountering Neumann's essays, I found them bulky, disorganized, repetitive, and complicated. In the eco-psychology course I took at Pacifica in the spring of 2016, I was assigned to read an article written by Neumann (1953/1994), "The Meaning of the Earth Archetype for Modern Times." I found myself struggling with the reading, trying to get to the depth of his ideas, nevertheless, something in this article was fascinating enough to call my attention and my previous analyst, Debora Kutzinski (2016) came to my mind as possible help. Debora (who is now almost 100 years old) was Neumann's analysand, student, mentee, and friend during the last seventeen years of his life in Tel Aviv. Although she is a Jungian analyst, trained personally by Neumann, she is probably the first "Neumannian," if such may be defined, loyal to Neumann's writings and teachings as an amplification of Jung's theory. Debora came to my mind as a possible source for help in grasping what was difficult for me. I reached out to her, initially intending to read together with her just the assigned article. She gladly agreed, and we started learning.

This was the "crack" through which the light of Neumann's writings entered my mind. We started with this article, and I was so fascinated that I then asked Debora if she would be willing to read another article from the same book with me and then another; before I knew it, I was hooked on Neumann. The developmental aspect of his writing deeply resonated with my own insights and understandings, and his description of the uroboric *participation mystique* of mother and baby was accurate in terms of my lived experience. From this point on, destiny took charge of my dissertation, and the process of research came naturally and in the right order.

I discussed the possibility of using Neumann as a primary resource for my dissertation with my professor, Dr. Susan Rowland, who approved the idea as "potentially good." Then a few weeks later I met with Erel Shalit in his home in Tel Aviv. I told him about my growing fascination with Neumann's work and my natural attraction to the developmental aspects of his writing, leading to my thought of using him as a primary source of my research, which back then was still centered on archetypal motherhood. Shalit was excited with me, encouraging me to situate Neumann as a central source for the research and prove his worth as a primary source. Three months later, in November 2016, Shalit gave a presentation in Pacifica, following the publication of what was (at the time) the unpublished work of Neumann (1934/2015), *Jacob and Esau*, which Shalit edited and provided with a comprehensive and inspiring introduction.

The presentation Shalit gave at Pacifica was a major changing point in my relationship with Neumann's writings. I was deeply impressed by the depth and complexity of the idea of confronting the shadow, of becoming one with the Self, as Neumann articulated it in his analysis of *Jacob and Esau*, and by the relevance of his tremendous insight today, even though the text was written more than eighty years ago. Hence, what was initially expected to be a few meetings with Debora, studying one article, became almost three years of weekly meetings, reading and studying many pages written by Neumann. Debora was generous enough to allow these sessions to be recorded, which enabled me to revisit them again and again, refining my understanding and articulating my remaining questions. It is not an exaggeration to say that this path that I took spontaneously, which progressed naturally according to my growing interest, changed the course of my life. Initially, I made a decision to welcome Neumann into what I then thought would be my dissertation; however, once this plan was accepted and approved, I became even more devoted to my learning sessions with Debora, and eventually my immersion in the material evolved into what I believe to be an alchemical process. The *prima materia* was my initial interest in research on Neumann's writings, which entered its dark phase, manifested as confusion, doubts, and contemplation of how central Neumann would be in my dissertation. Subsequently, the process reached a critical point when I realized that the subject of interest in which I was immersed (and thus my real and actual research) was Neumann's writings, which by then had already overridden the theme of motherhood. I got to hold the boon, in the form of the certainty I previously longed for: I knew exactly what I was researching, and the title was inherent in the research. Without any shadow of a doubt, at the center of my interest, research, and professional life were Neumann's writings, in particular, the developmental and relational aspects.

I intend to revive interest in Neumann's writings by presenting them as a cohesive theory, rephrased in an accessible language and presented as a developmental relational theory that is of great value to both theoretical understanding and therapeutic practice. Fortunately a new fresh breeze is blowing upon the old papers on which Neumann hand wrote his ideas, and I am hoping to be among those who blows this fresh air.

Chapter 1
Introduction

General Intro

Erich Neumann is a theoretician whose promising future was never fully realized. Due to his early death, his writings were left orphaned; his poetic writing style is challenging, even for readers of the original High German let alone for readers of other languages. Significantly, they lacked the author's attention, cultivation, and clarification and therefore arguably they were at times misunderstood and thus misjudged. His intellect was cultivated during his youth and student years in Germany, by intellectualism, existentialism, and Zionism. These influences, together with his phenomenological and developmental perspective, served as the fertile grounds for his Jungian and archetypal formulations in such a way that they elevate C. G. Jung's theory toward metapsychology, extend it to early life development, and elaborate the advanced stages of individuation.

The importance of Neumann's work, which singles him out as a particularly important theoretician in Jungian psychology, is anchored in Jung's undoubtedly solid support. This statement is supported among others, by the recent publication of Neumann's correspondence with Jung (Jung & Neumann, 2015), in which are found indications of Jung's appreciation of Neumann's work. In the foreword Jung wrote to Neumann's *The Origins and History of Consciousness* (1949/2014), he explicitly described Neumann's work as an elaboration of his own and as a map to the territory he had newly discovered. In a letter Jung wrote to Jolande Jacobi with regard to Neumann's first Eranos lecture, in which he explored mysticism from the developmental perspective, Jung insisted that Neumann presented the theme in a structural account. This is a hallmark of Neumann's writing; the tendency may be rooted in the systematic structural nature of the High German language Neumann spoke and used in writing. In any case, Neumann presented his ideas in a developmental and structural manner while using diagrams to add visual dimension and clarity. At the Eranos conference of 1952, Neumann's lecture was titled "The Psyche and the Transformation of the Reality Plans: A Metapsychological Essay" (1952/1989), indicating the metapsychological nature of the essay. From this point on to the last article he presented in the summer of 1960, "The Psyche as the Place of Creation" (1960/1989), all his Eranos lectures had a metapsychological component. In those articles Neumann described, in a structural account, aspects of psychology that are beyond empiricism and typical of metapsychology, thus elaborating on Jung and elevating his formulations.

Neumann's first depth psychological manuscript was his 1934 essay *Jacob and Esau* (1934/2015), in which he interpreted the biblical story as an account of Jacob's individuation, in which confronting the shadow is the central theme. During the Second World War and the Holocaust, he wrote *Depth Psychology and a New Ethic* (1949/1990). (Although dated 1949, the book was in circulation in Zurich as early as the end of 1948 and was completed by the end of 1945, when he first sent it to Jung). In this manuscript, he deepened the theme of the confrontation with the shadow while he articulated it in a developmental formulation, as the advanced stage of individuation. Therefore, in both these respects, the metapsychological and the advanced individuation, Neumann's writings supplement, elaborate, and amplify Jung's theory.

In addition, the importance and relevancy of Neumann's formulations stem from the lack of early life developmental theory within Jungian psychology, and from the complementarity between Neumann and subsequent leading theoreticians of the field of depth psychology and other fields. Neumann's theory about early life psychological development appears mainly in his last written and posthumously published book, *The Child: Structure and Dynamics of the Nascent Personality* (1963/1990), which is the most neglected of Neumann's writings, probably due to its posthumous publication in an intentionally unedited form, which left the material in its raw state, repetitive, and with loose ends. His theory about early life also appears in some of his Eranos lectures, and this part of Neumann's work is an underexplored supplement to Jung's theory, an archetypally based description of the normal and healthy early life psychological development from the nascent personality to its maturity. Presented in this way, Neumann's theory manifests a developmental relational theory that is relevant and useful to depth psychology's theory and practice.

To be truthful to Neumann's theory, and to avoid under-estimation of his contribution, it is important to emphasize two aspects. The first is his formulation of the ego-Self axis, a centra concept in his theory, which is described in length in this book and especially in the second part. The ego-Self axis also became central in the conceptualization and dialogue of the analytical world in general, and in Neumann's theory, the seeds are recognizable in the early writings. The second aspect is the call for redemption of the Feminine. This subject came to the forefront of his correspondence with Jung as they both matured. The Feminine is a thread running throughout Neumann's writings, creating the fertile grounds and foundations for his thinking and ideas: Self, unconscious, Great

Mother, anima, shadow, creativity and art, mysticism, and earth. In all these themes—Neumann wrote and theorized—the Feminine is called fourth, accordingly, he coined the term *matriarchal consciousness* to describe the aspect of the Feminine in need of redemption, which is a very interesting concept and deserves further attention, beyond its short appearance at the end of this book.

Source Material

This book is an outcome of a dissertation research, conducted over about 6 years and 3 continents, countless hours of readings, face to face learning and conversing, email correspondences, interviews, and inner contemplations. Many people took part of this process in varies ways, some in concrete knowledge, and others in general support. One source strikes as significant - the weekly reading and learning sessions, more then 50 hours of recorded conversations about Neumann's writings and theory I conducted in-person and in-private with Debora Kutzinski (February 27, 2016–November 14, 2018), at her home in Tel-Aviv. I will forever cherish these hours, as they hold enormous significance in cultivating my Neumannian thinking.

This manuscript traces the developmental theory that emerges throughout Neumann's writings and is amplified by metapsychology. In addition, as is apparent from the writing, there is also a development within Neumann's thinking about human psychological development, which culminates as it reaches the relational aspect in his last written book about the child. This manuscript follows the chronological order of the publications while claiming that the order sprang from the events of Neumann's personal life and was in accordance with them.

The following sections describe written books and articles, interviews in private communications, and weekly sessions, referenced as sources as they are used throughout the manuscript. All of which, contributed to the research conducted for the seed of this book, the dissertation. However, the main source material are the books that are at the center of Parts I and II: Neumann's first written (and only recently published) book, *Jacob and Esau: On the Collective Symbolism of the Brother Motif* (referred to subsequently as, *Jacob and Esau* ,1934/2015); his evocative book *Depth Psychology and a New Ethic* (*New Ethic*, 1949/1990); his magnum opuses, *The Origins and History of consciousness* (*Origins*, 1949/2014) and *The Great Mother* (1955/1991); and his posthumous book, *The Child: Structure and Dynamics of the Nascent Personality* (*The Child*, 1963/1990).

Part I

At the center of this part are Neumann's initial writings: manuscripts and letters to Jung. In the manuscripts, he described the advanced stages of the psychological process of individuation. First is *Jacob and Esau* (1934/2015), in which he analyzed the biblical story of the hostile twin brothers as the process through which Jacob individuates, confronts his shadow, and achieves psychic unity. Neumann never published the manuscript, and it was only in 2015 that Erel Shalit edited it, and brought it to publication. Nevertheless, unfortunately, like Neumann, Shalit died prematurely at the beginning of 2018 and therefore did not have enough time to promote the book as he would have.

The next book comprising the direction of advanced stages of individuation in Neumann's initial writings is *New Ethic* (1949/1990). This book was widely misunderstood by readers, who to this day commonly believe Neumann advocated for a new ethic. Nothing can be further from the truth, and this can never be stressed enough, although Neumann tried in every possible way and failed to clarify what he really was advocating. Neumann described the new ethic as an advanced ethical stage, a step beyond the old ethic; therefore, it was not intended to replace the old ethic but rather to include it within the new, as an advanced stage of individuation.

In addition, like any theoretician, Neumann was influenced by personal and collective historical circumstances. In order to take those into consideration, and describe them for the reader to evaluate, the research conducted for this manuscript included published sources of Neumann's biographical background. Those including indications that Neumann was an appreciated and original theoretician who elaborated and supplemented Jung's theory and was accepted, approved of, and supported by Jung.

The central source is the book *Analytical Psychology in Exile: The Correspondence of C. G. Jung and Erich Neumann* (Jung & Neumann, 2015). This book, a part of the Philemon Foundation Series, edited and introduced by Martin Liebscher (2015a), includes the correspondence of the two men throughout the twenty-seven years of their acquaintance. Following the publication of this book, Liebscher (2016a) wrote an article titled "The Challenges of Editorship: A Reflection on Editing the Jung-Neumann Correspondence," in which he explained the necessity for the meticulous introduction and annotations:

> The dialogue between the correspondence partners remains often vague and enigmatic to an outside reader who does not know the events, persons or topics discussed. This is where the introduction and annotations come into play for without a proper historical contextualization a published correspondence will only be of value to a few initiated scholars. In the case of the letter exchange between Jung and Neumann this consideration is especially pertinent as most of the material concerning Neumann was not known before the publication of the correspondence, and the archive material was not even accessible. (p. 159)

These words make it clear that, without the thorough research Liebscher conducted in the process of editing the correspondence, the publication would not be as effective as it is in reviving Neumann's work. Throughout the article, Liebscher demonstrated how crucial his historical perspective and contextualization were to the editorial work and how deeply he researched in order to reveal the broader context in which the letters were written. Liebscher's account of his research process is important as it validates the book as a reliable source and strengthens the validity of the material coming from the correspondence, which manifests a first-hand and written testimony of the nature of the two men's relationship in its depths, as opposed to what was apparent on the surface.

A good example is the controversy around Neumann's (1949/1990) book, *New Ethic*. On the surface, when spoken in front of the Zurich Analytical Institute, Jung failed to firmly support Neumann, which caused Neumann deep hurt and disappointment. However, in a personal letter to Neumann, Jung wrote, "Your formulations are brilliant and of incisive sharpness; they are therefore challenging and aggressive, an assault troop in an open field" (Jung & Neumann, 2015, p. 237). Reading these words by Jung suggests a new interpretation of this incident, and it is apparent that his weak support of the book was due to his stance at the Institute and the inner politics involved rather than his opinion of the text itself, which in this case, as evidenced by the letter, was rather high. In aiming to indicate the relevancy and importance of Neumann's writings, it is crucial to know, by means of Jung's personal correspondence with Neumann, how Jung greeted him, the words he used to relate to Neumann's theoretical thinking and formulating, and the extent to which he was willing to promote Neumann and his work.

In addition to the correspondence between the two men, Liebscher's (2015a) introduction is an essential source in its own right. In his acknowledgments, Liebscher described his thorough research, including visits to "obscure archives and libraries around the world" (p. vii). In addition to the two men's correspondence, his research bears the fruits of various testimonies, adding information to and affirming from different angles details about events and aspects of their relationship that are apparent in the letters. This correspondence book is the first published work to claim and affirm Neumann's relevancy and importance to Jungian psychology, and it is likely the engine behind the revival of Neumann's work and theory.

Following the publication of the correspondence and as a continuation of it, a conference held in Israel in 2015 may be seen as another step in reviving Neumann's legacy. The presentations at the conference were later edited and published in the book *Turbulent Times, Creative Minds: Erich Neumann and C. G. Jung in Relationship (1933–1960)* (Shalit & Stein, 2016). The anthology includes articles, letters, and memorials all related in one way or another to Neumann's relationship with Jung and thus of paramount importance as a source for researching Neumann's theory and its relevancy. In addition to an article by Liebscher (2016b), whose research and expertise was already mentioned, this book includes an article by the current scientific secretary of the Eranos Foundation, Riccardo Bernardini (2016). His article "Neumann at Eranos," provides a detailed background account of the Eranos conferences.

As described in Shalit and Stein's (2016) introduction, Eranos was central to Neumann's career and writing. Much of his thinking and theory was developed in the years he was occupied with preparing the lectures for the summer gatherings in Eranos. At Eranos, he met and became close friends with Frobe-Kapteyn, and at her request, he took on the project of writing an introduction to the Eranos picture archive, which later became *The Great Mother* (Neumann, 1955/1991). As an expert on Eranos, Bernardini (2016) based his article on the interesting testimonies in letters as well as conversations held at Eranos regarding Neumann's work and presence there. Two relevant facts mentioned by Bernardini are that "Neumann was the first analytical psychologist after Jung to speak at Eranos" (p. 202) and that he "usually lectured at Eranos as the keynote speaker . . . [and] had a large circle of followers, as he always touched on points of central interest" (p. 203). For these facts and others, Bernardini provided support from several different sources. His article is therefore a highly reliable source on how Neumann and his work were perceived and accepted by the attendees at Eranos, which included some of the most brilliant minds of Europe at the time. As Bernardini wrote, "Eranos brought together some of the most influential scholars of the twentieth century" (p. 200).

Last, but not in any way least among the selections in *Turbulent Times, Creative Minds* (Shalit & Stein, 2016) is the very short commentary by Kutzinski (2016). The commentary includes some personal potent remarks about Neumann's personality as a writer. As an example, she stated that "Neumann writes that artists are the Great Mother's most beloved children. Erich was surely one of them. If you read his essay. . . you cannot avoid hearing the artist, no less than the psychologist" (p. 310). Neumann's artistic tendency is relevant to his theory about matriarchal consciousness, discussed toward the end of chapter eight. Kutzinski concluded her commentary with these heartfelt words:

> His last Eranos lectures were his greatest work, especially "The Psyche as the Place of Creation.". . . In this essay he went very far. He went further than Jung. Sometimes I ask myself a painful question: Could it be that he paid for this with his life, dying so early, at age fifty-five? Did he come too close to the Great Mother? And she as the goddess of death, loved him not wisely, but loved him too well, and took him away into her arms. (p. 311)

These words are moving and enlightening, as they shed light on the intensity of Neumann's relation to the Great Mother, a relation that clearly went beyond a mere writing subject, adding a sense of destiny and calling to the theory Neumann wrote.

In addition to the two books reviewed thus far, articles by Adler (1960/1979) and Lori (2005) serve as reliable biographical sources on Neumann. His lifelong friend Adler (1960/1979) wrote his memorial article, "On Erich Neumann: 1905–1960," shortly after Neumann's death. Adler testified to having known Neumann for more than forty years, beginning with their student days in Germany. As mentioned in the introduction, Adler illuminated several of Neumann's personality traits that relate to the way he is seen as a theoretician today. Like Kutzinski (2016), Adler (1960/1979) pointed to Neumann's artistic nature, tracing it back to their early days together, during which Neumann wrote a novel and many "beautiful" poems (p. xii). He added that Neumann had a profound artistic nature, and his written works on the art and the artistic process are themselves testimony to his participation in this process (p. xiii). Important themes of Neumann's theory are his call to redeem matriarchal consciousness, the origins of art, and the relatedness element so lacking in modern societies. Another aspect of Neumann's personality to which Adler testified was his determination to achieve his goals, which came into play in his career at several junctures presented hereafter in the biographical material. The most significant example of Neumann's commitment and determination playing a central role in his work was the publication of his book *New Ethic* (1949/1990) despite the controversy and critiques it engendered in Zurich.

Additional biographical information on Neumann is presented in Lori's (2005) article "Jung at Heart," which was published in an Israeli newspaper upon the centennial celebration of Neumann's birth. Based on interviews with Neumann's son, Micha, and daughter, Rali, Lori's article, although subjective, provides some important facts about Neumann's life and background. The interviews with his children clarify that Neumann's passionate Zionism was a part of his childhood background and not an ideology adopted in adulthood. The relevance of this fact is that it indicates that Neumann's feelings were drawn to the Promised Land even when it was clear that this might potentially harm his career.

Part II

Central to this Part are two of Neumann's books: his magnum opus, *The Origin and History of Consciousness* (*Origins;* 1949/2014), and his posthumous book, *The Child: Structure and Dynamics of the Nascent Personality* (*The Child*; 1963/1990). His magnum opus, *The Great Mother* (1955/1991), is also used to illuminate aspects of the Mother archetype in early life. His edited volume, *The Fear of the Feminine and Other Essays on Feminine Psychology* (1950—1959/1994), and his interpretation of the mythology, *Amor and Psyche: The Psychic Development of the Feminine* (1952/1971), are used in describing the psychological development of the female. In addition, and in the purpose of presenting Neumann's writings about early life as a cohesive theory, Part II synthesizes these books with other of Neumann's publications, in particular with four of his published articles. These articles were written before or concurrently with the posthumous book, and unlike that book, they were published by Neumann himself; therefore, they manifest a clear and undoubtable statement of his theory.

It is important to note that Neumann's Eranos lectures are known to be tremendously deep in terms of the theoretical psychological insights they offer and revolutionary in terms of transforming psychology to the realm of mysticism and metapsychology. This significant element of Neumann's writings is worthy of further research and publication. Therefore, it is important to emphasize that the presentation of these Eranos articles is within the parameters of this book only and should not be seen as a reductive simplification of Neumann's revolutionary ideas but rather as a tribute to them. The articles used in Part II are "The Psyche and the Transformation of the Reality Planes: A Metapsychological Essay" ("Reality Planes";

1952/1989); "The Experience of the Unitary Reality" ("Unitary Reality"; 1955/1989); "Narcissism, Normal Self-formation and the Primary Relation to the Mother" ("Narcissism and Self-formation,"1955/1966), first published in German in 1955; and "The Significance of the Genetic Aspect for Analytical Psychology" (1959). Complete titles of these publications are included on first mention; thereafter they appear in abbreviated form.

In addition, and to indicate the relevancy and value of Neumann's formulation to the developmental relational analytical dialogue, Part II refers to Michael Fordham's works and to those of two of his followers, "The Emergence of Fordham's Model of Development" (Astor, 1990) and "De-integration and Re-integration in the First Two Weeks of Life" (Sidoli, 1983), as well as to personal communications with Brian Feldman, who was under Fordham's direct supervision. Fordham's theory is presented in a limited and succinct form, to the extent needed to indicate the essential points of agreements with Neumann, as they support one of the purposes of Part II, the articulation of a unified Jungian theory of early life development. Lastly, in order to indicate the complementarity between the Jungian archetypal perspective with the Freudian individual perspective, Part II refers to and draws from Donald W. Winnicott's works and in particular his "Primary Maternal Preoccupation" (1956/1984) and "Communication Between Infant and Mother, and Mother and Infant, Compared and Contrasted" (1968/1987).

The research conducted for this part also included personal communications with two senior Jungian child analysts in Israel. One is Batia Brosh, currently the chair of the Jungian Institute in Jerusalem. Talking with her was relevant to the understanding of how Neumann's theory found its way into institutional work in Israel. The second is Rivka Lahav, an expert on Sandplay Jungian work with children and for many years worked at the unique boarding school

Hamaon of Neve Tze'elim, which practiced Neumann's theory and will be mentioned at the end of chapter eight.

Other highly important resources for Part II are the recorded conversations with Debora Kutzinski (February 2016–November 2018), Neumann's analysand, student, and close friend and colleague, now almost 100 years old and the oldest Jungian analyst in Israel. My private communication with her spanned almost three years during which time, through reading and discussing his books and articles, my own foundational and substantial learning of Neumann's theory took place. Although Part II refers to some of her illuminations of Neumann's theory, the significance of these conversations extends far beyond any specific remarks, as they were the *temenos* from which the research leading to this book, was born. These conversations opened my deeper understanding of the theory, a precise comprehension of the original ideas, and an immersion into Neumann's way of thinking.

Erich Neumann: Biographical Background

Neumann (1905–1960) died early and suddenly. He was still young and at the peak of his career. After years of ordeals, he had finally arrived at the rewarding experience of being the keynote speaker and central figure in the Eranos conferences. He became a popular lecturer, and the future was promising. Sadly however, future did not arrive, and the promise was never fulfilled. Neumann died, leaving loose ends of articles and books, some of which were published unedited. Some writing waited over 80 years to be edited and published, and some are still waiting in varies places, not well archived.

Neumann's work was a product of intellectual and highly educated German-speaking Central European culture, that main-tained an existential world view. Born in Berlin on January 23, 1905, he was the youngest of three children, and was the only one among his family who was drawn to Judaism. His close life-long friend Gerhard Adler (1960/1979) reported that, even as a young student in Berlin, Neumann belonged to "a circle of friends who were deeply interested in all the problems of life, . . . among them, philosophy, psychology, the Jewish question and, last but not least, poetry and art" (p. xi). Indeed, Neumann's creativity was prominent early on. He wrote some poetry and a novel in the years 1921 to 1929. From 1923 to 1926, Neumann's studies at the University of Berlin included psychology, philosophy, pedagogy, history of art, literature, and Semitic studies. Then, in 1926, he enrolled in a program of philosophical and psychological studies at the University of Erlangen in Nuremberg, where he received a PhD in philosophy, with a dissertation, published in Berlin with the subtitle *Ein Vergessener Romantiker* (The Neglected Romantic) (p. xii, footnote). On a personal note, it has been synchronistically interesting to find this detail of Neumann's biography while conducting research that presents the neglected aspects of his writings.

In 1928, when Neumann was 23 years old, he married his wife, Julie, with whom he shared the passionate Zionism (19th-century Eastern European Jews' aspiration, ideology, and movement to return and settle in the homeland while reviving the language and Israel as a people). Having read both Freud and Jung during his later studies, Neumann's interest in psychology grew, and in order to take it up as an occupation, he started his medical training at the Friedrich Wilhelm University in Berlin and completed it in 1933. His friend Adler (1960/1979) testified that it was very typical of Neumann to be thorough, dedicated, and committed to his goals, and his personality traits in later years played a significant part in influencing his career. Although Neumann completed his medical studies and submitted his papers, he could not take the internship due to anti-Semitism and race laws in Germany at that time, and thus he was not granted a medical degree. His son Micha reported that he eventually received his degree before his death.

During this time, in addition to his formal studies, Neumann was very interested in Judaism and Hasidism (18th century's Eastern European Judaism's spiritual teachings and commentaries on the Bible and the Cabbala), and Zionism became the leading ideology in his life. In 1933, upon completion of his medical studies, after being prevented from entering the profession, he and his wife Julie took their one-year-old son Micha and started the journey to the Promised Land, immigrating from Europe to the Middle East. Earlier the same year, due to his interest in Jung's psychology, Neumann attended Jung's seminar on dream analysis in Berlin and was fascinated by Jung. On their way to Palestine, Neumann and his family stopped in Zurich. This visit was a crucial changing point in Neumann's career. Adler (1960/1979) wrote that it was in Jung's approach Neumann found a conjunction of his humanistic interests with a potentially practical profession in which he could make a living.

Presumably, Neumann asked for a meeting with Jung, but only Jung's letter responding to the request has been found. In this letter, the first in their correspondence, Jung wrote to Neumann, "I have reserved an hour's appointment for you on Tuesday, 3rd October at 4pm" (as cited in Liebscher, 2015a, p. xi). This first meeting was then followed by seven months of training and analysis by Jung himself and then by Toni Wolff. In May 1934, Neumann left Zurich and did not revisit until after World War II in 1947 (Liebscher, 2015a).

Another significance of this first meeting between Neumann and Jung is apparent in Kron & Wieler's (2013) claim that Neumann brought his essay on Kafka's "The Trial" (Neumann, 1933/1979) with him to this first meeting (although this claim is not supported by evidence). Although Neumann wrote the essay as a philosopher, his innate psychological perspective is apparent in it, and thus, symbolically it is his first oblation to Jung. Whether he brought the copy to their first meeting, or it was sent a few days later is not as important as the idea that Jung read it upon acquaintance with Neumann and it became Jung's first impression of Neumann. This first impression was likely positive as evidenced by their subsequent meetings in Zurich, as by the time Neumann was about to leave for Tel Aviv, Jung had already appreciated him deeply enough to grant him a copy of *Seven Sermons to the Dead*. Liebscher (2015a) noted that Jung had printed it limitedly and privately, and "gave copies to a selected few of his students and friends. . . Neumann's copy holds an inscription by Jung: 'zur freundlichen Erinnerung. C. G. Jung' (in fond memory. C. G. Jung)" (p. 22, note 179). Therefore, before Neumann left Zurich in 1934, Jung had already perceived him as a strong-minded theoretician.

On leaving Zurich, Neumann joined his wife and son (who had arrived a few months prior to him) in Tel Aviv, where he established a practice in his small house. There were not enough patients, and Neumann needed the income to support his family; therefore, he also gave lectures in his living room. As a dedicated Zionist to the Promised Land, Neumann faced a disappointment. He was an intellectual European scholar and expected to find some old acquaintances in Tel Aviv, but what he found were blue collar workers and simple people. Therefore, during the eleven intervening years between his visits to Europe, Neumann was safe from the Nazis in Tel Aviv, but as he confessed in a letter to Jung, he nevertheless was intellectually isolated. This isolation had both positive and negative influences on Neumann's work and theory. On the negative pole, as he wrote to Jung, he was prevented from discussing his ideas, and consequently he also lacked the feedback any theoretician craves. In addition, and critically, this isolation suggests that he had no editors and translators with whom to work and therefore wrote his depth psychological ideas in the German language while living in a Hebrew-speaking community and likely editing his own work.

On the other hand, the positive pole of his isolation was described by Neumann as the precondition and accelerator of his independent thinking and thus his development as a theoretician. These ideas are supported by his friend Adler's (1960/1979) assertion that during the isolation years Neumann read and studied intensely, activity that bore fruit in later years through his writings. It is also interesting to note that Neumann's ideological passion, which both created a strong bond with the Promised Land as a physical place and caused his severe isolation, presumably influenced his understanding and writing regarding the Great Mother and Earth archetypes, possibly in the direction of what currently is seen as an eco-psychological perspective.

Neumann's correspondence with Jung began in 1934 when he first arrived in Tel Aviv, and was encouraged by Jung to write what turned out to be his first book (yet next to last to be published), *Jacob and Esau* (1934/2015). The correspondence between the two men ceased during World War II and was resumed in October 1945 with a letter sent from Neumann to Jung, followed by a manuscript. During the years of the war, between 1940 and 1945, while isolated in Tel Aviv, Neumann wrote a manuscript entitled *The Origins and History of Jewish Consciousness*, later published under the title *The Roots of Jewish Consciousness* (Neumann, 1940–1945/2019). Neumann himself did not publish this book. One possible reason was that he felt he was not knowledgeable enough regarding the Jewish aspect of the work, referring to Hasidism. Another factor in Neumann's decision was his acknowledgement in a letter to Jung that his psychological state upon completion of this manuscript had changed, and he had returned to what he believed to be "pure psychology" (Jung & Neumann, 2015, p. 160). For Neumann, as for any other writer, the act of writing about the themes that are at the center of his personal life and at the core of his psychological contemplations became therapeutic writing and thus, once completed, the manuscript was likely not perceived as publishable.

Neumann wrote to Jung that his return to pure psychology manifested in writing *New Ethic*. He referred to this manuscript as "my small book" (Jung & Neumann, 2015, p. 254) and sent it to Jung along with the letter resuming their correspondence in 1945. Presumably, although Neumann was unaware of it when he presented *New Ethic* as signifying his return to pure psychology, writing the book could also have had a therapeutic element, making it personal. The book was heartfelt and written without much consideration about the effect it would have on his readers at the time. On the one hand, the emotional significance of the book magnified the importance of its publication for Neumann; on the other hand, it resulted in critical rejection and evoked anger in Zurich. In a letter Neumann wrote to Jung in 1949, a few years after the completion of the writing, and amidst the storm around the publication of the book, he confessed that it was written from his heart rather than head, and it was made of "personal core material" (p. 254). Nevertheless, together with these two manuscripts, another product of the years Neumann was isolated, and was what later came to be known as Neumann's magnum opus, *Origins and History of Consciousness* (1949/2014).

After leaving Europe in 1934, Neumann revisited in 1936 and returned after the war in 1947. It was Adler who was the bridge connecting Neumann with Switzerland, Europe, and the Jungian circle after the war was over. In a letter sent to Jung dated December 12, 1945, Adler praised Neumann's work and asked whether Jung could invite him to present at Eranos. Supporting his request, Adler was convinced that not only would Neumann's presentation be of great value and interest to the audience, but it would also suggest some original ideas, and it would be helpful for Neumann to both get the feedback he so desperately needed and to find a publisher. This attempt by Adler, a manifestation of his lifelong friendship with

Neumann, bore fruit a year later in the summer of 1947 due to Jung's significant efforts to convince the immigration authorities to allow Neumann entry into Europe.

Adler (1960/1979) wrote that he invited Neumann and his family to stay at his summer house in Ascona, where he introduced Neumann to Olga Frobe-Kapteyn, the founder as well as the heart and soul of the Eranos conferences who became Neumann's close friend. This first meeting between Neumann and Frobe-Kapteyn in 1947 was pivotal for Neumann's career. Frobe-Kapteyn was so impressed by him that she consulted Jung and invited Neumann to give a lecture the following year. In the summer of 1948, Neumann gave his first Eranos lecture, "Mystical Man" (1948/1989), and then lectured annually at Eranos until 1960, when he presented "The Psyche as the Place of Creation" (1960/1989) a few months before he died.

The conferences in Eranos were annual 10-day gatherings of the best minds from different fields of the humanities disciplines in Europe. The current scientific secretary of the Eranos Foundation, Riccardo Bernardini (2016), described Neumann as a leading figure as well as the most dominant participant after Jung retired. The nature of the gatherings in Eranos—the physical place on the lake, the participants, the conversations, and the themes—fostered the background through which Neumann expressed his existential, phenomenological, and metapsychological thinking into the writing known as his Eranos articles.

Not only did Neumann become a central Eranos figure, Eranos also became central in Neumann's life. With much warmth, he wrote to Frobe-Kapteyn, "Eranos has become a friendly island for me to which I belong" (as cited in Liebscher, 2015a, p. 1). An indication of the nature of their relationship is found in the personal dedication Neumann wrote to Frobe-Kapteyn in the first edition of *The Great*

Mother in which he mentioned their common deep connection with the Great Mother (as cited in Bernardini, 2016, p. 210).

Adler (1960/1979) wrote that in October 1960, after he had given his last lecture at Eranos in August, doctors in London told Neumann he was dying and that the courageous manner in which he and his wife accepted the news indicated their spirit. Neumann died at his home in Tel Aviv on November 5, 1960. On November 24, 1960, his wife Julie Neumann wrote a long letter to Frobe-Kapteyn in which she described Neumann's growing weakness in the last few weeks of his life, thinking that it was a kidney illness and luckily suffering no pain. Julie wrote that only after his death was kidney cancer diagnosed and concluded with "he passed away softly on Saturday, November 5, at 11:20 p.m. I was with him" (cited in Bernardini, 2016, p. 237). Might it be, as Neumann described the mature and psychologically developed personality, that his peaceful death manifested the final and ultimate surrender of the ego to the Self?

Erich Neumann and C. G. Jung - Evolving Relationship

The relevance and importance of Neumann's theory to the field of depth psychology lays on a fourfold argument. The first relates to Jung and Neumann's personal relationship to indicate how Jung perceived Neumann—a perception of his worth as a thinker and a theoretician that increased over the years and was reflected in their relationship. The second presents Neumann's writings as an elaboration of Jung's theory, and the third is that his writings are a necessary supplement and addition to Jung's theory which lacks attention to early life development. Finally, the fourth draws on supporting as well as opposing literature to Neumann's formulations and writings, which are additional indications of the relevance and importance of Neumann's theory to the contemporary field of depth psychology.

However, the foreword that Jung wrote for Neumann's (1949/2014) *Origins* serves as a concise testimony of Jung's appreciation of Neumann's work as a theoretician. This written testimony, providing clear support by Jung, rises above all arguments and overrules objections and attempts to minimize the importance of Neumann's work. When Jung wrote this foreword in 1949, he had already been acquainted with Neumann for fifteen years and had read his previous poignant and evocative book, *New Ethic*. Also, he had read Neumann's first Eranos lecture, "Mystical Man" (1948/1989), which he praised using the words "my admiration" and "excellent representation" (Jung & Neumann, 2015, p. 232). In addition, Jung defended Neumann and his work in response to the objections this lecture aroused among Jung's followers. The foreword to *Origins* (1949/2014) was written quite a while after Neumann first requested it, arguably indicating that Jung gave some thought to the superlatives he eventually used. This suggestion is supported by Liebscher's (Jung & Neumann, 2015) research which indicated the existence of different versions of the foreword, changed by Jung to reach its final version (p. 252, note 471). Critically, this can be seen as the way Jung chose to clearly and firmly support and promote Neumann's work publicly. In this foreword, Jung not only stated that in Neumann's work he saw a continuation of his own work, but he also wholeheartedly thanked Neumann for the way he presented and supplemented his work. Jung leaves no doubt in the reader's mind that he fully supported the book, the content, and the writer; furthermore, he deeply appreciated the achievement. The reader is strongly encouraged to read the foreword in full.

If you read the foreword, it becomes clear that Jung left no doubt as to the depth of his appreciation of Neumann's work, not simply as a theory in its own right, but rather as a Jungian theory, elaborating supplementing, and deepening his initial ideas. In addition, Jung made an important clarification in this foreword when he expressed his appreciation of Neumann's presentation of the material in a structural form. He thus distinguished it from creating a system, as Neumann was accused, first by Jacobi and later by Michael Fordham and Wolfgang Giegerich. Furthermore, this foreword, seen as Jung's statement of support, situated Neumann as a relevant, important, and original thinker and theoretician of depth psychology and critically as his "second generation" and thus, as Liebscher (2015a) wrote, "effectively declaring Neumann to be his successor" (p. xliv).

In addition to Jung's foreword, the perception of Neumann as Jung's successor is based on letters, private communications, and overall impressions reported by people in the close circle surrounding Jung. However, the question of Neumann as Jung's successor is only one aspect of the relationship between him and Jung and is prone to interpretation, while the essence of the relationship—its nature rather than the facts of definition and public recognition—is of the utmost importance. Even if Neumann was not clearly appointed as successor, he was effectively treated as one. Jung saw him as a most promising theoretician, and therefore his writings are significantly relevant to depth psychology. Furthermore, in the maturity of the two men's relationship, at the time when Neumann had already lectured at Eranos, the correspondence between the two indicates that Jung perceived Neumann as a colleague and importantly as an equal. In the spirit of this consideration, the term *relationship* here refers to the way the two men perceived one another throughout the years.

As mentioned previously, Neumann first saw Jung in person at the dream seminar held at the end of June 1933 in Berlin. Three months later, at the beginning of October, their first meeting occurred in Zurich where Neumann stayed for another seven months of training and analysis. Also as mentioned before, Adler (1960/1979) noted the professional significance of Neumann's acquaintance with Jung and his theory. Nevertheless, for Neumann, there was a much deeper and personal aspect to this meeting, as evidenced in his letter to Jung, dated July 1934, shortly after arriving in Tel Aviv. As Neumann (Jung & Neumann, 2015) confessed,

> Before I came to you, I was rather sad that I was not able to go to a Jewish authority because I wanted to go to a "teacher" and I found it typified precisely the decline of Judaism that it had no such authoritative personality in its ranks. With you, I became aware of what was prototypical in my situation. According to Jewish tradition, there are Zaddikim of the nations, and that is why the Jews have to go to the Zaddikim of the nations— perhaps that is why they do not have any of their own left. This Jewish situation, the beginning of an exchange, of an understanding *sub specie dei (under the sight of God)*—this is what makes this "letter exchange" so important to me. (p. 35)

It is understood therefore that meeting Jung was a profound experience for Neumann, who found in Jung the illuminated teacher he sought for and a spiritual authority. These facts indicate that Neumann developed a high appreciation, presumably admiration, and probably also an idealizing transference toward Jung. A sign of the positive transference Neumann developed and held toward Jung throughout the years is found in a much later letter, written in 1950, when Neumann had already gained many years of perspective on the relationship. Neumann wrote to Jung, "I know that you have been my inner leader in it all" (Jung & Neumann, 2015, p. 267), which is a very deep and meaningful statement. Neumann could feel so strongly toward Jung only if there was enough in Jung's attitude to evoke this feeling.

A hint as to the elder Jung's first perception of young Neumann may be found in the fact that, at the end of January 1934, after Neumann had had only four months of psychological studies, Jung referred a patient to Neumann. It is known that in the early days of analytical psychology training was not a long procedure; nevertheless, four months is a short time, and though not unusual, suggests Jung's positive impression of Neumann. As suggested earlier, this positive impression was cultivated, at least partly, by the essay Neumann wrote prior to his first meeting with Jung about Kafka's "The Trial" (Neumann, 1933/1979), which Jung read upon meeting Neumann. In this essay, Neumann expressed his innate psychological archetypal perspective, and if Jung did read it, he recognized the transpersonal archetypal aspect embedded in the essay and thus in its author's perspective, and his appreciation of Neumann as a thinker and as a theoretician must have been positively influenced.

However, despite Neumann's fascination with Jung and Jung's appreciation of Neumann, there was between them from the very beginning as early as 1934 the question of Jung's anti-Semitism. Jung, of course, did not perceive himself as racist or anti-Semitic, but his writings at the time had a distinct aura of racism (a subject discussed at length in chapter 2). Given the overall situation in Europe and the race laws in Germany, Neumann could not ignore Jung's attitude toward the murderous persecution of Jews. Even though Jung's statements were ambiguous and ambivalent, his remarks about Jewish psychology at such a critical time were seen as negative. Neumann thus wrote long letters to Jung, pleading with him to state clear support for the Jewish people. His first letter was written while still in Zurich, and Liebscher (2015a) thoughtfully interpreted it: "That Neumann felt it necessary to use the written form instead of talking to Jung personally shows the shocking impact that Jung's race-psychological remarks must have had on him" (p. xxiv). Significantly, this letter was written while Neumann was still seeing Jung for analysis, when he could have raised the subject in person (see Shalit & Stein, 2016, p. xiii). Because their relationship was initiated with the one-sided admiration of Neumann for Jung, the way Jung expressed his views in writing might have been an early disappointment (or "de-idealization") for Neumann and an awakening realization of Jung as a flesh and blood person with a shadow.

Jung's suspected racism and anti-Semitic attitude were an open subject discussed between Jung and Neumann in Zurich, and the discussion continued after Neumann left Europe and arrived in Tel Aviv. James Kirsch, another Jungian analyst who arrived in Tel Aviv prior to Neumann and left for England shortly after, wrote an article that also criticized Jung's racism. When Jung wrote to Kirsch with regard to this critical article, he mentioned his work with Neumann and asked Kirsch to greet Neumann and remind him that Jung was waiting to hear from him. This request can be seen as an underlying marker in the relationship as it stood at that time; not only was Neumann eager to meet with Jung but also Jung sought communication with Neumann (although it is possible that Jung also used his acquaintance with Neumann against Kirsch). At this point, however, Neumann was not necessarily aware of Jung's growing interest in him. Liebscher (2015a) pointed out a meaningful confirmation Neumann received from Jung in response to an open letter that Neumann had published as a reply to the article by Kirsch: "I thank you particularly for your intelligent and proper elucidation of Kirsch's article" (p. 51). With Jung's personal expression of such sentiments, Neumann received direct confirmation of his mentor and teacher's high opinion of him.

The next significant event in Jung and Neumann's relationship regards the essay Neumann wrote about Jacob and Esau which stands central to the next chapter and was initiated by a review Neumann wrote about Hugo Rosenthal's (1934) article (also discussed in the next chapter). After writing the review, Neumann discussed the subject in his letters to Jung, who was so impressed by Neumann's elaboration on the subject that he recommended Neumann publish the review as an article (Liebscher, 2015a). Jung also urged Neumann to present the work to the Zurich Psychological Club in 1933–1934, a suggestion that Neumann rejected, feeling not yet ready to present it (Liebscher, 2016b). However, this act by Jung of encouragement and trust surely indicates that very early in their relationship, Jung recognized how promising a theoretician Neumann was.

Jung and Neumann's relationship did not significantly change over the next ten years, during which they continued to correspond for the first five years and then ceased corresponding during the five years of World War II. Some aspects of their written correspondence may indicate underlying elements in their relationship, as Liebscher (2016b) pointed out when he referred to Jung being thirty years older than Neumann, indicating "a huge imbalance in professional and scholarly experience" (p. 26). Liebscher also drew attention to the difference in the length of the letters between Jung and Neumann as a sign of the initial imbalance, being in Jung's favor at the height of his career while Neumann was still making his first steps (p. 26). In addition, a close reading of the opening and closing greetings in the two men's correspondence (Jung & Neumann, 2015) sheds some light on the way they perceived and presented their relationship to one another. Evidently, right after their first meeting, Jung marked his respect to Neumann by greeting "Dear colleague" and a few months into their correspondence he greeted Neumann, "My dear colleague" and further "My dear Neumann," clearly marking a personal element into their relationship, a fact strengthened by his conclusion of the letter with "Your always devoted" and alternatively "Your always loyal" or "Faithful." The first time a difference is apparent is at the end of 1938, when Europe was burning with hatred, and Jung found it necessary to end a letter with "I remain your always loyal" (p. 147), possibly indicating his attempt to show sympathy to Neumann as a Jew and his wish to assure him that their relationship was unchanged. However, Neumann was in a different position, as most of the time he was in need of Jung, and expressed this position by beginning one of the letters in 1939 with the words "Thank you very much for your letter that has shown me once again you continue to have patience with me and once again have engaged with my problems that I know could not be your own" (p. 120). In a further letter, at the end of 1939, Neumann explained that he was suffering from isolation: "It is almost unhealthy to almost only have oneself to check things out with, so that this letter is a bit too much like an 'analytic session'" (p. 153). After this letter, there was one more letter from Jung to Neumann, in 1939, and then a silence between them for five years.

As noted earlier, during the years of the war between 1940 and 1945, the two men did not communicate, but Neumann—who was both intellectually isolated in Tel Aviv and longing for what was once "his" Germanic culture, which had now severely betrayed him— wrote creatively and prolifically. The next communication between Neumann and Jung was, as mentioned, initiated by Neumann after the war in 1945, when he sent Jung the manuscript of *New Ethic* (Neumann, 1949/1990) followed by a letter. The circumstances surrounding this book, including strong critiques and the Jung Institute's refusal to publish it, were disappointing for Neumann, as Jung failed to support him publicly in this matter. Liebscher's analysis of the way Neumann was affected by this reaction to his book indicated that, although Neumann was deeply disappointed, he was able to withhold his anger by differentiating Jung as the president of the offending institute from Jung as the person whom he admired and who defended his work (p. xlvii). Indeed, after receiving all those letters from Jung before the war, which were signed using the words "devoted" and "loyal," Neumann was probably hoping for much empathy from his mentor, who knew the horrors of the war and their effect on Neumann's Jewish soul. The manuscript was written from his bleeding heart, from the depths of his pain, and as previously suggested, presumably had therapeutic qualities. Therefore, despite his deep and personal involvement with the theme of the book, Neumann was able to maintain his depth psychological and archetypal perspective to theorize about the call for modern man's ethical development, a fact that indicates his psychological maturity and leadership capabilities.

Another significant effect of the controversy surrounding the *New Ethic* was the establishment of Neumann's reputation as an important depth psychology theoretician. If, until that point, he was the gifted and promising psychologist-to-be, now the promise was fulfilled. The time gap presumably had a kind of reset effect on his and Jung's relationship and thus enabled a change in the way Jung perceived Neumann, who had psychologically and professionally matured during those terrible years while he developed as a theoretician. The transformation in the way Jung perceived Neumann is possibly reflected in a letter he wrote to Neumann in 1948 with regard to *New Ethic*:

> Your formulations are brilliant and of incisive sharpness; they are therefore challenging and aggressive, an assault troop in an open field, where there was nothing to be seen in advance, unfortunately. . . . Your writings will be a *petra scandali, (rock of offence)* but also the powerful impetus for future developments. For this I am most deeply grateful to you. With best wishes, Your very devoted, C. G. Jung. (Jung & Neumann, 2015, p. 237)

Jung acknowledged the significant theoretical achievement of Neumann's work as a brilliant formulation and thus acknowledged Neumann as a theoretician in his own right. Although Jung failed to support Neumann publicly, his words in this letter served to differentiate his public attitude from his personal one. Nevertheless, this difference exposed Jung's weakness, and it is understandable that Neumann was greatly and painfully disappointed. Neumann later shared with Olga Frobe-Kapteyn, a good friend, the way he came to perceive Jung as a very dear and loving friend who occasionally exposed his weakness and made painful mistakes (Liebscher, 2016b, p. 39).

Neumann withdrew neither the manuscript of the *New Ethic* nor himself as a theoretician of Jungian psychology. This important and controversial book was published at the end of 1948, a few months before his second book was published. Almost immediately after sending Jung the manuscript of the *New Ethic,* Neumann also started to send Jung parts and drafts of his other work, known today as his magnum opus, *Origins* (Neumann, 1949/2014), which, unlike the first book, was warmly accepted by Jung. Jung's perception of Neumann shifted after reading the manuscripts, as Jung began to engage with him theoretically as an equal, as is evident in their correspondence (Liebscher, 2016b, p. 30). The foreword Jung wrote to Neumann's (1949/2014) *Origins,* is effectively the warmest foreword/introduction Jung ever wrote for another theoretician. Jung praised Neumann's work with superlatives and approved it as an amplification of his theory. As noted, Liebscher (2015a) pointed out that in this foreword Jung not only praised the work and was generous in his words, but he also stated that Neumann's work was a continuation of his own, and therefore effectively singled Neumann as his successor. Liebscher pointed that this foreword was the pivotal point in Jung and Neumann's relationship, as these written words were the means through which Jung declared Neumann as the next-generation theoretician.

One more significant event noted in Jung's and Neumann's correspondence is the Eranos conference in the summer of 1947. With the efforts of his friend Adler, Neumann arrived in Europe again in that summer. This visit was enabled by the extraordinary help of Jung, who wrote to the immigration authorities applying for a visa for Neumann and then wrote to them again to expedite the process. It seems that Jung went out of his way to make sure Neumann arrived at Eranos.

At this point, as Liebscher (2015b) pointed out, Jung had already read the draft of Neumann's latest work and now perceived him as more of an equal. As mentioned before, at this 1947 Eranos conference which Neumann attended as a listener, where he originally met his friend Olga Frobe-Kapteyn. At this conference, upon meeting Neumann, Frobe-Kapteyn invited him to give his first lecture at the following year's conference. In the autumn of the same year, already having a very positive impression of Neumann, Frobe-Kapteyn received Jung's recommendation of him as the prospective writer of the introduction to the Eranos picture archive. This recommendation met an attentive ear, and history tells us that Frobe-Kapteyn suggested the appointment, Neumann accepted, and the introduction became his second magnum opus, *The Great Mother* (Neumann, 1955/1991). Jung's recommendation indicated his belief that Neumann was the best man for the task and thus added relevancy and validity to his writing.

The first lecture Neumann gave at Eranos in 1948, "Mystical Man," evoked extreme responses, the most relevant being Jolande Jacobi's because it elicited Jung's high appreciation of Neumann. Jung did not attend this conference (although he read Neumann's lecture), and therefore Jacobi wrote to him about what occurred. Her letter strongly and brutally criticized Neumann and conveyed a sense of jealousy. Jung at this point undoubtedly appreciated Neumann, and thus the extreme negativity toward his apprentice presumably evoked Jung's emotional involvement. Although no emotions are apparent in his response, it would be reasonable—due to his own professional life experience—to assume that Jung easily identified with Neumann as the "unwelcomed" one. "Uniqueness" and "otherness" in theorizing, indicating free thinking and creativity, were surely traits appreciated by Jung, who was excluded from the Freudian circle due to his being a unique and creative thinker. Thus, he presumably recognized that Neumann possessed these characteristics, as is evident in his passionate defense of him:

I think that Neumann's work is excellent. It is not a dogmatic system, but a structured account thought through in minute detail. Admittedly he does not take the feelings of his audience into consideration. That is the reason why he does not mention the positive aspect of the damaged. But it is certainly not unknown to him. . . . His style of presentation must have had a particularly unfortunate effect. But his intellectual achievement is outstanding. . . . With Neumann it is more complex. One needs to think with him, otherwise one is lost. I even recommend a careful reading of his lecture. . . . According to my opinion Neumann is a scholar of the first order, and it is up to my students to prove that he does not teach a dogma, but attempts to create a structure. (Liebscher, 2016b, pp. 33–34)

These words indicate that Jung was clearly proud, in favor, supportive, and appreciative of Neumann and his work, recognizing his unique way of thinking and writing, and most critically, describing his theory as an outstanding intellectual achievement. The last sentence of this quote is at the root of the importance of Neumann's theory to the field of depth psychology. In this statement, Jung first embraced Neumann as a writer of Jungian theory; secondly, he legitimated Neumann's "outstanding achievements"; and thirdly, he laid it on the shoulders of next-generation Jungians, presumably including me as the researcher and author of this manuscript a third generation to "prove" that Neumann was not dogmatic but rather attempted "to create a structure."

Eranos is the place where Neumann blossomed. From the first lecture he gave in 1948 to the last in 1960, he lectured every year and thus effectively, as Liebscher (2015a) wrote, "in the case of Eranos Jung's successor was Neumann" (p. 1). As an honored successor, Neumann became a keynote speaker at the Eranos conferences, and a circle of followers was established around him (Bernardini, 2016).

He soon became "one of the most important figures at Eranos" (Adler, 1960/1979, p. xiv). Aniela Jaffé reported that the discussions during the breaks became significantly different when Neumann started to attend Eranos (Liebscher, 2015a).

For Jung's 80th birthday in 1955, Neumann (1955/1979) reflected on the more than twenty years of his relationship with Jung:

> C. G. Jung is the only really *great man* [emphasis added] I have met in my life. As teacher and friend for more than three decades, he has constantly provided me with new and vital substance for both love and vexation—like Nature herself, the lover of leaping, the superior of man. And when, in this man with all his weaknesses and all his greatness, I struck upon that which is greater than man, yet in which all human qualities are grounded—that was for me a decisive and profoundly orientative experience. . . . Often years later, it would dawn upon me how essentially right he had been, and how he had bypassed my ego, as it were, and had spoken directly to the center of my psyche. . . . He often has the effect of a giant among dwarfs, who always has to stoop a little to make himself understood. . . . It was in this way, when I came to him as a young man, that he gave me, like a gift from a higher power, the courage to be myself myself. (pp. 255—256)

This long note of gratitude from Neumann to Jung captured the way he perceived Jung in this important point in their relationship. Neumann clearly acknowledged here the deep and profound effect Jung had in his life. He described the positive transference he developed toward Jung as an admired figure with the use of the term "great man." Neumann's choice of this term is significant and relevant to this discussion, as it casts light on how highly Neumann valued Jung. The term "Great Individual" is central to Neumann's theory, and he used it to describe a creative man upon whose shoulders humanity's development relies.

For his part, Jung wrote to Neumann on the same occasion in 1955, and while thanking Neumann for his generous words, Jung also complimented Neumann's work when he wrote, "I would like to sincerely thank you. . . for that greater thing that you are achieving in your life's work" (Jung & Neumann, 2015, p. 310). Moreover, he concluded his letter by declaring, "Men like you are *rarissimae aves (rare birds)* whose perspective the world needs" (p. 311). Jung's words seem to indicate the mutual deep appreciation in which the two men held each other in their later days. Evidently, in these words, Jung made clear how highly he thought of Neumann as a theoretician and how he perceived him as a relevant writer.

This discussion of Jung and Neumann's relationship concludes with the words of Jung, recalled by F. Elkisch in 1976, many years after Neumann's death: "I have . . . only two real friends with whom I can speak about my own difficulties; the one is Erich Neumann and he lives in Israel and the other is Father Victor White in England" (as cited in Liebscher, 2016b, p. 44). Undoubtedly therefore, the relationship between Jung and Neumann had much more significance than a mere teacher-student relationship. Owens (2018), who provided an in-depth description of the mutual relationship between the two men, wrote, "Neumann's encounter with Jung, begun in 1933 at age twenty-nine, was the transformative event in his life. But to a degree, the influence eventually went both ways; Neumann evoked new perceptions in Jung" (p. 134). Owens then described how significant and important for Jung was Neumann's opinion and how highly he considered Neumann as a reader of his most personal written material. Therefore, Neumann was clearly important to Jung beyond a mere student. In any case, with no other student was Jung so appreciative of his theorizing, so involved with his writing, and so invested in his career. Jung praised Neumann in an uncompromising way, which leaves hardly any doubt that it is only due to Neumann's early death that his promising future was never fully fulfilled.

Critic and Support of Neumann's

The introduction to *Origins* (Neumann, 1949/2014), written by Neumann in 1949, may be seen as the way he introduced his current and future work to the world. He began the introduction with these words:

> The following attempt to outline the archetypal stages in the development of consciousness is based on modern depth psychology. It is an application of the analytical psychology of C. G. Jung, even where we endeavor to amplify this psychology, and even though we may speculatively overstep its boundaries. (p. xv)

Here, Neumann left no doubt that his writings are both archetypal and developmental, and the distinct developmental aspect is a supplement to Jung's archetypal theory. Neumann notably retained his modest and humble approach to his teacher, Jung, when he stated his loyalty by declaring his work an "application" of Jung's theory; by adding "endeavor" and "to amplify"; and lastly, by admitting that he "may speculatively overstep analytical psychology's boundaries." It seems that Neumann anticipated a possible criticism and provided the answer beforehand in this introduction. Another very humble anticipation of criticism was expressed by Neumann five years later in his second book, *The Great Mother* (1955/1991):

> Our conscious classifications and schematizations are always attempts to arrive, through abstraction, at an orientation within the reality of life. But this living reality, with its crests and troughs, progressions and regressions, irruptions and anticipations, is at every moment spontaneous and unformulable. . . . In the reality of an

> analysis . . . and . . . in real life, every step is individual, every dream is unpredictable, and it is only in the most general sense that transformation can be correlated with a scheme of development. (p. 83)

Clearly Neumann here questioned any theory and any attempt to fully know the psyche, as he recognized it as multiple, unique, and impossible to be described in full.

Neumann's anticipation that his writings might evoke criticism was not in vain, and few Jungian writers are known to be very critical of Neumann. The first, while Neumann was still alive, was Jacobi, whose letter to Jung was discussed previously with regard to Jung and Neumann's relationship, noting that Jung responded with firm support for Neumann. The two other known Jungian critics of Neumann are Fordham and Wolfgang Giegerich. Fordham's first published critique of Neumann's formulations appeared in his book *New Developments in Analytical Psychology* (1957), where he devalued Neumann and attacked him for not supporting his assertions with evidence (pp. 28–29). Neumann (1959) commented on this critique in his article "The Significance of the Genetic Aspect for Analytical Psychology," published a year before he died, stating that he never wrote of any "law" that required scientific evidence (p. 132). In this sense, Neumann differed from Jung (1954/1990c), who wrote "I am an empiricist, not a philosopher. . . who always takes it for granted that his own disposition and attitude are universal" (p. 75). In these words, Jung "legitimated" what Fordham misunderstood as Neumann's dogmatic style in writing when he contended that Neumann presented his theory as a "fact." As Jung pointed out, Neumann was a philosopher rather than a scientific empiricist. Fordham's (1981) second critique was aimed at Neumann's formulations in his posthumous book *The Child* (1963/1990) and was written more than twenty years after Neumann died. Fordham's critique and partial aspects of his work (1957, 1969/1994, 1981) are discussed in Part II.

The second critic, Giegerich (1975), also focused on Neumann's formulations in *Origins* (1949/2014) fifteen years after Neumann's death and fourteen years after Jung's. Therefore, neither Neumann nor Jung could respond to defend Neumann's work and its loyalty to Jungian theory.

These critiques cannot be faulted for being written post-humously, as Neumann died young and unexpectedly. Nevertheless, they created a loose end as no one could defend Neumann as well as he could and would have defended himself. A moving example of the way Neumann courageously countered his opponents among the Jungians was found in a letter he wrote to Jung discussing *New Ethic* and the institute's objection to publishing it. Neumann wrote politely, but very firmly and courageously. On the one hand, he assured Jung that he would withdraw the book from publication through the Institute, but on the other hand he promised to prove that he was worthy of the agitation around the book and added a small and significant cynical remark, referring to his opponents as "pussyfooters" (Jung & Neumann, 2015, p. 241). Neumann demonstrated responsibility and as previously mentioned, his friend Adler (1960/1979) testified that he was determined to achieve his goals. Although he did not want to harm Jung or the Institute (and thus withdrew the book from publication there), he was determined to publish it elsewhere.

On the other hand, some notable figures did support Neumann's work, and the three strongest advocates were Jung; Olga Frobe-Kapteyn, who was the highest authority of the Eranos conferences; and the Bollingen Foundation, which published Jung's *Collected Works* (1957–1983). These three were also the most pertinent sources of support in the Jungian world during the years when Neumann was active as a writer, theoretician, and lecturer.

Regarding Jung's support, in addition to all that was already described, another factor is suggested to have played a part in Jung's deeper understanding of Neumann's psyche: the unconscious levels of the relationship between the two men. This suggestion, although speculative, is based on biographical facts. In *Memories, Dreams, Reflections*, Jung (1961/1989) wrote, "Under my treatment a pagan becomes a pagan and a Christian a Christian, a Jew a Jew, according to what his destiny prescribes for him" (p. 138). Among Jung's first-generation followers, Neumann was the one most challenged by what his destiny prescribed for him and most pious in following his destiny (disregarding Jacobi, who converted from Judaism to Christianity). It may be assumed that Jung's appreciation of Neumann's personality was partly due to Neumann's dedication to his destiny. As described earlier, Neumann's personal life was firmly rooted in the German culture and Europe, yet he was following a deeper and a more profound ancestral call rooted in the soil of the Promised Land.

At the beginning of the 20th century, being a Zionist meant privileging the collective Jewish people over oneself as an individual Jew. Neumann's journey to the land of Israel and his first ten years there were his quest, manifesting a central theme of his writings— the Hero's Journey. Reflecting on his biography from the hero's perspective, Neumann was the classic hero: He left his homeland and the known world to travel far away on a journey he felt destined to take, he met his inner demons in extreme isolation, and he also fought the dragons of the outer world, consequently winning the boon and returning to the place from which he departed—Europe—where he blossomed at the Eranos conferences. Presumably therefore, on an unconscious level, Jung recognized Neumann's heroic life and sympathized with his heroic journey.

The second devoted advocate of Neumann's work was Frobe-Kapteyn, identified here as such because the encounter with her at

Eranos was pivotal for Neumann's career. Following his first visit, a close and robust bond was established between him, Frobe-Kapteyn, and the physical estate of Eranos. Bernardini (2016) suggested an aspect of this strong bond when he pointed out that the Great Mother archetype was central to Eranos as much as it was central to Neumann's thinking and theorizing. As previously mentioned, Neumann and Frobe-Kapteyn had a close friendship during the ten years that followed their first encounter until Neumann's sudden death. Bernardini pointed out that two years after Neumann died, both Frobe-Kapteyn and Swiss biologist and zoologist Adolf Portmann acknowledged Neumann as "perhaps the only follower of Jung's to establish his own school of followers" (p. 203). Bernardini also referenced an unpublished letter, in which Frobe-Kapteyn wrote,

> I suggest [to the Bollingen Foundation] that after my death, the estate be offered as a loan to Dr. Erich Neumann for the duration of his life, so as to enable him to carry on his work in Europe from a permanent residence. This solution would give him the opportunity of continuing *his creative work, based on C. G. Jung's psychology, but reaching forward into fields as yet unexplored by psychology. I need not stress the fact that he is obviously the next psychologist of great importance in the sequence Freud-Jung, and that he too is a pioneer, as I know that the Bollingen Foundation realizes this* [emphasis added]. (as cited in Bernardini, 2016, pp. 226–227)

In this letter, Frobe-Kapteyn effectively recognized Neumann's contribution to depth psychology to be as important as Freud's and Jung's. Given that the letter was written prior to Neumann's death, it leaves no doubt as to the significance he held (and presumably still holds) for the field of depth psychology in general, and in particular for Jungian analytical psychology. Bernardini (2016) additionally mentioned that in 1947, during his first visit in Eranos, not only did

Neumann meet and become close friends with Frobe-Kapteyn, he was also introduced to John David (Jack) Barrett, Jr., who was then the editor of the Bollingen Series. Therefore, when Frobe-Kapteyn wrote those words, she probably knew they would meet attentive eyes. Bernardini described how, at the Bollingen Foundation, Neumann was seen as the best of Jung's followers and the only one to continue his work. Effectively, the amount of written work published by Neumann is second only to the amount published by Jung himself (p. 224).

A Note on Terminology

A clarification is needed with the use of the capital letter *S* in the word *Self*. In his writings, Neumann (like Jung) wrote *self* with a lower-case letter. Nevertheless, he was definitely referring to the archetypal Self. In later years, the distinction between *self* and *Self* among Jungian writers grew out of the need to separate the Jungian archetypal perception of the Self from psychoanalytical self-psychology's perception of the self. Later Jungian writers differ; some continue to use the lower-case letter and others use the capital letter. This manuscript situates itself among those who adhere to Neumann's notion of the Self as the archetypal Self and thus use the capital letter.

Another terminological distinction is important: Neumann was criticized by his opponents for his interchangeable use of the terms *stage* and *phase*. Close reading of Neumann's work indicates that the different usage of the two terms was intentional, and this manuscript follows what presumably was Neumann's distinction. Neumann (1949/2014) wrote that "stage refers to a structural layer" (p. 41) and therefore this term is used with reference to the succession of psychic psychological development (for example, "the child's development at this stage" [p. 25]). The term *phase* is used to indicate a more comprehensive psychological perspective that reflects the nature of psychological reality and the world-related layer (for example, "in the uroboric phase of the primal relationship" [p. 25]). Therefore, stage holds perspective of time, while phase is more of the psychological experience. Neumann repeatedly emphasized that the use of these two words, the description of development in phases and stages, is required for clarity. Nevertheless, psychological development is fluid and not exact. Most importantly, as Kutzinski (personal communication) clarified, the consciousness grows as a circle that becomes wider and thus encompasses more within it; therefore, it also includes all that was prior and not discarded as a prior "stage" or "phase."

PART I

ADVANCED STAGES
OF INDIVIDUATION

Chapter 2
The Burning Themes:
Shadow, Voice, and Earth

The seeds of Neumann's well-articulated ideas and formulations in his magnum opus are to be found already in his initial writings. In these early writings, Neumann effectively described the highest stages of consciousness development achieved by the process of individuation, which may be seen as his oblation to Jung's theory. This chapter presents Neumann as a creative Great Individual—as he likewise described Jung—and from the current perspective, an ecological social and political activist.

Jung, Neumann and the Great Individual

In an appendix to his book, and here already in the abbreviated form - *Origins* (1949/2014), with regard to consciousness development, Neumann wrote about the Great Individual, of whom he also wrote in *Depth Psychology and a New Ethic* and already abbreviated - *New Ethic* (1949/1990). His description of the Great Individual draws from and elaborates on Jung's concept of the mana-personality. Neumann described the Great Individual functioning in a sense as the Self and the creative center of a group, with enough ego strength to be exposed to the group's unconscious contents that are transmitted to him by the revelation of the Voice. The religious use of the term "Voice" refers to the voice of God; therefore, from the psychological perspective, it is the voice of the Self. Indeed, Neumann described the Voice as "the individual expression of psychic truth" (1949/1990, p. 35), that is, an ethical orientation from within.

As Neumann's description of the Great Individual was in developmental terms, he described three levels of Great Individuals who are distinct from one another in two aspects: the degree of their conscious participation in the revelation and the scope of the contents revealed to them by the Voice. The first and lower one is the Great Individual who passively carries the group's unconscious projections, which means that he has no conscious relation to the projected contents; these Great Individuals are carriers of gods' and goddesses' symbolism, mostly from the earthly realm, such as beauty and fertility. To the second level of Great Individuals belong those prophets and shamans whose personality is archetypally possessed with spirit, such as demons and God. These Great Individuals are unconsciously carrying the projections of the group, and thus their ego is passive in the process of the collective assimilation of these unconscious contents. The Great Individuals at these two first levels are similar to the mana-personality described by Jung as an ego endangered by inflation—such as a magician, hero, chief, or saint who identifies with the archetypal contents projected upon him.

The decisive common element of the mana-personality as described by Jung and the two first levels of greatness as described by Neumann is their unconscious identity with the projections. Nevertheless, the fundamental difference between the mana-personality and the Great Individual of the third level manifests in their terms; the first represents mana and the latter greatness, and the first is personality and the latter individual. Therefore, presumably, for the mana-personality there lurks the danger of identifying with the negative and shadowed projections, whereas Neumann's Great Individual, seems to refer to the manifestations of the positive pole. Nevertheless, it seems that in describing the Great Individual of the third level Neumann drew from Jung's (1933/1965) writings in his essay "The Spiritual Problem of Modern Man" and his descriptions of a "modern man." Jung wrote that, in order to develop, the modern man must be proficient in his roots and tradition so that he can break free from them and outgrow the past stages of consciousness and their duties imposed on him by his world. Indeed, Neumann (1949/2014) theorized that the third and higher level of the Great Individual characterizes those whose "conscious mind actively participates in the process and adopts a responsible attitude toward it" (p. 425). Conscious responsibility is a decisive aspect of Neumann's formulation concerning the advanced stages of individuation, especially regarding the assimilation of the shadow. Nevertheless, at this point the conscious responsibility at this level of greatness entails an ego that is strong enough not only to participate but also to participate responsibly and actively, with the content invading from the unconscious. Hence, the Great Individual becomes creative, as through him the human qualities of ego-conscious formation manifest.

Insightfully, Lance Owens (2018) suggested that this is exactly the process through which Jung created what is known as the *Red Book*. His ego was strong enough to process and assimilate the invading unconscious contents and thus he performed as a Great Individual. Furthermore, Owens suggested that possibly, during their time together in Zurich, Jung told Neumann about the experience and about the books (*Black Books*) and thus planted the thought in Neumann's mind. In later years, in his Eranos essay "The Psyche and the Transformation of the Reality Planes: A Metapsychological Essay," Neumann (1952/1989) described the Great Individual who differs from the common man in that he is able to experience a "larger area of the world" (p. 50). Here he referred to "extraneous knowledge," which he theorized stems from the archetypal-field and the deeper Self-field. Neumann made clear reference to Jung's writings about synchronicity, describing it as carried out by "absolute knowledge" that extends beyond ego-conscious perceptions of space and time. Importantly and significantly, Neumann (1949/2014) asserted that this level of Great Individual serves as a prototype of the development of individuality as the hero represents the prototype of the development of consciousness. In his later article "Mystical Man," the first that he presented at Eranos, Neumann (1948/1989) wrote of the Great Individual as a highly mystic man manifests as a precursor of the individuation process. Interestingly, in a note, Liebscher (Jung & Neumann, 2015) pointed to remarks by Neumann in a seminar on Hasidism, given in Tel Aviv, in 1939–1940, where he talked about the image of the Zaddik and said exactly the same thing:

> And when you look at a Zaddik, he actually stands beyond the law and all limitations. Everywhere in everything that we will come to hear of the teaching of the Zaddik it can be said that this is the prototype of the doctrine of the individual. He is the only one who is able to be an authentic human being. *This is the precursor of that which appears in the process of individuation as finding one's own way to the law.* (p. 12, note 134; emphasis added)

In a talk presented to a Jewish audience in Tel Aviv, Neumann described the Zaddik (Jewish term for a righteous, pious, just, and innocent man) in much the same way that he described the Great Individual of this third level and later as the high mystic. Furthermore, as previously mentioned in a letter to Jung, Neumann (Jung & Neumann, 2015) used the word "Zaddik" to describe Jung, writing that he saw him as an authority and a teacher and thus a manifestation of the Jewish concept of the "Zaddikim of the nations" (pp. 35–36). Neumann's underlying thought was that the Great Individual of the third level is the archetypal representation of the achievement of a well-advanced individuation process. Supporting this, in an appendix to *Origins*, Neumann (1949/2014) wrote of "the great individual . . . who really is a great man in the sense of being a great personality" (p. 426). Five years later, on the occasion of Jung's eightieth birthday, Neumann (1955/1979) wrote, "C. G. Jung is the only really great man I have met in my life" (p. 255). He then very movingly described Jung's greatness as an ability to relate to one's very being and admitted that:

> he had bypassed my ego, as it were, and had spoken directly to the center of my psyche. . . It was in this way, when I came to him as a young man, that he gave me, like a gift from a higher power, the courage to be myself. (p. 256)

Neumann wrote those things retrospectively, but as they stand here, they will shed a different light on some of the events, at the genesis of Neumann's career, in which he needed the courage to be himself. There is no doubt therefore that for Neumann, Jung was much more than a mere teacher; he was a Great Individual and a Zaddik and manifested the perfect vessel for Neumann's projection of his own greatness.

Neumann (1949/2014) described the Great Individual as the archetypal manifestation of the psychologically advanced personality, whose ego has achieved full maturity and independence. In that sense, the Great Individual of this level represents a psychological stage in which the shadow is assimilated; thus, there is no split into a negative and a positive pole, as such an individual has achieved a high level of psychic unity. Furthermore, Neumann clarified that, as ego conscious development belongs to the patriarchate and masculinity, the gender symbolism is psychological rather than biological or sociological. Thus, "feminine people" bear masculinity and "masculine people" bear femininity, and it is always far more a question of relationship than of definitions. In order to elucidate his formulation, Neumann asserted that, although the figure of the

Great Individual is a common projection of the male group, it is not confined to it; the corresponding figure of the female group would be, beautifully and simply, the Great Mother.

Neumann, a Political, Social and Ecological Activist

In December 1933 Jung, in his opening address after assuming the presidency of the General Medical Society for Psychotherapy, demanded an end to the confusion between Jewish and Germanic psychology, claiming that "The differences which actually do exist between Germanic and Jewish psychology, and which have long been known to every intelligent person are no longer to be glossed over" (Jung, 1933/1970, p. 533). His article "The State of Psychotherapy Today" (Jung, 1934/1970, pp. 157-173), published a month later in January 1934, was no different. Outrageously, Jung wrote that the Jews (like women) due to their physical weakness became accustomed to finding their adversary's weakness and vulnerabilities, referring to their need to defend themselves and thus find the weaker spots of the adversary. In addition, he claimed, as they are a much older civilization than the Arian, they are generally speaking more conscious of the negative and shadowed aspects of things. And in a determined way, as if it were a fact, he added,

> The Jew, who is something of a nomad, has never yet created a cultural form of his own and as far as we can see never will, since all his instincts and talents require a more or less civilized nation to act as host for their development.
> (pp. 165–166)

In response, Neumann cleverly reacted in three different channels. The first and immediate one was a personal letter in which he strongly attacked Jung; the second was published soon after as a rejoinder to Kirsch's article which was much calmer and somewhat protective of Jung; and the third was the manuscript about Jacob and Esau, a deep reflection into the history and future of the Jewish soul, in which the central theme is the integration of the shadow. This manuscript was Neumann's way to defend Jewish psychology; to present it as highly and strikingly close to analytical psychology, which was at its infancy; and to draw Jung's attention to his ignorance about it. Effectively, the manuscript was the beginning of Neumann's life's work, and his theorizing about depth psychology, a task he never ceased to pursue.

Beginning with the first among Neumann's reaction, Liebscher (2015a) believed that Neumann's personal letter to Jung was written while Neumann was still in Zurich and was seeing Jung regularly. He also suggested that the fact that Neumann wrote to Jung rather than speaking to him in person indicates how deeply he was shocked by Jung's writings about race psychology. This letter is significant for the theme of this chapter as it contains both the seeds of Neumann's later writings and the indication of his "greatness" and activism.

At the beginning of the letter, Neumann (Jung & Neumann, 2015, N4) confessed, "I feel I simply must take issue with you on a matter that goes far beyond any merely personal concerns," therefore, the letter is written by a man fighting for his people, a leader and presumably a political activist. It is the first sign of what later became very clearly a characteristic of Neumann, that is, his willingness to fight for a cause and bear the consequences as a "truth warrior." Then, Neumann proceeded and was angry enough to write,

> *Where I come from, great men* have always been called upon
> to exercise discernment and to stand against the crowd—
> and it is precisely my conviction about the uniqueness of
> your own nature that causes me now—(*not only in my own
> interest*)—to ask you if this easy affirmation, this throwing
> yourself into the frenzy of Germanic exuberance—is this
> your true position or do I misunderstand you on this point?
> [emphasis added] (p. 12)

Here clearly Neumann appears as an activist who was willing to risk the personal domain (as at that point his career was already invested in Jung's theory) for the higher cause, the support of his people, and this kind of social activism is relevant to his later formulations about a new ethic. Therefore, this first letter that Neumann wrote to Jung established the grounds for Neumann's later theorizing. In the letter are the seeds of Neumann's perception of the Jewish people's relationship with the external world and the non-Jews. He soon after elaborated on this theme through deep interpretation of the story of Jacob and Esau, in which the central theme is the integration of the shadow previously projected on the "other." This interpretation, less known among Neumann's writings, is the foundation for his later work just recently published, *The Roots of Jewish Consciousness* (Neumann, 1935–1945/2019). More importantly it manifested a forerunner for the *New Ethic* (Neumann, 1949/1990), also dealing with the integration of the shadow and furthermore with the ego's mature responsibility to make choices and take action as a further developmental phase of individuation. These works in turn led to his magnum opus about the development of consciousness, from its embryonic stage to the level of the mystic, creative, Great Individual.

Neumann's second way of addressing Jung's racist remarks was the rejoinder to Kirsch's article, in which he appeared much softer and defended Jung, claiming the Jews are generally more conscious, thus aware of the shadow. Nevertheless, he described this trait in Judaism as a "fundamental fact of its *moral instinct.*" He posited that as the individual needs to integrate his shadow, so do the Jewish people, and Zionism need to become "conscious of the negative" and "only then will an ultimate and deeply grounded development of Erez-Israel and a rebirth of the Jew that emerges from his creative foundation be possible" (Jung & Neumann, 2015, p. 356). Therefore, in this rejoinder, a very early and initial publication dated 1934,

Neumann already clearly linked shadow, earth, and current Judaism. Importantly, one needs to know what Erez-Israel means for the Jewish people in order to grasp the depth of what Neumann wrote here. Erez-Israel directly and explicitly relates to the land, the soil, and the physical portion of the Holy Land on earth. This may be seen as Neumann's interpretation of the roots and psychology of anti-Semitism, suggesting that it is anchored to the Jewish projection of their own shadow, and in that sense, Jews bear some responsibility. Obviously, this is not to ignore the anti-Semitic objective of guilt and blame but rather it indicates an aspect of his personality and his maturity—that he was able to recognize fault on the side of his own people, even in the extreme circumstances of rising anti-Semitism.

In Tel Aviv, Neumann wrote another letter to Jung describing his personal experiences with Erez-Israel and the encounter with his anima, and shared his sense of mission.

Therefore, the psychological encounter with the themes of the repressed and the shadowed, together with the anima and the land on the one hand and the sense of mission or attending the call of an inner voice on the other hand, evoked Neumann's inherent activism. Activism is a way of being in the world for the Great Individual and manifests the seeds of his later articulation of the progressive stages of individuation and his ecological activism and eco-psychological orientation.

Also in this second letter, Neumann mentioned the two writing projects he was immersed in at the time, during the first weeks of his new life in Tel Aviv. One was the rejoinder to Kirsch's article, and the second, and much more important historically to Neumann's theory, was his elaboration of Hugo Rosenthal's (1934) article about Jacob and Esau, which was the third channel of reaction to Jung's remarks.

The historical facts, revealed and described by Liebscher (2015) indicate that in the aftermath of the publication of Jung's racist article "The State of Psychotherapy Today" (Jung, 1934/1970) and the attacks against him by Jewish authors, Jung added a Jewish author's contribution to a collection of essays, *Reality of the Soul* (Jung, 1934, as cited in Liebscher, 2015, p. xxviii). The Jewish author was Rosenthal (1934), and his essay, "The Type-Difference in the Jewish History of Religion" (Liebscher, 2015, p. xxix), triggered Neumann's thinking. He published a review of Rosenthal's article, "On the Jewish History of Religion" (cited in Jung & Neumann, 2015, Appendix 1), in which alongside expressing agreement with the principal idea of exploring the polarity of extraversion and introversion within the biblical story of Jacob and Esau, he suggested that Rosenthal didn't follow the idea to its ultimate depth. Generally, Neumann's criticism was that Rosenthal kept too close to the internal Jewish perspective and thus missed the wider implications of Jewish introversion and its opposition to the extraversion of the non-Jewish people in the diaspora of two thousand years. The diaspora is a meaningful concept for the Jewish soul, related to the exile of the Jews from Jerusalem for over two thousand years, when they lived scattered throughout the world. Therefore, Zionism entails returning to the Promised Land and reestablishing the Jews as the people of Israel on its land. Neumann therefore pointed to the potential depth of the biblical story in light of the relationship between the introverted Jewish people and the non-Jewish extraverted world throughout which they were scattered. Highly intrigued by the subject as he was, Neumann later wrote a much longer commentary and shared it with Jung. Effectively, this was the first psychological analysis Neumann was engaged with and thus it became the departure point of his career, the first step toward his magnum opus, and his other writings. After reading Neumann's long commentary and corresponding about it, Jung (Jung & Neumann, 2015) complimented Neumann's ideas and recommended an elaboration: "Your material is very fine and interesting. It would be worth developing the symbolic contribution further" (p. 58). Upon receiving this recommendation, Neumann wrote,

> I will pursue your suggestion of elaborating on the "Symbolic Contribution" to the Jacob-Esau problem, perhaps with a general introduction. The great difficulty is the rather depressing impossibility of a publication—but first of all it should be finished. (p. 62)

Sadly, Neumann was right regarding the impossibility of publication of a book concerning Jewish psychological perspective in times of rising Nazism. Nevertheless, in the spirit of Zionism and motivated to reflect on Judaism and the "Jewish problem" as well as by his activist's sense of mission, he embarked on the task. Jung's recommendation is dated July 1934, and by December 1934, Neumann wrote to Jung that he had concluded the writing. As Neumann intuitively and cleverly anticipated, the manuscript remained unpublished for more than eighty years until 2015, when it was revealed, translated, and published by Erel Shalit as *Jacob and Esau* (Neumann, 1934/2015). Shalit not only edited the manuscript into a cohesive book, but he also added a remarkably elucidating introduction as he recognized the importance of this manuscript to the understanding of Neumann's thinking and future theorizing.

Neumann, a Hero's Journey on the Path of Individuation

During his first months in Palestine in the spring of 1934, when Neumann was only 29, as encouraged by Jung, he wrote the insightful manuscript of *Jacob and Esau*. Neumann brought up the issue of Judaism in his dialogue with Jung at a time when he, as a young man, was defining his new identity as a Jewish-Zionist-Jungian psychologist, as well as an immigrant who was in a way a refugee and a newcomer to the state, which was not yet established, and to a society still struggling to define itself. Under these challenging circumstances, in his second letter to Jung Neumann wrote:

> The chaos here becomes not only bearable to me, but I also feel myself to be infinitely closely bound up with it; I emerge out of this to my own "people." I must though, confess that I am quite often afraid at the same time. (Jung & Neumann, 2015, p. 19)

What Neumann here described as an experience of emergence was due to his maturity despite his young age, an indication of his individuation process. When one considers his life during those years, it appears that he underwent a hero's journey: leaving home for an unknown land, fighting dragons (the obstacles he faced), and releasing the anima to finally return (to Eranos in Europe) as a hero, holding the boon of recognition as the most promising theoretician following Jung. Although the individuation process continued throughout his life, at the time he wrote this letter he was already into his journey. Accordingly, his writings in the following years indicate that he was occupied by themes and processes that belong to the advanced stages of the individuation process—assimilating the shadow, following the inner voice, and redeeming the feminine aspect—all emerging from his own psychological contemplations and effectively becoming his theory.

In his letter to Jung, Neumann (Jung & Neumann, 2015) described at length the chaos referenced in the above quote as the bursts of repressed shadow that were carried by the Jews throughout the thousands of years of repression and oppression in the diaspora and that now, when the Jews were finally settling on their own land, were "liberated." As shown, in their correspondence, Neumann agreed with Jung that the Jews had the tendency to see the negative and shadowed side of things and to raise it to consciousness; nevertheless, he attributed this tendency to the Jewish characteristic moral instinct. Therefore, as Shalit (2015a) wrote, Neumann at the time of his initial writings had "an astute understanding of the shadow . . . of the need to attend to the inner voice, and of the tension between the spirit and the earth in Judaism and Zionism" (p. xvii). These three themes—shadow, inner voice, and tension between spirit and earth—belong in Neumann's theory and to the more advanced stages of individuation that he described in his initial writings. Apparently, he was occupied by these themes during those first years of theorizing, as he shared with Jung in the first letter he wrote from Tel Aviv (Jung & Neumann, 2015, 5N). These themes found their way into Neumann's writings, mainly his initial efforts and particularly *Jacob and Esau* (Neumann, 1934/2015) and *New Ethic* (Neumann, 1949/1990), which are at the focus of part 1.

Chapter 3
Jacob and Esau –
A Story of Individuation

General

In one of the first letters in their correspondence, Jung agreed with Neumann, affirming that, in the biblical story of Jacob and Esau, "Jacob is the *quintessence* of the Jew" and therefore the story represents "an individuation on a collective level" (Jung & Neumann, 2015, p. 54). Indeed, in *Jacob and Esau*, Neumann (1934/2015) interpreted the story as the Jewish version of symbolic representation of an individuation process, anchored in his explanation that the forefathers represent the experience of the entire Jewish people and therefore Jacob represents both the Jewish people and an individual Jew. Nevertheless, he was aware of the need to validate the story as relevant—beyond the Jewish people—to the human soul, and therefore he attempted to indicate that Jewish symbolism is embedded in the symbolism of all humanity.

Neumann was acquainted with Hasidism from his previous studies and from his earlier days in Berlin. Jewish mysticism was a genuine interest of his, and even more important to him was the renewal of the Jewish spirit as a reaction to the rising anti-Semitism. Therefore, Rosenthal's article (see p. 52) intrigued him, and he was drawn to write a psychological analysis of a biblical story, one which would illustrate both the depth and the progressive psychological aspect of the forefather's account and its role as a

Jewish (elevated) mythology. Following the midrashim, Neumann presented the original mythological opposition between the sun and the moon, heaven and earth, and the hostile brothers, emphasizing its fundamentality to the human psyche. Using Jungian typology, he analyzed Jacob's introversion and his shadowed extraversion in the image of Esau, articulating the psychological experience of Jacob's encounter with evil and the catharsis of acknowledging evil as the "other" face of God.

The Framework

As described earlier, Jung added Rosenthal's article to his publication as a way of compensating for his suspected racism and anti-Semitism. Neumann found Rosenthal's analysis of the biblical story of Jacob and Esau to be too literal and superficial, and he also wrote that it "suffers from its negative stance towards the text, which, just as Bible criticism does, often simply contradicts instead of illuminates it" (1934/2015, p. 20, note 36). Neumann believed that in order to penetrate the depth of the meaning of the core text, one needs to follow the midrashim surrounding it. Thus, he suggested an illumination of the story of Jacob and Esau through midrashic literature and exegesis. Midrash originates in the Hebrew word *doresh*, which translates as "inquires." In traditional readings of the Bible, there are four levels of understanding the text: the literal (simple), which is the breadth; the allegoric (hint), which is the length; the seeking (search), which is the depth; and the mystical (hidden), which is the height. In Hebrew, the third, seeking/search, is *drash*; therefore, midrash belongs to this level. As the midrash offers an amplification and elucidation of the literal story into the depth of its meaning, each biblical story may be interpreted differently by several midrashim, each presenting another aspect of meaning when the differences in interpretation would usually imply layers of depth. Shalit (2015a) suggested that the Jewish custom of exegesis and the existence of midrashim manifest a psychological approach to the reading and prevent the danger of literalness and concreteness.

Neumann wrote that the midrashim "constitute a unified, pervasive, and absolutely unequivocal symbolism, which belongs to the archetypal heritage of the Jewish people in particular and of humanity in general" (1934/2015, p. 19). In saying this, he gave a universality to his manuscript, which was not necessarily Jewish oriented, although it originated in the Jewish canon. Similarly, although his analysis retains a Jewish perspective, it is relevant for depth psychological discussion about consciousness development— assimilation of the shadow and dissolvement of its projection—as well as the individuation process. Neumann was qualified to analyze the biblical story as a psychological inquiry as he was highly knowledgeable of Jewish midrashic literature (although he believed himself to be insufficiently proficient) and he had a strong and solid footing in the field of depth psychology, especially when encouraged by Jung to elaborate.

In the biblical story of the hostile twin brothers, Neumann found the path of further consciousness development and individuation through which the shadow (which was once cast out, repressed, and suppressed as was Esau) becomes integrated within Jacob's newly achieved psychic unity. In his manuscript, Neumann emphasized the universal nature of the central theme of the biblical story. It concerns a fundamental issue of the human psyche, arising with the conflict of the opposites and culminating with the problem of the shadow. This was the first time Neumann articulated the process of individuation beyond the stage of shadow assimilation and toward psychic wholeness. The initial theoretical attempt was done in terms of a process and progression, as Neumann held a developmental perspective. Moreover, he believed that the motif extends "to the fundamental tension between the spirit and the earth" (p. 33). This is presumably the first time that Neumann linked the themes of the shadow to the tension between spirit and earth, which became one of the key aspects of his theory and later appeared as the focus of the article "The Meaning of the Earth Archetype for Modern Times" (Neumann, 1953/1994), supporting the claim that Neumann's theory has eco-psychological characteristics.

To fully penetrate the depth of the biblical story from the psychological perspective and to indicate its importance and relevancy, Neumann needed to situate it both as a forefather's account and as an individuation path on the axis of human consciousness and psychological development. To achieve that, he explored the story and the midrashim regarding the story through mythology, as an indication of the consciousness developmental level implied by the interpretation of the midrash. There is evidence of his developmental orientation even in this first attempt to theorize; the development of human consciousness is embedded. Moreover, in both this first manuscript and his magnum opus, *Origins* (Neumann, 1949/2014), a decade later, Neumann embarked on his journey through literature, starting with mythology, to which he assigned significance.

Jacob and Esau (Neumann, 1934/2015) was published post-humously, as an edited book made of three articles, each make a chapter. Therefore, the order of the chapters was carefully decided upon by the editor, Erel Shalit. Nevertheless, with the aim of presenting the developmental orientation of Neumann's writings, the following is a developmental description as it emerges from the text, not necessarily in order of the edited published book. As well, for the purpose of emphasizing the relevancy of Neumann's theory, his analysis of the psychological developmental aspects of the biblical story of Jacob and Esau will be amplified by lectures delivered by Jonathan Grossman, an Israeli university professor, expert of biblical literature analysis.

Consciousness Levels in Encountering the Shadow

In accordance with his developmental perspective, Neumann analyzed humanity's encounter with the archetypal shadow, and accordingly with one's own shadow, recognizing and describing three levels of consciousness development. His deep analysis of each level, supported by Jung's original writing. Found here is a summarized version (full version in Appendix I), which is enough to move with the flow of the central theme of this chapter: the unavoidable stage of the individuation process, that of encountering one's shadow.

Neumann described humanity in its infancy, the initial consciousness stage, as collective, implying that man had no individuality yet and his perception was collective. As such, in the absence of any individual form, inward and unconscious content was projected outward. Accordingly, the mythology was that of gods and deities, like Sun and Moon, not yet recognizable people with faces. The lack of consciousness also led to a mythological perception of the conflict of opposites projected outwardly, the "not yet shadow" was perceived as the archetype of salvation, allegedly leading to the redemption of the original state of unity. Still at this early and initial *mythologizing* stage and at the edge of transition to the next, when human consciousness started to emerge, differentiation was enabled, and the conflict of the opposites ensued. At this further stage, the negative side was projected and concretized via rituals, such as the scapegoat. Once human consciousness emerged and became stable enough in the light, the outward projection of the negative was replaced by splitting the inner opposites into ego-conscious and shadow. In this later stage, corresponding to modern man's conscious development, the shadow, which is split off from the personality, is projected on the "other" as an outside object. This is the departure point for the analysis of the story of the hostile biblical brothers, Jacob and Esau.

A Biblical Story and the Midrashim
as a Level of Interpretation

The biblical story at the focus of Neumann's (1934/2015) exploration considers the forefather Jacob. Neumann suggested that some may question whether a biblical story can be a subject of psychological inquiry. Therefore, he found it necessary to situate the forefathers on the line between objective mythological figures and a subjective family story. On the one hand, no doubt there is a mythological aspect to the images of the forefathers and the prophets as they "contain the experience of an entire people" (p. 2). On the other hand, their stories include concrete and historical components typical of family stories. Neumann suggested that the forefather's life story was carried down the generations by his family and descendants and that it was shaped by their experience of him and his life: "The renewed and vivid preoccupation with the forefathers brings forth within the people experiencing these figures another, namely, mythological figure of the forefather" (p. 2). Hence, in this aspect, the biblical story is a mythology; nevertheless, the people's preoccupation with the forefathers' account brings forth the midrashic text:

> It is precisely the intimate and vivid relationship between the people and the forefathers that adequately explains why it is fruitful to consider midrashic literature and the biblical text together. Ultimately, the account of the forefathers and its specific formulation, from which the noncanonical text later emerged, both stem from the soul of the people remembering and processing those events and experiences. (p. 3)

By remembering the story of the forefathers and by carrying it across generations, when their experience of the forefathers and of their story is woven into the story that is carried across generations, the people are also psychologically processing the forefathers' account.

When it is presented this way, the midrash and the Jewish act of exegesis around it become like the analytical act. In his introduction to Neumann's work, Shalit (2015a) wrote,

> In fact, this is exactly what Neumann himself does: he carries the people's story further by processing it. The psyche, both individual and collective, is involved in the process, implying a psychological approach rather than a literal reading of the scriptures. (p. xix)

Shalit pointed to the fact that Neumann himself was deeply and psychologically engaged by, and immersed in, the material when he wrote of the midrashim as the people's engagement with the forefathers' lives. As Neumann was a depth psychologist and a man of his times, his analysis of the biblical story, using midrashim from various times, manifests a midrash, stemming from the collective psyche of the Jews of the twentieth century, of which Neumann was a part. This also indicates that Neumann had the qualities of a Great Individual, as he described him: an individual who suspends his ego in order to consciously draw from the collective unconscious. Indeed, Neumann was an activist, motivated by the interest of his people rather than his own interest, therefore he suspended the personal domain and drew from the collective psyche of his people and humanity at large.

It seems that reading, learning, and remembering the biblical story are not enough; the exegesis in the midrashic text provides the processing of the collective psyche of the people. In turn, the midrashim manifests the discussion that occurs in the people's unconscious and thus reflects the fundamental problems occupying the people in terms of symbolic language. This explains why a midrash about the motif of Jacob and Esau, which reflects the conflict of the opposites in the people's unconscious, would use the symbolism of moon and sun. The symbolism of the moon and the sun originates in the archaic mythologizing layer; the midrash uses this mythological symbolism to discuss the motif of the hostile brothers, and an account of the forefather as a historical individual. Neumann (1934/2015) termed this merger of a historical individual's account with collective mythological material *secondary mythologizing* (p. 67). He explained that "the actual purpose of drawing upon midrashic literature is to reveal the close linkage between archetypal symbolism and the fundamental text" (p. 20). Thus, he presented the midrash as the bridge between the mythological collective perspective and the individual forefather as a personal perspective. Accordingly, Neumann saw the close relationship between the forefather's account and the midrash as "astonishingly intimate" (p. 20) and therefore found it critical that the midrash take the literal details into account.

In this assertion Neumann relied on Jung who "once remarked that myths could be considered to be the dreams of the people" (p. 19). As with dream work, we pay attention to all details as the unconscious is never wrong or accidental, and thus every detail in the dream bears some significance to the dreamer. Likewise, when the forefathers' accounts are perceived as the dream of the people across generations, each detail is of importance and needs to be interpreted in the midrash. On the other hand, each midrash was written by an individual, a disadvantage compensated for by the fact that the language used is symbolic, which makes this individual anonymous. Similarly, the experience of the forefathers and the prophets originates in the "anonymous primal source of the collective unconscious" (p. 23), and therefore it is to be seen as a mythological family story. Once this theoretical foundation of Neumann's interpretation is established, the analysis of the story as an individuation path can be better understood.

The Plot

Jacob and Esau are the biblical twin brothers, sons of Isaac and Rebekah. Esau was the first to be born, hairy and red, and in Hebrew, his name indicates that he was "ready" and "done." Jacob was born second, and in Hebrew, his name indicates that he is the one who follows and was holding Esau's heel. Isaac favored Esau, who grew to be a skillful hunter and man of the field, thus extraverted; while Rebekah favored Jacob, who became a herdsman – quiet tent dweller, introverted.

Esau agreed to exchange his primogeniture with Jacob for a dish of lentil soup and thus lost his birthright to Jacob. With the help of Rebekah, and in an act of deception, Jacob got Isaac's blessing and thus enraged Esau, who now hated his brother and wanted to slay him. Thus, the twins became hostile brothers. Jacob was fearful and fled to the wilderness. He slept there on the ground and dreamt the 'big dream' (known as the Ladder Dream) of a ladder between earth and sky, in which God assured him that he was the chosen one and carried the blessing. In return, Jacob vowed to reunite with his family.

After twenty years in "exile" in Harran, Jacob decided to go back and to encounter Esau. The night before encountering his brother, Jacob was detained by a stranger, with whom he struggled. He finally realized that the stranger was an angel of God, and that his adversary, inner and outer, was God. This transforming event influenced his reencounter with his brother Esau, who was no longer perceived as his adversary, but rather his twin brother.

Neumann's Analysis of the Biblical Story as an Individuation Path

When Neumann wrote *Jacob and Esau*, his sources were limited to the books he had at home, the knowledge in his mind, and maybe some research he was able to conduct. There is no doubt that his analysis was psychological, and thus, was not comprehensive from the Jewish perspective, as it was intended to elaborate on the original article by Rosenthal (1934) and centered on typology. In addition,

Neumann had an objective limitation, as does anyone who reads the Bible in translation: he was hindered by the Bible's extensive use of implied connections between words and their double meanings in the Hebrew language. Research conducted by a Hebrew speaker must consider further material currently available. From the wealth of Jewish and religious interpretation found in Hebrew, this chapter refers to the work of Jonathan Grossman (2017, 2018), an Israeli university professor of biblical studies, which offers a meaningful support, addition, or amplification to Neumann's line of analysis, that is, Jacob's psychological development, his individuation path.

Jacob and Esau as Opposites

Neumann (1934/2015) followed Jung in defining the fundamental problem of the human psyche as that of the opposites, manifested by the opposition between conscious and unconscious, which in his analysis is approached through the conflict between Jacob and Esau. He presented the story as it embodies the principle of the opposites, a twofold opposition within the human psyche—between conscious and unconscious, and the polarity within the unconscious itself—between the equal sides of creation and destruction, good and evil.

Understanding the midrash as an amplification of the forefathers' account into its mythological and symbolic meaning, Neumann embarked on his analysis using three midrashim (Hebrew plural of midrash) as the means to establish the symbolic opposition between Jacob and Esau as hostile twin brothers.

The first midrash describes the twins in their mother's womb and the division into two worlds, when Jacob says to his brother,

> Esau, my brother, there are two of us, and two worlds lie before us, one world on this side, another beyond. One world is where people eat and drink, a world of commerce and change; the otherworld, however, has none of this. If

it is your will then take this world, and I shall keep the otherworld for myself. (Neumann, 1934/2015, p. 3)

This symbolic conversation in the womb corresponds to the mythological original unity and the first division into the opposites. The unity of the twins is the one world, and the opposites are the primal division into two worlds: this world and the other world. Therefore, the division in the womb transforms the twins into the motif of the brothers. In addition, the opposition is between the outside world with its symbolism representing Esau and the inner "other" world with symbolism representing Jacob.

The second midrash Neumann uses is rather simple: "When he created the world, the Lord decided that the sun world be Esau's kingdom and the moon Jacob's" (Neumann, 1934/2015, p. 3). Neumann uses this to establish Jacob's connection to the moon and Esau to the sun. He indicates how the moon is significant for Jacob as the representation of the Jew.

The third midrash refers to the two faces of Isaac. Esau drew strength from the one turning outward as profane; the other face, Jacob drew strength from, is sacred and turning inward. Shalit (2016), who spoke the Hebrew language, explained that one needs to be acquainted with the Hebrew language to fully grasp the imagery embedded in the midrashim. He suggested a further elaboration of the last midrash Neumann uses when he pointed to the uniqueness of the word "face," *panim* in Hebrew. Unlike most Hebrew words which are gendered, *panim* refers both to feminine and masculine, singular and plural. In addition, with a minor change, the word *panim* becomes *pnim*, which means inward or *ponim*, meaning "to turn." Therefore, the use of the word "face" in this midrash is charged with meaning beyond the literal. Lastly, Shalit pointed to what Jung (1921/1990) wrote in the definitions of *Psychological Types*, "I call the outer attitude, the outward face, the *persona*; the inner attitude, the inward face, I call the *anima*" (p. 467). Along this line, Esau represents the outer persona whereas Jacob represents the inner feminine aspect, the anima.

As an indication of the origin of Neumann's subsequent theory (of a new ethic) is his analysis of the aspect of Isaac's inner face strengthening Jacob:

> Jacob, the Jew, looks inward, toward YHWH and his inner demand . . . YHWH is "inside" and appears only to the inward-facing gaze . . . it is precisely the demand for interioriz
> ation that is clearly Jewish . . . a decisive feature of Judaism. The radical prophetic demand for an orientation within the human heart toward the inner voice, toward the voice of God, toward the law that is placed within him. (Neumann, 1934/2015, p. 4)

Here Neumann points to the pivotal element of Judaism, which is also a pivotal aspect of depth psychology: the orientation inward, toward the inner world and into the depth of psyche. Neumann explains that the inner-looking gaze of Jacob as the Jew refers to the introversion of the Jews in opposition to the people of the world, of extraversion (the initial idea from Rosenthal's (1934) essay that Neumann further elaborated). The midrash used by Grossman (2017) teaches that for the Jewish people Jacob the forefather represents the Israelites in the diaspora.

In taking up the idea of inward orientation, Neumann establishes a key concept he returns to in *New Ethic* (Neumann, 1949/1990): the Jewish concept of the *inner voice* as the voice of God, which in Jungian terms would be the Self, calling from within to orient oneself to one's true path. Neumann emphasized that the orientation to within, to the voice of God, is also an orientation to an to an inner authority, inner law. In his theory, this is exactly the essence of the new ethic, a law springing from within, from the inner voice, and directing one toward the true deed, at times in complete opposition to the outside law. Neumann (1934/2015) writes: "Also part of this context is the crucial task of safeguarding this inner orientation and this chosenness, along with the tendency not to commingle with the world and not to lose oneself to it" (p. 4). Neumann refers to the uniqueness of Jacob as the chosen one, an aspect that became even more important in his formulation of a new ethic. The voice that the chosen one is called to follow is a call for individuation and separation from the refuge of the collective's morality.

As a testimony to the way these ideas lived and developed in Neumann's thinking, ten years later, in 1943, in a lecture titled "Stages of Religious Experience and the Path of Depth Psychology" (Neumann, 1970/1988), he emphasized that this orientation inward is not to be seen as an inferiority: "Only gradually it became clear that the turn inward, introversion, was not a step backward, a regression, but the way to another world whose reality was equally valid to that of the outside world" (p. 13). These thoughts may be seen as an echo of Jung's assertion (1928/1972a) that the psychic movement of regression is not to be seen necessarily as involution or degeneration; rather as a developmental phase.

Neumann (1934/2015) then used another midrash in which God admits to the moon that the other world is greater than this world. If so, the moon asks, should he (the moon) be accordingly greater than the sun? In response to this wish for power, God punishes the moon by causing him to be much smaller than the sun. The midrash says that God did this because he found the moon's craving for power to be "doing evil against the sun" (p. 6). The moon and the sun, Neumann suggested, are the original introversion and extraversion; thus, the smallness of the moon becomes the inferiority of the introvert. As the moon is the introverted Jacob, his introversion becomes his inferiority in face of Esau's extraversion. In this sense, Jacob and Esau as the pair of opposites represent the opposition between the inner voice and the outer hand of action as in the biblical story: "The voice is Jacob's voice, but the hands are the hands of Esau" (Gen. 27:22). In summary, Shalit (2015a) wrote that it is "the sense of inferiority, fear and threat that invisible interiority experiences in relation to the hands of action and the skills of the extraverted" (p. xxii). I suggest that Isaac perceived the two opposites existing in one entity as a biblical manifestation of the symbolic possibility of unity existing in man.

The Shadow

Moving toward the essence of confronting the shadow, Neumann (1934/2015) presents another midrash in which a much deeper interpretation of the difference in size is found between the moon and the sun. As in the previous midrash, the moon asks God whether the two worlds he created are equal, and God replies by making the moon smaller. Nevertheless, this midrash goes further when the moon accuses God of dividing the world and of "breaking" the unity, an accusation addressed in the text as a "true word" (p. 8). Since the moon did speak a "true word," God offers a consolation. Neumann writes, "The consolation that God offers the moon—that it shall rule day and night—evidently does not appease the moon" (p. 8), and the rejection of the consolation causes God to demand the sacrifice of a goat at each renewal of the moon.

This midrash contains a twofold elaboration of the opposition conflict. In the first instance, the subject at hand is elevated to a higher level, beyond the personal matter of the moon. The "true word" introduces the opposition of the two worlds, and thus the conflict is between the sacred inner world and profane outer world. In the second instance, the conflict becomes a matter between the sun as consciousness and the moon as the unconscious, and the question of who is greater is solved as the moon will rule day and night. To indicate the depth of this statement, Neumann pointed to

Jung's assertion and quoted from his letter (Jung & Neumann, 2015, p. 58), saying that the sun, as the exterior, has a great power indeed, whereas the moon, the inner as the invisible, only seems powerless but actually is the ruler and is as powerful as the sun. Consequently, from this assertion by Jung, Neumann (1934/2015) arrived at his important formulation: "Incidentally, this fact can be appreciated only by those who have grown aware of the extent to which the outer stems from the inner, and who see through the outer to the inner standing behind it" (p. 9). Neumann follows Jung here with the symbolic use of the words. The inner represents the introverted unconscious moon, which seems smaller than the outer representing the extraverted conscious sun. The inner is concealed and thus seems smaller and weaker, although in fact it is much powerful.

Shalit (2015a) suggested in this statement that we can see the seed of the thought that led Neumann formulating the important concept of the *ego-Self axis* (p. xxii). Indeed, the essence of the ego-Self axis, which is central to Neuman's theory and to Part II, is that the ego emerges out of the Self to forever remain dependent upon it as a source. Throughout Neumann's initial writings, the development of this idea is apparent, first evolving into formulations of the relationship between ego and Self, and finally arriving at the term *ego-Self axis*, which is Neumann's profound contribution to the analytical dialogue of child developmental theory. Neumann (1934/2015) points to one more relevant aspect of this midrash: "Since God's remorse did not return the moon to its original size, this suggests that the moon has raised a correct question, a question that remains to be answered" (p. 9). As the moon plays a central role in the Jewish sacrifice ritual, Neumann approaches the answer through the ritual of sacrificing the goat. In the plea made while the ritual took place, he finds an unexpected new motif: "Besides the diminution of the moon, which is related to the opposition between the moon and the sun, there in now the problem of its darkening, its opacity" (p. 11).

This inner opacity of the moon needed to be elucidated and so Neumann follows relevant Jewish literature that Shalit (2015a) described as "tying together the symbolism of Jacob, the moon, the angels (both good and evil) and Esau, and the ritual sacrifice, as well as the banishment of the goat, the scapegoat" (p. xxiii). Neumann refers to the Jewish Atonement Day ritual (performed at the temple in Jerusalem), which deals with the projection of evil and shadow. The essence of the ritual was that much was drawn to determine the fate of two goats; one was to be sacrificed to God, and the other was the scapegoat carrying the people's sins to the desert, Azazel, where the demons reside. The ritual indicates a yet undeveloped consciousness, as it entails a projection and concretization of the evil and sins on the goat (Neumann, 1934/2015, p. 53). In addition, Neumann points out that embedded in this ritual is "a polarity between YHWH and Azazel" (p. 13), referring to an early consciousness developmental stage in which the division between positive and negative prevails. Neumann theorizes that the rituals were practiced when humanity was still at the collective unconscious level. In this case, it is a *participation mystique* with an animal, a concretization via projection of inner content—the evil, sins, and shadow within on an outer world object—in this case, a goat. Therefore, the moral conflict is resolved by the sacrifice of the goat.

Neumann (1934/2015) returns to the opacity of the moon and explains that as the moon represents Jacob, the opacity is within Jacob. He theorizes that this motif of the opaque moon shifts the problem from the outside to the inside as a moral problem, and the darkening by evil becomes an inner Edom. In the Hebrew language *Edom* means red, symbolizing sin, and Esau was red; therefore, an inner Edom is one's shadow. Neumann (1934/2015) explores the connection between the diminution of the moon, as a representation of the two worlds, and its opacity as a moral problem, as the answer to the moon's "true word." He finds the answer in the text itself; that is, the opposition between Jacob and Esau also exists within Jacob. Indeed, the unconscious has both positive and negative aspects, creativity and destruction, and therefore, as Jacob represents the introvert, the unconscious as moon, the opacity of the moon is the shadow within Jacob. This means that, for Jacob, there is an outer Esau brother, an opposition that is a real threat to the promise and the blessing; nevertheless, there is also an inner Esau, an opposition within, an obscuring shadow. Neumann (1934/2015), like Rosenthal (1934), reverted to Jung's typology:

> For there is no such thing as pure introvert or extravert, because each of these attitudes is one-sided and incomplete. Instead, all persons carry within themselves an attitude in opposition to their dominant one. This opposition attitude, however, is undeveloped and primitive, at work as an inferior function. (p. 15)

Therefore, Jacob the introvert clearly carries an inferior extraversion in the image of Esau. Moreover, Neumann emphasized that the inferior function always resides in the darkness of the unconscious, as the other half of the conscious personality, and therefore in the shadow. In a later work, Neumann (1948/1989) returned to Jung's typology to illuminate the extent to which the introvert is threatened by the outside world and therefore is doomed to project his own shadow on it:

> The introvert's fear of the world and inability to live in the world becomes ascetic world renunciation; he projects his own inferior, extraverted side into the image of a world that has all the qualities of hell, a world surrendered to the devil . . . a God-forsaken world. (p. 399)

This explains how negative and powerful the image of Esau was for Jacob, as it was indeed a combination of an objective introverted fear from the threatening world, which Esau represented, with the subjective projection of inner shadowed content on him. Important to notice that in the original biblical story, Jacob is the hero and Esau's story is told in only a few sentences. Indeed, the Jewish biblical story presents Jacob's perspective, but essentially it does not dehumanize Esau.

As the opacity of the moon represents the moral problem of the inferior side, Neumann (1934/2015) concludes that "Christianity and Judaism both sought to resolve (the moral conflict) by sacrificing the inferior, by exterminating evil, and by the sacrificing of the goat" (p. 17). This is, of course, Neumann's critique, claiming that both Judaism and Christianity offer the resolution of the conflict originating with problem of the opposites on the lower level of consciousness development, implying a projection and concretization of the shadow. As the concretization ritual is to be performed until the messianic era, the moral process of projecting and splitting becomes infinite.

Neumann arrives at his main point regarding projection in the story of Jacob and Esau to posit that psychologically one projects his inferiority mostly and preferably on those closest to him. At first, Jacob does not experience his own inferiority. Instead, he projects his inner Edom-Esau on the outer Esau-Edom. The moral problem, symbolized by the opaque moon, is the first and initial step in overcoming this projection as it marks the emerging of awareness of the one-sided position and the possibility of similarity between what one sees outside and does not see inside. Along the same lines, Neumann (1934/2015) continues his analysis of the biblical story: "As soon as this (projection) does not happen and one confronts one's own problem, the projection is withdrawn and the actual image of the Other becomes visible" (p. 18). Here Neumann suggested that the powerlessness of the moon, that is, Jacob's powerlessness, has a moral cause; it is due to his inner weakness. This brings the discussion into the personal realm once again as now it is no longer an issue of two worlds but rather a moral problem of the introvert. Neumann asserts that with this conjunction of the personal with the suprapersonal (or in Jungian words, the personal with the archetypal), that is, when Jacob the individual addresses the archetypal problem of opposites, he takes the second step toward overcoming his primitive experience of Esau. This statement made by Neumann strongly echoes what is true in Jungian analysis when the ability to symbolize and relate to the archetypal level becomes the foundation of psychological transformation.

The psychological implication of this part of Neumann's analysis entails overcoming the split and the projection of the shadow by addressing the moral problem and the problem of the opposites. Previously, the analysis of the story revealed that the opposition between the worlds also exists within the psyche as the opposition between conscious and unconscious. Proceeding from that, Neumann describes the relationship between the conscious and unconscious as having a twofold significance. He describes a central concept of his theory, the ego-Self axis. This entails a form of relationship in which the inner is greater than the outer and stands behind it; that is, the ego emerges from the Self and forever remains dependent upon it. On the other hand, by following the midrashic symbolism, he describes the other aspect of the opposition within, that of the shadow. In the early stages of consciousness development, both for humanity and an individual, a split between inner and outer entails the projection of the cast-off inner on the outer. The psychological meaning of this stage is a distorted perception of the other, as an anchor of projection, just as Jacob perceived Esau as a representation of the outer real threat of the world and at the same time a carrier of Jacob's projection of his shadowed inferiority. To overcome the projection, Neumann asserts, one needs to confront the moral conflict, acknowledging his own inferiority in order to recollect his projections and enable an objective perception of the other.

The Scheme and the Flight

As Neumann (1934/2015) continued his analysis, he attended to the contradictory combination of Jacob's inferiority and his chosenness. Although Esau was first to be born, Rebekah, his mother and the feminine figure, intuited and recognized Jacob's inherent right to the blessing and therefore helped him receive it by deception. Neumann interpreted "Rebekah's instigation" (p. 24) to be activated by her son Jacob's inferior shadowed side, as he was her favorite son and she identified with his projection on Esau. Therefore, although Neumann did not mention this, it is interesting to note in this part of the story Jacob's shadow becomes significant to the process as, like Prometheus and other heroes, he is compelled to act cunningly and faultily in order to attain what he needs to proceed on the path of individuation. The act of breaking the law symbolizes the departure and separation from the collective, a necessary act to become an individual and thus a milestone of the individuation process.

To add significance to Rebekah's role, Grossman (2017) pointed out that both Isaac and Rebekah sent Jacob away from his home and family of origin, each using a different name for the same destination. Rebekah knew Jacob was in danger and encouraged him to flee as a refugee to Harran. Unaware of Rebekah's scheme and thinking of Jacob as Esau, Isaac proudly sent him on his journey to Paddan Aram (the same place but with a different name). When the scripture describes Jacob's departure, the destination is given the name Rebekah used, Harran, indicating that Jacob departed on his journey perceiving himself from his mother's perspective as a refugee and therefore having a mentality of weakness and helplessness. Grossman also points out that, although Jacob could rest the night in a guesthouse, the scripture says that, "when he reached *a certain place*, he stopped for the night" (Gen. 28:11, emphasis added), meaning that the place is not named to indicate its insignificance. Also, preparing to sleep on the ground, Jacob used "one of the stones" (Gen. 28:11), indicating that the stone he put under his head was also indefinite. At the lowest point of his life, feeling mentally weak and helpless and as a refugee in the wilderness resting on the ground with a stone under his head, Jacob fell asleep and dreamed.

Jacob's Ladder Dream

In the dream, there is a ladder between heaven and earth, with "the angels of God ascending and descending on it" (Gen. 28:12–15). God is above it, and he makes a clear, specific, and detailed promise to Jacob, leaving no doubt that he is the chosen one, the blessed one, who carries the promise. Moreover, as Grossman (2017) explained, God's promise in this dream is identical to his promise to Abraham, which is more comprehensive than his promise to Isaac. In summary, Neumann (1934/2015) wrote, "If there is any doubt about Jacob's entitlement to primogeniture, to the promise and to the blessing, then this legitimacy is confirmed once and for all by his famous dream at Bethel" (p. 20).

Jacob's ladder dream is what in Jungian psychology is termed a 'big dream,' which Jung (1928/1972b) described as instinctively recognized for its significance and its origin from a "different level" (1946/1991, p. 118). In Neumann's later work written in 1943, "The Stages of Religious Experience and the Path of Depth Psychology" (Neumann (1970/1988)) describes the process of analysis in terms of ego revelations and experiences with regard to the progressive stages and referred to those kinds of dreams as a religious experience, typical of a forefather:

> Only rarely, and then at times of great crisis, does the editor (Self) disregard a lack of understanding in consciousness and break through the defensive barricade of the ego. Then, suddenly, a "great dream" breaks into the life of a

man who "never dreams" and now, startled by this address, begins to listen attentively. (p. 24)

Jacob's dream is precisely the kind of dream Neumann describes here; it appeared at a time of extreme distress and it manifested a life changing event in the sense that Jacob was called to attend, own, and mostly fulfill his chosenness and blessedness.

The first notable elements in the dream are the ladder and the angels. Neumann (1934/2015) interprets the angels ascending and descending between heaven and earth as the emergence of the creativity within the shadow amid the movement "between the son's ego-consciousness on the one hand and the mother's collective unconscious on the other" (p. 51). Thus, Neumann describes the essential idea of the axis between ego and Self, which he later termed the ego-Self axis. In this dream, although he had not used the term yet, he describes the ladder as such that is the axis. When well structured, the axis enables a free flow of contents to move between consciousness and unconscious, ego and Self, and vice versa. In addition to these two elements of the dream, there is also the fact that Jacob experienced it while on the run. As noted earlier, Neumann believed that every detail of the story is relevant, that is, if we take it as mythology and treat it as a dream. Therefore, he drew attention to the fact that in the narrative of the story, Jacob experienced the dream while he was at the lowest point of his life thus far:

Jacob flees to a foreign land as an utterly forlorn, miserable, and defenseless individual. He is exposed to a world that is unimaginably hostile, and this experience doubtless fills his consciousness. Under these circumstances, his dream . . . provides him with crucial and magnificent compensation . . . It is precisely his powerlessness that plainly reveals to him the central position occupied by the one who bears the promise. At this moment, he realizes that as the chosen one, as the bearer of the promise, he and also later his people will always be inferior to the multitude. (p. 21)

The significance of the encounter with a big dream at a time of distress, explains Neumann, is the understanding that being chosen and carrying a promise comes with a sense of fear and foreignness. The understanding emerging from this interpretation may have held personal significance for Neumann, who at the time was a foreign immigrant, and somewhat in fear, who was called to lead as he testified in his letter to Jung. Neumann suggested that this dream had a psychological compensatory element for Jacob as he experienced such a significantly positive and confirming big dream in a time of negative circumstances. This psychological assertion by Neumann is confirmed by Grossman (2017), who used midrashic text to analyze the use of the Hebrew language and elucidate it: In English the scripture says "then Jacob continued his journey" (Gen. 29:1), which seems insignificant. Nevertheless, in Hebrew the sentence is constructed to indicate that Jacob was feeling light, and he easily walked away, supporting Neumann's psychological interpretation and corroborating the compensatory element of the dream.

Grossman (2017) noted that, upon waking up the next morning, under the influence of the confirming dream, Jacob acknowledged that what he thought to be an indefinite place in the wilderness actually was "the house of God, this is the gate to heaven" (Genesis, 28:17), and the wild indefinite stones he "set it up as a pillar" (Genesis, 28:18). These two transformations are significant as they both relate to the theme of the two worlds, the sacred and the profane, and the transformation between them. They also indicate the profound influence of the dream on Jacob.

From a close reading of the scripture, Grossman (2017) asserted that, although God's promise to Jacob was as big and comprehensive as his promise to Abraham, Jacob's vows were much narrower and somewhat scanty, relating to his immediate life and not to his distant future, thus indicating his distressed situation. Concerning the dream, Grossman (2017) said, "This is not just another revelation of God, this is *a* revelation, and Jacob ignores the historical drama embedded in it" (author's translation). Whereas God promises Jacob his descendants' survival and the concrete land, Jacob, who was troubled by his conflict with his brother, limited his wish to return to his family of origin, to his vows, and the aid he sought from God was thus minimal as opposed to the big promise. This point has a twofold significance: it amplifies the theme of the opposites—heaven and earth, sacred and profane—and, it indicates that Jacob wanted to reconcile with Esau and he knew he needed God's help in order to achieve this reconciliation.

In terms of individuation, it seems that the dream suggests that once given a meaning, the profane reveals the sacred within it. In psychological developmental terms, this would mean the revelation of the Self by the ego. In addition, one needs to define his individuality and uniqueness as a separation from the collective, whether represented by one's family, community, nation, or culture.

Interestingly, although not a psychologist by profession, nor a Jungian, Grossman (2017) nevertheless, holds a Jungian perspective, and thus, concluded his lecture asserting the importance of the dream: "We learn, that one should remember, particularly at times of extreme distress, that a wider history awaits, and eventually, also a ladder between earth to heaven" (author's translation).

Reencountering Esau

The culmination of Jacob's individuation process is the transformation he undergoes through the events surrounding his reencounter with Esau. Although the years following the ladder dream were not interpreted by Neumann (1934/2015), he did mention what is obvious from the literal story, "that his encounters with the outside world are all negative. The world confronts him as his fiercest, wildest, and most daunting antagonist in the guise of his brother Esau" (p. 23).

Jacob had a challenging life story, which Neumann describes as leading to his fear of Esau both as the real older, stronger brother he was, representing the extraverted world threatening the introvert, and as a projection of the inner Esau, that is, his fear of his own inferiority and shadow. In Jacob's story, the traces of his shadow are easily recognized, beginning with receiving the blessing from Isaac and ending with his deception of Laban with the sheep. Therefore, Neumann pointed to a discrepancy between Jacob 'the promise' and his personality, which at the time was yet undeveloped, one-sided, introverted, and still splitting and projecting the shadow. Here Neumann drew extensively from Jung's typology to describe Jacob's experience of the world: "The introvert repeatedly and unforgettably experiences how great is the danger of what most matters to him being destroyed, even annihilated, by the pointless violence of worldly events" (Neumann, 1934/2015, p. 24).

After twenty years with Laban and realizing Laban had taken advantage of him, Jacob decided to pursue the fulfillment of God's promise by returning to Canaan with his wives and children. Neumann observed that, "For Jacob, whose inner life has for decades been concerned with the dream at Bethel, Esau must have become a more serious problem than his family" (p. 24). This, on the one hand, explains the significance of reencountering Esau for Jacob, yet on the other hand it explains his fears and anxiety. Indeed, using midrashim and current Jewish interpretations, Grossman (2018) described Jacob as confused and in turmoil. Moreover, knowing that his brother was coming with 400 people, he was, as the scripture says, "in great fear and distressed" (Genesis, 32:7). As Jacob was unsure about the nature of the expected encounter, he prepared himself for both a fight or a reconciliation.

Grossman (2018) points to a highly important and significant aspect of the next event, which is apparent only through close reading of the text in Hebrew. Although the English version twice says that Jacob "spent the night," which does not necessarily mean he went to sleep, the Hebrew scripture twice notes that Jacob went to sleep. Then both English and Hebrew scripture say that he woke up in the middle of the night and moved the camp of his loved ones across the river. Grossman elucidates this is an indication of Jacob's troubles, as he went to bed but couldn't sleep. Furthermore, using midrashim and further interpretations, Grossman describes a map of the rivers at the point the scripture mentions to show with a very high probability that Jacob was not moving the camp toward Esau but rather, he was moving away from Esau in order to use the river as a barrier against Esau's troops in case of a fight. According to Grossman, "these interpretations are telling us that Jacob was fleeing. He was so very nervous . . . about the expected confrontation that he could not sleep and at the middle of the night decided to flee with his camp" (author's translation).

Grossman explains that since Jacob was on the run again, God had no other choice but to make sure he was detained from the flight, and he confronted Esau saying, "this is the proof of God keeping his promise, he symbolically says to Jacob—I will not let you run away from this conflict" (author's translation). This rather modern interpretation sheds a different light on the encounter with the stranger, supporting Neumann's psychological analysis. On the one hand, the stranger was indeed a threat to Jacob as he was physically holding him and preventing him from running; thus, as a concrete threat the stranger was a representation of Esau. On the other hand, this is a meaningful aspect of the journey of all heroes—the call to "confront" the dragons, as one cannot develop unless he confronts his greatest fears.

The struggle with the stranger was a physical encounter, and it is clear Jacob was not defeated. Thus, to prevent him from running away, the stranger, as God's executor, was compelled to wound Jacob. The wound itself and the following dialogue between Jacob and the adversary/stranger were interpreted differently by Neumann (1934/2015) and Grossman (2018), presumably due to Neumann's limited sources at the time of writing. Neumann (1934/2015) interpreted the wound as a negative outcome of the struggle, although he did point out that "the fact that Jacob limps is an archetypal trait— one that he shares with an array of mythological heroes" (p. 27)— and assumed, as the text is commonly read, that the stranger asked to be let go and Jacob asked for a blessing in return.

Based on reading the text in Hebrew, Grossman (2018) introduced another linguistically equal reasonable possibility. In this alternate interpretation, it was not the stranger but rather Jacob who asked to be freed to go, and he greeted the angel rather than blessing him (in Hebrew, the same word is used for greeting and blessing— and it is for the reader to choose between the different meanings). Grossman's interpretation emphasizes Jacob's experience of the revelation. On the one hand, the dawn alerted Jacob, who understood that he could not run from Esau—it was too late; the stranger had detained him. On the other hand, Jacob knew that the encounter with Esau was a part of his promise and vow, and lastly the "stranger" had avoided revealing his name. This was therefore the moment of revelation in which Jacob collected his projections, integrated and assimilated his shadow, and saw the adversary "other," the stranger, as the individual he was. At once, Jacob realized he was struggling with God, and the realization was fundamentally transformative, as the angel renamed Jacob as Israel.

In his later work, Neumann (1948/1989) wrote, regarding the numinous experience, "The scope of the revelation in which the numen can manifest itself is contingent on the scope of the personality which receives the revelation" (p. 394). Therefore, Jacob was psychologically ready for such a meaningful revelation and the next stage of his individuation process. In addition, as Jacob's transformation was so radical, Neumann (1934/2015) asserted that the struggle with the stranger was more than just Jacob's personal confrontation with his moral problem. This struggle embedded a collective level of meaning from which emerges "an altered notion of God" (p. 25). Jacob surmounts the opposites by recognizing the stranger as Esau, the inner, and the outer as God.

Expanding on Neumann's assertion, Shalit (2015a) wrote, "Jacob's personal shadow has here merged with the archetypal antagonist. Shadow and Self have merged and become one" (p. xxvi). Once Jacob realized that he had been wounded by God, the wound became a concrete touch by God. Neumann elucidated that the physical wound reveals how real this experience is, and Grossman (2018) postulated that Jacob's limp became the evidence of this numinous experience, in which he incarnated the encounter point between heaven (God) and earth (body). A touch by God, as a numinous experience, must lead to a transformation. Jacob as forefather is both a mythological figure and a person. Therefore, the renaming as Neumann suggested, indicates both the reality of the event and its significance in terms of the personality transformation that occurred.

Neumann (1948/1989) developed the idea of Jacob's trans-formation beyond the forefathers' accounts into an individual's numinous experience, describing its transformative effect on the ego: "In every confrontation of the ego with the numinous, a situation arises in which the ego goes 'outside itself'; it falls or is wrenched out of its shell of consciousness and can return 'to itself' only in changed form" (p. 381). This is the essence of the transformation in terms of the relation between the ego and the Self. It is the highest point of the event, and it is exactly here that Neumann (1934/2015) recognizes the radical change in relation to the shadow, which up to this point was projected and sacrificed, and from this point forward was assimilated. He writes, "Whereas the customary Judo-Christian solution to this problem is to sacrifice the inferior and negative, here something fundamentally different, indeed crucially opposite, happens" (p. 26). It is through this aspect, the step beyond the projection and sacrifice, that Neumann presents the biblical story as an individuation process. Interestingly, the fundamental difference is embedded in the text. Not only does Neumann's interpretation indicate a crucial stage of individuation, but it also significantly elevates the common reading of the story. Presenting this advanced developmental stage as Jewish psychology, could have been (had the manuscript been published) a very good counterpoint to the anti-Semitic perception at the time.

Regarding Esau, Grossman (2018) explains that the midrashim illuminated Esau's perspective, indicating that he was unsure about the nature of the encounter and that he had used the four hundred people as a security shield. Nevertheless, interestingly, those midrashim interpret Esau as having been influenced by Jacob-Israel's transformation, as in a sense the angel was Esau, and thus he was transformed as well. In psychological terms, that would mean that the fact that the projection was withdrawn allowed Esau to withdraw his projective identification (i.e., his negative and threatening traits had ceased, and it was easier for him to act differently). Neumann (1934/2015) elucidates the way the encounter was affected by Jacob's transformation:

> The way in which he avoids moving on with Esau is also cunning, but it is no longer a partly malicious case of fraud, an unconscious inferior function at work. It is instead a conscious human action, that is, a successful adjustment to a fully recognized reality. Esau is a factor that Jacob must

deal with, a different kind of human being, rather than a demon and a fear-inspiring brute. (p. 27)

When encountering Esau in the morning, Jacob, who was still under the strong influence of the night's occurrences, was already transformed and acted consciously and responsibly according to the reality that he now objectively perceived. This description was echoed in Neumann's later writings about the new ethic. Surprisingly for Jacob-Israel, the story says, "But Esau ran to meet him and embraced him and fell on his neck and kissed him, and they wept" (Gen. 33:4). Jacob-Israel received a warm welcoming hug from his brother and a gentle rejection of his gifts. Surprised and transformed as he was, Jacob-Israel said to Esau, "for I have seen your face, which is like seeing the face of God, and you have accepted me" (Gen. 33:10). This is the highest point of Jacob-Israel's transformation, when he recognized that the shadow, the adversary, is God.

About this culmination point, Neumann (1934/2015) writes,

The conscious assimilation of the shadow side leads partly to its sacrifice, to its detoxification, and to its disempowerment. The acknowledgment of the principle of duality has weakened Jacob's shadow and its negative assertiveness, on which he has been forced to rely on various occasions. This reliance can be felt in Jacob's humility toward Esau, along with the important fact that he stands in awe of Esau as a symbol of his experience of the other side of God. (p. 28)

In these words, Neumann describes Jacob as the mature "individuated" personality who encounters the revelation as a numinous and humbling experience, having been exposed to the shadow in such way that its assimilation within his psychic unity enabled the termination of his projections. For years preceding the writing of this manuscript, Neumann (1952/1989) described this kind of numinous experience as one that is enabled by the ego-Self axis of the Great Individual, whose personality sphere has sunk into the Self-field (p. 56).

The Conclusion of Jacob's Journey

Neumann (1934/2015) saw Jacob-Israel as the Jewish example of a forefather, manifested as a Great Individual who was able to go the further step and progress beyond projection. To signify the importance of this final step he wrote, "only the shadow, and the compulsion to accept it, turns the bearer of the principal of consciousness into an individual" (p. 52). Nonetheless, Neumann was not blind to his people, and although he saw Jacob as a representation of both the Jew and the Jewish people, he also analyzed him as a forefather and a mythological figure, which represents that which we aim at rather than that which we are.

In the story of Jacob and Esau, God fulfills his promise and appears as the Almighty. Neumann was indeed a Jew, proud of his origins and faithful to the future of his people, but he was not blind to the shadowed parts of his heritage or to the anti-Semitism prevailing in Europe. In one of his first letters to Jung, written from Tel Aviv at the end of 1934, Neumann (Jung & Neumann, 2015) passionately and critically defended the Jewish perception of God:

> The Old Testament is an incredibly "liberal-minded" book, definitely not written by demeaned and insulted men. The fact that it repeatedly has as its central points the inner aspect, the efficacy of Y.H.W.H., is no revenge for defeats. The emphasis lies on the efficacy of Y.H.W.H. in world history, in world events in general. This is not to be understood in the primitive sense in which the good always win through, it was never intended in this way, but in the way that the structure of the world and of man

centrally aims at "meaning." If the destiny of the individual is recognized as meaningful through individuation, then this is the same thing in microcosmos. Even here the issue is that there is no dualism for the processing, but that every negative and meaningless thing is made meaningful through its incorporation into the life context that has become meaningful. In this way, "evil" is only a "servant of God." The negative external aspect is precisely being dependent on the world. (p. 65)

This is a very deep and mature perception of YHWH, and astonishingly, these words were written when Neumann was only 29 years of age.

The following years were the black days and the abyss of the history of modern man. During the Second World War, about 40 million civilians, minorities, and marginalized communities were murdered. Six million of Jacob-Israel's descendants, Neumann's father among them, were cruelly and brutally slaughtered in an attempted annihilation, in what seemed to be the worst possible manifestation of evil. Was Neumann writing these things about the Jewish Y.H.W.H, as a mystic prediction of what was coming? Or were they the seed and the forerunner of his "small book" (Jung & Neumann, 2015, p. 254), *New Ethic* (Neumann, 1949/1990), written before, during, and after—presumably not least as a consequence of—the massacre of the Holocaust?

Chapter 4
Attending the Inner Voice - New Ethic

The Background
From *Jacob and Esau* to *New Ethic*

The psychological analysis of the biblical story of Jacob and Esau was Neumann's first step as he embarked on the journey into the realm of a much wider framework emerging from his psyche as a part of his individuation process. At the peak point of his analysis, Neumann articulates the psychological experience of Jacob's encounter with evil and the catharsis of acknowledging evil as the "other" face of God. For Neumann, interpreting evil in terms of psychological processes was an acute revelation before articulating this theme in later writings. In a letter to Jung regarding *New Ethic*, he confesses: "this small book was not really conceived from the head" (Jung & Neumann, 2015, p. 254). Neumann revealed the intimate relationship he had with the written content, which was for him much more than theory. The book was the precursor of what was destined to occupy him during the coming decade, and it was what Jung and he referred to in their correspondence as "Jewish psychology."

Neumann wrote *Jacob and Esau* (1934/2015) when he first arrived in Tel Aviv, and Jung's writings were new to him but nevertheless very familiar. Throughout the text, Neumann constantly referred to Jung as his psychological source. This becomes significant when trying to trace the seeds of his theorizing about a new ethic and where they were planted in Neumann's mind. When discussing the relation between the forefather and the people, Neumann cited Jung from his foreword to the article "On the Psychology of the Unconscious," originally written in 1917. Clearly, Neumann had read this article in which, interestingly, Jung discussed morality as a human instinct (1943/1972, pp. 26–27). Jung's articulation in this article seems to be the seed that later grew to become Neumann's formulation of the new ethic, indicating that he had assimilated this content. Neumann's later elaboration in the manuscript of *New Ethic* (1949/1990) was written through his developmental lens. The four paragraphs written by Jung (1943/1972, para. 28–31), summarize Neumann's later formulation, and they point to the affinity between Jung's writings and Neumann's elaborations, and therefore, explain Jung's passionate support of Neumann's.

Nevertheless, it seems that there might be an even deeper seed of a new ethic in Neumann's mind, and it is rooted close to his acquaintance with Jung. As mentioned earlier, although Neumann wrote his analysis of Kafka's "The Trial" (Neumann, 1933/1979) prior to becoming a depth psychologist, it is a depth psychological account. Kron and Weiler (2013), who read the original German version, elucidate Neumann's use of a German word emphasizing the idea of "a dialog with oneself, with an other or more others. It means an effort to listen to the other side even when opinions are opposed, to come to understanding and wishing to find a solution respecting both sides." Therefore, Kafka's article dealing with contemplations, law, judgment, and court evoked Neumann's thinking in the direction of his later writings. Already in this early essay are found embedded the ideas of Other, integration of shadow, inner dialog, and inner voice. This was Neumann's fertile psychic ground on which Jung's theory was cultivated during the following years.

As described earlier, the analysis of Jacob's and Esau's story was one of Neumann's reactions to Jung's racist remarks: he was passionate to prove Jung wrong by illuminating the depth and wisdom of the Jewish exegesis and tradition. Presumably, the combination of his profound interest in the material he was articulating, the depth of the psychological perspective he had just lately acquired, his passionate nature, and the growing anti-Semitism in Europe all came together in his further writing about Judaism. Shalit (2016) reflected, "The interface between analytical psychology and Jewish exegesis was a flame that kept burning at Neumann's desk for years to come." Indeed, since writing about Jacob and Esau was rather a small project and did not consume much time, Neumann simultaneously (1933–1934) embarked on his next project, occupying him for the next decade and throughout the World War II: the two-volume book *Jewish Consciousness* (Neumann, 1935–1945/2019), which he decided not to publish at that time, but was eventually published in 2019. (*The Roots of Jewish Consciousness*, Neumann, 1940–1945/2019).

As time went by, the anti-Semitic atmosphere worsened, and the situation of the Jews in Europe became unbearable. Neumann and his wife Julie both had close family members still in Europe and thus for Neumann it was an extremely personal and acute experience of evil. A critical event in Neumann's biography, undoubtably influential but rarely mentioned, is the vicious murder of his father. In 1937, Neumann's father was investigated by Gestapo, during which he was severely beaten, to the point of brain hemorrhage, causing his death a few hours later. (Micha Neumann, private communication) This must have been devastating news for Neumann, who had settled safely in Tel Aviv. Beyond the loss of a father and the terror of the barbarian violence, it was a painful betrayal by his beloved Europe and a terrible, most painful personal encounter with evil, challenging his philosophical perspective of existential wholeness and the equality of evil in it, as evidenced in *Jacob and Esau*.

From a psychological perspective, it is impossible not to notice the interface between Neumann's inner and outer worlds. While Europe was burning in the hatred of Nazi anti-Semitism, Neumann demonstrated a passion to revive and elevate the depth, wisdom, and beauty of Judaism, which Ann Lammers (2019a) described as "an act of existential resistance" (p. xxvi).

Possibly, another powerful force at work under the surface as it relates to Neumann's passionate nature and strong activism, is what he referred to as his "Mars" (Jung & Neumann, 2015, p. 15). Since Neumann wrote that he saw himself as a warrior, it is understandable that his psychic defense mechanism was a tendency to attack rather than to retreat. I suggest that this tendency was at the root of a fundamental difference between Jung and Neumann in their perception of evil. These differences manifested in Neumann's formulation of a new ethic and Jung's "corrections and amendments" (Jung & Neumann, 2015, Appendix 3, pp. 361–369), as will be shown towards the end of this chapter.

At the end of 1945, after five years of silence, Neumann renewed his correspondence with Jung by sending him a letter and the first copy of *New Ethic* (1949/1990), which he wrote in 1942–1943 (Jung & Neumann, 2015, p. 191). Jung initially liked the book, approved it, and was willing to write a foreword and promote its publication; however, things moved slowly. In December 1948, Jung wrote to Neumann that his manuscript "stirred up the dust" in Zurich. Nevertheless, he wrote that Neumann's formulations were "brilliant and of incisive sharpness" (p. 237). In the next few weeks, the objections to the book among Jung's follower in Zurich were so extreme that Neumann withdrew it from publication through the Institute. Jung's followers and students in Zurich all had good, although unconscious, reasons to resent both Neumann and the book. First, Neumann was often envied due to the attention Jung gave to him and his work and the way he complimented Neumann's formulations. Second, the manuscript was easily misunderstood as a critique rather than a call for progression and development. Lastly, and significantly, a single note of blame could not be ignored in Neumann's (1949/1990) manuscript. In the introduction he wrote

> Those who saw and failed to act, those who looked away because they did not want to see, those who did not see although they could have seen, and those, too, whose eyes were unable to see—each and every one of these is actually in alliance with evil. We are all guilty—all peoples, all religions, all nations, all classes. Humanity itself is guilty. (p. 26)

Neumann blamed humanity. He wrote, "The murdered are also guilty—not only the murderer" (p. 26). Nevertheless, for most of Neumann's readers, this truth was too heavy to bear, and the guilt was projected on Neumann himself, just as he brilliantly described in the content following the introduction. In the first letter he wrote to Jung after their silence, he described the manuscript of *New Ethic* as his return to "pure psychology" (Jung & Neumann, 2015, p. 160). Presumably, although Neumann was not aware of it and surely did not describe it this way, the work on *New Ethic* was therapeutic for his psyche.

In February 1949 Neumann wrote to Jung that he had found a publisher. (Although the book's official publication date is 1949, it was already in circulation at the end of 1948). He asked Jung to write the foreword to the English edition. A month later, in March 1949, Jung wrote to Neumann that he agreed to write the foreword on the condition that Neumann accept more than a few of the changes he demanded, as mentioned above. Jung excused his demand by saying, "But it is very important to me that your text on the *Ethic* comes out in an *acceptable form* for its Anglo-Saxon audience" [emphasis added] (Jung & Neumann, 2015, p. 247). Presumably this indicates that Jung was not as interested in the book's innovation and new formulation as he was in its acceptance by the Anglo-Saxon audience.

Liebscher (2015a) referred to an interesting letter written by Jung to Cary Baynes in May 1949, in which he admitted having written the foreword but not sending it to Neumann yet because he demanded corrections in the text. He also admitted that Neumann did not accept most of the changes that he (Jung) presented as suggestions. Indeed, in the English edition, which was eventually published in 1969, Jung's foreword is dated March 1949. Jung both strengthened Neumann's argument but he also complimented him, saying, "The ethical aspect of this process of integration is described with praiseworthy clarity by the author" (Neumann, 1949/1990, p. 17). Apparently, Jung highly valued Neumann's formulations and even supported them, but he nevertheless was not as brave as Neumann and failed to stand by his promising student as firmly as was needed.

One last aspect about Neumann's personal relationship with the subject of *New Ethic* (1949-1990) and evil concerns the horrifying historical events of the time. Neumann knew beforehand that his manuscript about Jacob and Esau would not be published for circumstantial reasons. Therefore, once it was completed, he left it in his drawer and moved on with writing the two volumes of *Jewish Consciousness* (Neumann, 1935–1945/2019). The second volume, subtitled *Hasidism*, was written between 1935 and 1940 and was probably revised between 1940 and 1945, as Lammers (2019a, p. xxvi) suggested. Lammers' (2019b) hypothesis about the revisioning of the second volume may be at the core of *New Ethic*, which he testified was completed in 1943.

In a few copies of the second volume, the third chapter, "Life in This World," was missing. In this chapter Neumann presented the Hasidic teaching, which Jung also approved, that creation in its wholeness equally includes the shadow side, that is, evil. Lammers (2017) thoughtfully suggested that, by the time Neumann completed the second volume, the first and shocking photos from the Death Camps had come out, and, as an act of "empathic attunement" he chose not to speak this truth at that time. I suggest that Neumann needed some distance from this truth to be able to bear and assimilate it, as it confronted and contradicted his strong conviction about the role of evil, that it is equally as real as goodness and that both belong to this world. Moreover, from a psychological perspective, Neumann possibly needed to integrate his inner conviction about the equality of good and evil with the outer world impossibility of any goodness in the face of the horrific outbursts of evil. The integration of the two opposing realities meant finding a "third," in Jungian terms, which is indeed found in Neumann's formulations in *New Ethic*, in the form of what he described as an active approach of free will and ego-responsibility facing evil.

The Genesis of New Ethic

Almost ten years after *New Ethic* was first published at the end of 1948, Neumann recognized the influence of his formulation of a new ethic in Jung's published essay of 1957, "The Undiscovered Self" (Jung, 1957/1970). This must have been a victory for Neumann in view of the ordeals surrounding the publication of his manuscript. In a letter to Jung, Neumann wrote, "For if a reader of your work now asks himself, so what can actually be done, then he comes up against the problems that compelled me to this work back then in the Second World War" (Jung & Neumann, 2015, p. 324). Close reading of this sentence reveals that Neumann's primary motivation in his writings was that he needed to act in the face of evil. Neumann's warrior "Mars-like" nature manifested in his activism that sent him to fight, attack, and confront the negative aspects of life whether they were problems, obstacles, opponents, "hate of the pussyfooters" (p. 241) or the Nazis. In the same letter, Neumann revealed for the first time that the conception of the book and its genesis "were internal images where it was all about evil and the 'ape men' as destroyers, internally and externally" (p. 325). In saying this Neumann honestly revealed his personal encounter and realization of his own shadow. Therefore, these images and the way Neumann experienced them are relevant to understanding the psychic depth from which the idea about a new ethic sprang.

The Ape-Man Fantasy

In the next letter Neumann wrote to Jung, he referred to "a series of phantasies" and mentioned that they "roughly corresponded timewise with the extermination of the Jews, and in which the problem of evil and justice was being tossed around in me" (Jung & Neumann, 2015, p. 331). The time at which the fantasies appeared is of importance, as when interpreting a dream, the context of the reality of the dreamer is relevant. Whether these were images of daydream visions or night dreams is one and the same for the purpose of the interpretation, as in both cases they are products of the unconscious, which Neumann described as follows:

> I seemed to be commissioned to kill the ape-man in the profound primal hole. As I approached him, he was hanging, by night, sleeping on the cross above the abyss, but his—crooked—single eye was staring into the depth of this abyss. While it at first seemed that I was supposed to blind him, I all of a sudden grasped his "innocence," his dependence on the single eye of the Godhead, which was experiencing the depth through him, which was a human eye. Then, very abridged, I sank down in opposite this single eye, jumped into the abyss, but was caught by the Godhead, which carried me on the "wings of his heart."

> After that, this single eye opposite the ape-man closed and it opened on my forehead. (Bit difficult to write this, but what should one do) Working outward from the attempt to process this happening, I arrived at *The New Ethic*. For me since then the world looks different. (p. 331)

Had this fantasy been a night dream, it would be considered a Big Dream; and it makes sense to interpret it as such. The dream begins with a sense of mission, as if the dream-ego is acting upon a higher cause and not a personal one. The initial mission is to kill—which is the primitive way of eliminating—a hominin, as the most primitive inner aspect resides in the darkness of the depth. Then the dream reveals that this primitive image, representing a psychic aspect, has one crooked eye, which may symbolize a distorted consciousness, one-sidedness, or no perspective. Moreover, it can be amplified by the Cyclopes, the one-eyed, immortal, barbarous giants of Greek mythology, who dwelt in the belly of the earth (Graves, 1992, pp. 32, 37, 717). In this case, it becomes important to note that in the myth Odysseus, as the hero, fights the son of Poseidon, the Cyclops Polyphemus, whom he eventually blinds (pp. 718–719). The symbolic meaning is that the hero fights the instinctual primitive forces of the unconscious to overcome them by "blinding" them. In Neumann's 'dream' this is exactly when the surprising twist in the plot occurs, when the innocence and the involvement of the Godhead are revealed. Then the crucial transformative element of the dream appears, when first he discovers that the Godhead resides in this human abyss and significantly when he jumps, rather than falls, into the abyss. The act of jumping into the abyss rather than falling indicates a free will choice, which is a leap of faith and opposes logic. This is a crucial distinction that Neumann emphasized in the same letter to Jung and will define the difference between the two men in their approach to evil, as discussed later. In the dream once he jumps, he finds that he is caught and carried by the Godhead "on the wings of his heart," as its compassion, and the single eye is on his forehead, symbolizing that he now owns the qualities of the ape-man; thus, instead of killing it he understood that he was called to assimilate it.

Neumann's statement that after this fantasy the world looked different leaves no doubt as to its transformative effect and thus its numinous nature. In a lecture he described the effect: "the ego is encompassed by the nonego, that is to say, a change takes place in the personality" (Neumann, 1948/1989, p. 384). Understandably, he also stated that this fantasy led him to *New Ethic*, as he understood that his heroic intention was not to kill or blind the primitive within. Rather, as Neumann understood, his hero's journey entailed the transformation in which, instead of killing the primitive, he was called to realize that the primitive "out there" has no consciousness and is not responsible; it is the inner and is divine. In an act of free will that entails a leap of faith, the projection can be taken back, and one is carried by compassion. Indeed, *New Ethic* utilizes the image of the ape-man to elucidate its importance and positive influence on the ego:

> When the ego realizes its solidarity with the evil "ugliest man," the predatory man and the ape man in terror in the jungle, its stature is increased by the accession of a most vital factor, the lack of which has precipitated modern man into his present disastrous state of splitness and ego-isolation—and that is, a living relationship with nature and the earth. (Neumann, 1949/1990, p. 97)

Not only does evil reside in us but we need to own it as a legitimate part, and when we do this, ego expands and creativity is set free. These echo Jung's (1933/1965) assertion: "At first we cannot see beyond the path that leads downwards to dark and hateful things—but no light or beauty will ever come from the man who cannot bear this sight" (p. 215). In opposition to the assimilation of the shadow,

Neumann theorized that the rejection of the evil side results in a harmful psychic split. In addition, to clarify the image of the ape-man, Neumann (1949/1990) added a note stating that he referred to "a psychic image which appeared in this form and is projected" (p. 97, note 1) emphasizing once again that it is a psychological image. Neumann clearly saw the image of the ape-man as evil and the representation of the instinctual and earthly side, which is crucially missing from modern man's experience of himself. This is probably another one of Neumann's early expressions of his eco-psychological perspective, especially when considering the dream in which the earthly and the Godhead are connected and therefore pointing toward the integration of the worlds, heaven and earth.

New Ethic
Developmental Clarification

Neumann's writings on Jacob and Esau already indicated the developmental perspective of his work, and their relevancy was supported using reputable current interpretations that validate and amplify Neumann's perspective. Nonetheless, the manuscript of *Jacob and Esau* was not published upon completion and became available to his readers only recently. On the other hand, *New Ethic* (Neumann, 1949/1990) was Neumann's first publication, immediately followed by *Origins* (Neumann, 1949/2014). In *New Ethic*, Neumann obviously held the same perspective and the theorized in terms of development, a fact which is of the utmost importance as one of the reasons for the strong objections to the book by the hostile and envious readers among Jung's followers in Zurich was that the developmental perspective was overlooked. Of course, Jung himself already had a very high opinion of Neumann as a brilliant theoretician and was thus a supporter rather than an opponent, although his support was reserved and even concealed.

Had Neumann been more precise about his developmental perspective and had the opponents of the book read his second publication, *Origins*, before *New Ethic*, some of their objections might have been assuaged. Neumann would have avoided the unpleasant experience of being socially expelled from the Jungian circle and newly established institute in Zurich. In *Origins*, Neumann (1949/2014) emphasized that his explanation in terms of stages had two implications. The first was "their stadial succession" (p. xvi), and as the translator explained in a note, the word "stadial" means stage of development in the biological sense. Thus, Neumann borrowed the term to indicate the inherent aspect of the stages, that they follow one after the other in a sequence. Importantly, the second implication was that the stages are not fixed, and they somewhat overlap in the sense that one stage does not make redundant the previous stage nor is it layered over it; rather there are some overlaps between the layers. This would imply that the old ethic is a prerequisite for progressing toward the new ethic and cannot be neglected or bypassed. Unlike many others, Jung understood this aspect, as in the foreword to the English edition he wrote (Neumann, 1949/1990), "If the values of the old ethic were not seated in the very marrow of his bones, he [a person] would never have got into this situation in the first place" (p. 16). Further, Jung stated clearly what Neumann neglected to emphasize enough; that is, even when one is well adjusted to the old ethic, it is not necessarily the case that he will develop further to the new ethic:

> We might therefore define the "new ethic" as a development and differentiation within the old ethic, confined at present to those uncommon individuals who, driven by unavoidable conflict of duty, endeavour to bring the conscious and the unconscious into responsible relationship. (p. 15)

Jung well understood the depth of Neumann's argument: not only does the new ethic take for granted the assimilation of the old ethic but it is also a further developmental stage belonging to the advanced stages of individuation and attainable only by a minority. As suggested earlier, Neumann belonged to this minority, as evidenced by his writings. Jung's recognition of these developmental aspects of the new ethic is highly relevant as it supports Neumann's formulations of the further and advanced stages of the individuation process. Unfortunately, Neumann failed to emphasize what was needed to prevent the many misunderstandings of the text, which effectively harmed it and dimmed its brilliance. Ten years later, in 1959, in the preface to the Spanish edition, Neumann (1949/1990) wrote a clarification:

> One of the main lines of argument in this little book has been the attempt to establish the necessity for a hierarchal ethic—that is, to show that for men with different types of psychological make-up, different types of ethic are appropriate. At the same time, I have repeatedly stressed that the new ethic, with its changed attitude to evil, presupposes a man who is "moral" by the standards of the old ethic. The demands of the new ethic—if it is possible to speak of demands at all in this context—are higher and more exacting than those of the old. (p. 21)

Therefore, the manuscript of *New Ethic* is not, as is commonly perceived, mainly about the projection of the shadow, and it is not a threat to one's morality or a criticism of those who did not reach this further stage. Rather, and importantly for depth psychological developmental theory, it becomes a description of a further developmental stage, a goal that, although undoubtedly not achievable by all, should be attempted. This last aspect is an echo of Neumann's writings about Jacob's last transformation to the state of psychic wholeness, a state that is rarely achieved.

An indication that Neumann saw individuation as a process that begins in the second half of life and proceeds into later life is found in his next letter to Jung. In this response to Jung's letter telling him about objections to his book at the Institute, Neumann (Jung & Neumann, 2015), in his direct style, perhaps wanting to mock the members of the Institute for rejecting his book and himself so brutally, described them as "your students who always wish to anticipate the wisdom of the 'third half of life' before they have the struggles of the first behind them" (p. 239). Neumann here talks about wisdom that belongs to an advanced stage, one that is beyond that of the individuation—implying assimilation of the shadow and withdrawal of projections—of the second half of life, as Jung described it.

Neumann theorized about *New Ethic* in 1943 and published it in 1949. Its current relevancy will be supported using Lawrence Kohlberg's (1976, 1986) moral development theory that was first published as a dissertation in 1958 (Walsh, 2000, p. 37), which is the leading moral theory in the developmental psychology field. An important difference between Neumann's and Kohlberg's perspectives is that Neumann wrote about ethics and Kohlberg researched morality. This difference is relevant to this chapter as it is situated in the conjunction of Freud's personalistic perspective (represented by Kohlberg) and Jung's archetypal perspective, (represented by Neumann). In *New Ethic*, Neumann used both concepts, *moral* and *ethic*. The research conducted for this chapter leads to the conclusion that ethics is a philosophical reflection, manifested as an ontology whereas morality is a cognitive judgment and a behavior. Jung (Neumann, 1949/1990) suggested a definition of the relationship between the two concepts that supports this differentiation: "ethics represents a system of moral demands" (p. 15). As such, the ethical stages that Neumann theorized in 1948 are like an archetypal ethical layer that corresponds and to the three moral levels theorized by Kohlberg, in his dissertation, in 1958.

A Brief Description of Lawrence Kohlberg's Moral Development Theory

The domain of moral development research and theory is dominated by Kohlberg's six-stage model. A brief description of Kohlberg's theory will be used in the following analysis to support the validity and current relevancy of Neumann's theory. Kohlberg's theory refers to the process of moral reasoning as it originated from Jean Piaget's theory of the stages of logical reasoning. Like Neumann, Kohlberg (1976) described the stages of the development of personality; nevertheless, unlike Neumann, who described some overlap between the stages, Kohlberg described these stages as a path of progression, one step at a time, from bottom to top. Moreover, he theorized that regression or straddling is improbable, and interestingly, although he did not hold a Jungian archetypal perspective, he found that the sequence is "cross-cultural" (Spohn, 2000, p. 131).

Kohlberg grouped the six stages of moral development into three major levels, each encompassing two stages. The levels may be seen as the archetypal layer behind the stages, and Kohlberg defined them as preconventional (encompassing stages 1 and 2), conventional (stages 3 and 4), and postconventional (stages 5 and 6). The preconventional level of Kohlberg's (1976) theory refers to children, for whom the primary motivation is avoidance of punishment and obeying authority. The conventional stage refers to most adults, whose motivation is standing with the rules and social order. The postconventional stage is attained only by the minority, who are motivated by universal principals. Interestingly, supporting the assumption that his moral levels correspond to Neumann's ethical stages, Kohlberg suggested that the three levels may be understood through their representation of the "relationship between the *self* and *society's rules and expectations*" (p. 33). That is, the Self represents ethics, and society's rules and expectations represent morality. When viewed through this perspective, the preconventional involves a relationship with something external to Self; the conventional has to do with something with which the Self identifies; and the postconventional, applicable to the individual who has already differentiated himself from rules and expectations, concerns self-chosen principles. Here Kohlberg added a sociological aspect and went further to define a *"sociomoral perspective,* which refers to the point of view the individual takes in defining both social facts and sociomoral values, or oughts" (p. 33). This aspect of Kohlberg's theory is very important at this point as it describes the individual's relation to the group at each moral level, remarkably like the way Neumann's described it in *New Ethic.*

Carol Gilligan, who initially was Kohlberg's research assistant, presented in her famous book *In a Different Voice* (Gilligan, 1982) a feminine perspective of moral development. She claimed that Kohlberg's research is directed toward masculine participants and thus his theory reflects the moral developmental stages of the male psyche grounded in justice and fairness, whereas the female develops her morality differently, as it is grounded in relationship and care. Although she was initially perceived as a critic of Kohlberg, it is now commonly accepted that Kohlberg's and Gilligan's perspectives reflect two types of moral reasoning: Kohlberg's is motivated by justice, whereas Gilligan's is motivated by care (Jorgensen, 2006a, p. 179). The two perspectives are as complementary as the conscious and the unconscious. Justice is a conscious judgment, yet care is an instinct and an emotion thus originating in the unconscious.

One additional aspect of Kohlberg's theory relates to the unconscious process of reasoning. Although Kohlberg is well known for his six-stage model of moral reasoning, in his later years he arrived at a seventh stage. As noted, the six stages are grounded in logical processes; therefore, from the depth psychological perspective, the seventh stage is grounded in the illogical processes, that is, the unconscious. Of the seventh stage Kohlberg wrote, "I have also speculated about mystical forms of experience and religious or metaphysical concepts that articulate these forms of experience, conception I have referred to as a metaphoric *Stage* 7" (Kohlberg & Ryncarz, 1990, p. 191). Strikingly, these words echo Neumann's (1948/1989, 1970/1988) articulations of the mystical and religious experience, and it appears that, whenever one deals with moral issues from a nonlogical perspective, one arrives at religiosity.

While conducting the research about Kohlberg for use in this chapter, a very interesting detail came to light. Kohlberg was a German-speaking Jewish Zionist who visited Palestine as an activist on behalf of the Jewish settlers and apparently was there in 1948 (Walsh, 2000, p. 37). Neumann completed *New Ethic* by 1943 and at that time he earned part of his living by lecturing in his living room to a German-speaking audience (Lori, 2005). Neumann was twenty years older than Kohlberg. Therefore, based on nothing more than a hunch, I suggest the possibility that the young Zionist activist Kohlberg had listened attentively to the older Zionist activist Neumann's lecture, and a seed of thought was planted in his mind to later become his dissertation research.

In any case, Kohlberg was very careful about describing the seventh stage he theorized as he was aiming at a scientifically oriented reader for whom a mystical experience belongs to the occult. In the following analysis of Neumann's work, Kohlberg's six stages within the three levels of moral development will be used as a reference. The seventh stage ties Kohlberg's (1990) later work to Neumann (1949/1990).

Neumann's Stages of Ethic Development

In *New Ethic*, as in most of his writings, Neumann (presumably as evidence of his typology as an intuitive thinker) provided his reader with the big picture of the framework that situates the issue at hand—a new ethic—in the broader field. A leading line of his theory is the mutuality between ontogenetic (borrowed from biology and referring to an individual organism) and phylogenetic (a group of organisms) development: "Ontogenetic development may therefore be regarded as a modified recapitulation of phylogenetic development" (Neumann, 1949/2014, p. xx). Therefore, his theory of the ethical development of man is woven within this development in humanity; his descriptions apply to both the individual and the collective. Nevertheless, the nature of ethical development is such that only at the last stage of the new ethic does it become purely individual and therefore relevant to the individuation process.

Primal Unity

Neumann's description of the primal and lower ethical level is signified by its collective nature in which the individual has no moral stance nor ethical responsibility. One is but a member of a group, clan, or tribe, and as such, he is completely subject to its codes of behavior. Individual failure to follow these codes is seen collectively and results in punishment (which is collective as well) such as blood revenge.

Neumann (1949/1990) begins his description with the infancy of humanity, as he did in *Jacob and Esau,* where he described the original stage as a collective unconscious layer characterized by a *participation mystique* of man and nature, when unconscious contents were projected and concretized in rituals such as the Jewish scapegoat ritual. In *New Ethic*, regarding morality, he referred to this stage as the primal unity. He emphasized that the participation mystique implies that the collective psyche dominates the individual, who is undifferentiated from the group. The individual's ego is yet "an embryonic ego," still weak and subject to unconscious forces, that "lives in a condition of almost complete dependence on the tribe, the world and the collective unconscious" (p. 59). Critically, at this primary stage of ethical development, there is no individual conscious yet; there is also no ethical responsibility; and the individual is but a member of the group, which is collectively responsible to all its members. The group's common interests—group responsibility and group ethic—rule, which means that blood revenge belongs to this ethical level. Neumann pointed out that from this primal ethical level sprouted the Judeo-Christian perception of the descendants' reward and punishment. To substantiate that Neumann's theory is anchored in Jung's original writings, here again Jung's article from 1917 becomes relevant to Neumann:

> Morality . . . is a function of the human soul, as old as humanity itself. . . without which the collective life of human society would be impossible. . . the instinctive regulator of action which also governs the collective life of the herd. (Jung, 1943/1972, p. 27)

Therefore, Jung saw the archetypal role of morality as a function rather than an acquired trait, and he recognized its importance in regulating the life of the group. It seems that Jung referred here to what Neumann defined later as the level of ethic of the group.

Kohlberg (1976; 1986), who held a personalistic perspective, nevertheless termed the first level of morality as preconvention and described it as the phase of early childhood, which corresponds to Neumann's archetypal perspective of the Infantile-Childish ego. Also, like Neumann, Kohlberg posited that at this level one holds a concrete perspective. Rules and expectations are determined by the authority figure and thus are external to the Self and generalized without exceptions, whereas reward and punishment motivate moral behavior. Clearly, Kohlberg's first moral level is essentially the same as Neumann's primal unity stage, in which the individual has no ethical responsibility, and he subordinates to the group identity.

Neumann (1949/1990) theorized that, at the primal stage of group identity, the Great Individual has a profound role as the creative center of the group that functions in a sense as its Self. At this stage, Neumann is referring to a Great Individual from the second level, which implies that he is creative and active in his role as a "spiritual progenitor" (p. 62) while he follows the Voice and therefore establishes the group's set of values, that is, its ethic. Although in *Jacob and Esau*, Neumann referred to the Voice in the experience of the forefathers, in this case he explained that the experience of the Voice is not restricted to religion or to Judaism. It is a unique individual who is able and attentive enough to hear the Voice, however it appears, and thus becomes the founder of the group's ethic. Neumann theorized that the progression toward the next ethical level depends on an elite among the group, the first to follow the Great Individual, who becomes the Founder. His experience manifests a religious nature that does not necessarily relate to a specific religion but rather to numinosity, transforms him, and then the elite adopts his ethical attitude and imposes it on the group as collective values. At this stage, the members of the group are following the imposed law uncritically; they accept it without reflecting. Nevertheless, the fact that they can follow a law implies that the initial separation between the conscious and unconscious has already happened, and some consciousness has been achieved.

Old Ethic

Neumann's perception and description of modern man's current ethical level is one in which conscience is at the service of the individual, who recognizes and differentiates good and bad according to the accepted law. Accordingly, failure to follow the law results in punishment imposed on the individual by the group. However, at the early phase of the old ethic the individual blindly follows a collective set of roles, while at the current (written in 1943) phase of the old ethic, the individual is critical, reflective and responsible to follow the collective moral demands.

As opposed to the previous stage of primary unity, in which the unconscious prevailed, the early phase of old ethic coincides with the establishment of the collective ethic. In terms of consciousness development, it is the beginning of the separation between the system of conscious and unconscious, corresponding to the separation of the World Parents described in the mythological phase, and requires that some ego-conscious has already emerged from the unconscious. As discussed previously, the division of the worlds implies a division between good and evil—a dualistic perception: "The old ethic is based on the principal of opposites in conflict" (Neumann, 1949/1990, p. 45). The central problem of the ethical developmental stage of the old ethic is therefore the conflict between good and evil, light and dark. Obviously, the old ethic aspires to the good and the light, and therefore the hero fighting the unconscious dragon belongs to this stage. Neumann emphasized that initially the old ethic, which imposed a set of values coming from the singular Great Individual through the elite to the members of the group, liberated man to be the bearer of the drive toward consciousness. Moreover, as the process of accepting the "law" strengthens consciousness, this process is essential and crucial to its development and it lasts a long time, from the genesis of human conscious to the current day. Here is an essential element of Neumann's formulation in this book: the development from the early phase of old ethic which was still collective, to the current old ethic which bares individual responsibility is an achievement of modern man's developed consciousness and is not to be diminished. Neumann suggested what he theorized—out of a deep conviction—the next step that awaits humanity and the next developmental ethical stance—the new ethic.

To aid young consciousness, which needs to follow the collective ethic and overcome the unconscious forces, the psychic authority of conscience appears. Neumann described this formation as the manifestation of the individuation experienced by the group-man. Initially in the early phase of old ethic, man was but a member of a group and therefore, the contents dealt by the conscience were collective, as the ego was already capable of applying the collective values to itself and others as a part of the group. As consciousness developed further, the individual gradually separated from the group and his conscious separated from the primitive collective unconscious. It is at this phase that human development stands at a threshold, moving from the old ethic, that of current days, in which the former collective moral responsibility becomes an individual moral responsibility.

In this sense, although Kohlberg's perspective is personalized and not archetypal, it seems that essentially what he described as the second moral level is like Neumann's old ethic. In Kohlberg's theory, the second moral level is the conventional and characterized by the subordination of the individual to the group. He described it as "social system morality" (1986, p. 494), in which the active conscience leads one to act as expected by the group to which he belongs. Nevertheless, he emphasized that at this stage the terms "conscience" and "morality" may still refer to group rules and values. In this sense Neumann and Kohlberg both indicated that this is a stage of transition from group to individual identity, manifested by the direction of operation of the psychic authority of conscience. Neumann theorized that what was before (at the transition from primal unity to the old ethic) a blind acceptance of the collective value imposed by the elite at this stage. When this blindness become conscious, a conscientious responsibility to fulfill the collective ethical demands comes into being. Neumann described this phase as the classical form of the old ethic, which until the current day (written in 1943) was valid for most people as "an essential transitional stage" (1949/1990, p. 64), that is, the forerunner of the new ethic.

When the world view is dualistic at this stage, the ego-conscious is inflated as it identifies itself with the good. Neumann described two psychic methods enabling this identification and thus implementing the old ethic. One is conscious suppression and denial of what is unaccepted by the collective value, and the other is unconscious repression and exclusion of these contents, relegated to the shadow. The two methods are "two sides of one and the same process" (p. 41), as both are used to keep the ego's perception of itself as good while excluding the evil. Presumably, Neumann's use of the concepts of suppression and repression originated with Jung's (1946/1991) writings on neurosis and the psychic mechanism of all people (not only those who are neurotic) who naturally prefer to push "any inconvenience in himself . . . as far away from himself as possible in space and time" (p. 111). Although Jung wrote these words, originally in 1926 regarding neurosis, he later elucidated the connection between neurosis and moral conflicts. In the foreword to *New Ethic* he wrote, "The treatment of neurosis is not, in the last resort, a technical problem, but a moral one" (Neumann, 1949/1990, p. 13). Therefore, the things he wrote about suppression and repression are just as true regarding contents one perceives as immoral, evil, and shadowed.

In an article originally published in 1926, Jung (1946/1991) differentiated between the two methods of disposing of the inconveniences in oneself and diverting attention away from them: when suppression is a conscious switch of attention, one is able to return to the suppressed contents as "they are always recoverable" (p. 109). Repression, on the other hand, "is an artificial loss of memory, a self-suggested amnesia" (p. 109). Therefore, unlike suppression, repression is an unconscious act that leaves the contents out of reach of the consciousness.

Using the concepts as Jung described them, Neumann (1949/1990) theorized the method of suppression as the leading principle of the old ethic, through which the negative aspects of personality not consistent with the ethical values are suppressed by the ego. Therefore, suppression is a conscious act that involves asceticism, sacrifice, and suffering. In terms of the economy of psychic energy, the conscious involvement in this method uses energy therefore less is accumulated in the unconscious. Moreover, as the suppressed aspects remain available to the conscious, ego deflation occurs due to a sense of sin and guilt and at the price of flattened personality. In religious doctrine, suppression promotes the development of the conscious by offering a framework of orientation and, Neumann described the principle of suppression as "a conscious achievement of the ego" (p. 34), supporting its development by the demands entailing its strengthening and creating a persona.

Alternatively, repression, which is "the instrument most frequently used" (Neumann, 1949/1990, p. 35), excludes from the conscious all those unaccepted personality aspects that are not consistent with the ethical values; they are repressed and sent to the unconscious to be forgotten and withdrawn from the control of the conscious. Neumann emphasized that the repressed personality aspects become autonomous like complexes that work on the collective level, just as they do on the personal yet their effects are more dangerous than those of the asceticism resulting from suppression.

In terms of psychic energy, repression works differently from suppression and, Neumann theorized, is "destructive" (Neumann, 1949/1990, p. 49). As the shadowed contents accumulated in the unconscious are completely repressed, they have no contact with the conscious and are highly charged with repressed energy. They "become 'regressive' and subject to negative reinforcement. . . in regression more primitive forms of reaction are mobilized" (pp. 48–49). This is a significant remark as Neumann later revisited regression from another, more dangerous angle to be discussed hereafter. In describing modern man, Jung (1933/1965) wrote, "A higher level of consciousness is like a burden of guilt" (p. 198), as consciousness casts a shadow which activates guilt, an idea Neumann followed in theorizing about the way the old ethic confronts evil. He theorized that both psychic methods of handling the unaccepted aspects of personality—the shadow—entail guilt feelings. When the shadow is denied by a strong conscience, the guilt feelings are conscious; when it is darkened and forgotten in the unconscious, the guilt feelings are unconscious as well. Either way, guilt feelings are discharged by the projection of the shadow. As Neumann theorized in *Jacob and Esau*, evil is projected on an outer object, experienced as the "other."

The following extract from the book substantiates Neumann's activist perspective:

> The way in which the old ethic provides for the elimination of these feelings of guilt and discharge of the excluded negative forces is in fact one of the *gravest perils* confronting mankind. What we have in mind here is that classic psychological expedient—the institution of scapegoat. This technique for attempting a solution of the problem is to be found wherever human society exists. It is however best known as the ritual of Judaism. (Neumann, 1949/1990, p. 50; emphasis added)

On the one hand, Neumann harshly criticizes mankind and makes a clear reference to a projection on the Jews; nevertheless, being conscious and ethical, he admitted that the ritual was originally Jewish. Neumann was qualified to do so as he was both Jewish and the author of two other manuscripts describing and interpreting this ritual (Neumann, 1934/2015, 1935–1945/2019), explaining its primitive significance and its evolution. In his writing about the ritual, Neumann (1949/1990) coined the term "scapegoat psychology" as "an early, though still inadequate, attempt to deal with these unconscious conflicts"; adding that "this psychology shapes the inner life of nations just as much as it does their international relationship" (p. 51). Once again, Neumann indirectly criticizes European nations, evoking the rejection of his manuscript. He described the primitive level, as he did in *Jacob and Esau*, and he added that the rise of the shadow toward consciousness was achieved through the actual ritual, when concretization demanded that the eye would see the distraction of the evil. Nevertheless, at this stage evil is recognized as outside the individual. Therefore, the scapegoat psychology still operates under the collective ethic of group responsibility, the most primitive form of ethic. Neumann mentioned that Judaism had conceptually progressed to the stage in which everyone carries the responsibility for the collective when the sacrifice ritual was transformed to collective prayer ("God, forgive *us*, as *we* have sinned"), indicating group responsibility.

As in *Jacob and Esau*, Neumann describes the old ethic as the projection of the shadow, as the inner "other," on an outer object. As Jacob projected on Esau, so does the modern man of the old ethic project his shadow on minorities. Neumann noted that the energetic charge of this projection originates with unconscious guilt feelings and remarked that, once evil is "out there" as the other, then conversely the other "out there" becomes necessarily evil. Obviously, when Neumann wrote the book, the projection was on the Jews in the form of anti-Semitism.

Another important group that falls victim to the scapegoat psychology, asserted Neumann, consists of those with "outstanding personality," who are easily regarded as "other" although because of their superiority. It is more than possible that in this case Neumann referred to those who are Great Individuals, nonetheless rare in their existence.

Lastly, regardless of the method of implementing the old ethic, and possibly as a reaction to the Nazis, Neumann wrote, "In both classes we find, as a consequence of the denial of the negative, an unconscious reinforcement of the negative in practice to the point of *sadism and a bestial lust for destruction*"

(Neumann, 1949/1990, p. 55; emphasis added). Neumann then differentiated the stature of the leaders from that of the masses and added: "In the ascetic class, the sadism is nearer to consciousness and assumes a rationalized and systematic form, whereas in the repressive class, the masses, it is of the wildest emotionality and overwhelms consciousness" (pp. 55–56). If the Zurich Jungian circle was to be offended in anyway by Neumann's formulation, this surely can be seen as his directed attack.

Neumann asserted that, although the old ethic still prevails, in current days "the regression which disfigure this story of progress show quite clearly that the old ethic . . . makes excessive demands on the majority of human beings" (Neumann, 1949/1990, pp. 67–68). Therefore, on the one hand Neumann described the Great Individual as the motivator and creator of progress, and on the other hand he described mass regression. This puzzle is solved by Neumann's himself:

> The classical form of the old ethic, then continues to evolve in two directions. . . . The first leads, with the progress of individuation, to the "ethic of individuation," the "new" ethic; the second, to the collapse of the old ethic and to regressive phenomena which we have described elsewhere. (p. 66)

Here, it seems that Neumann's theory relied on Jung's (1928/1972a) assertion about psychic energy and the energic equivalence; accordingly, "the intensity of progression reappears in the intensity of regression" (p. 39). Therefore, Neumann concluded, if humanity is rapidly progressing, then a danger of rapid regression must be lurking in humanity. The regressive phenomenon is what Neumann referred to as the recollectivization process, which he described in *Origins* (Neumann, 1949/2014, Appendix II, pp. 436–444).

Recollectivization

As this process opposes development, due to its regressive nature, its relevancy to this book is limited to the aspects that support the overall understanding of Neumann's theory, although it has high relevancy to current social and political discussion.

Neumann asserted that the significant expansion of humankind changed the form of the old grouping so that the group today is a mass of unrelated individuals. In the past, groups were relatively small, and members were bound to one another on an emotional level, even if not personally. Currently, Neumann (1949/2014) theorized that, instead of the group—be it a clan, tribe, or village, for example—there is a mass of unrelated individuals: "his isolation in a mass which no longer offers him any psychic support becomes unendurable" (p. 439). The danger Neumann recognized resides in this isolation, in the lack of psychic support. The old type of group exists today mainly in the form of a family, while the bigger groups are the masses, in which the members are overly individualized and inflated, as explained earlier. He wrote, "From the point of view of the old ethic, masses are by nature inferior; they tend to revert to the primitive group-identity which involves no individual responsibility" (p. 70).

Interestingly, as mentioned earlier, Jung first read Neumann's manuscript between October 1945 and January 1946. In the "Epilogue to 'Essay on Contemporary Events'" (Jung, 1946/1970), Jung wrote, "the greater the aggregation of individuals, the more the individual factors are blotted out, and with them morality, which depends entirely on the moral sense of the individual and on the freedom necessary for this" (p. 228). Not only is this a verification of Neumann's formulation, but the final words refer to what presumably is Jung's attempt to excuse his and other's helplessness in confronting the Nazis. Interestingly, in "The Psychology of the Unconscious" (Jung, 1943/1972), originally written in 1917, which was mentioned earlier as the possible Jungian theoretical grounds of Neumann's formulation of ethical development, Jung touched upon the freedom needed for individual morality:

> With the growth of civilization we have succeeded in subjecting ever larger human groups to the rule of the same morality, without, however, having yet brought the moral code to prevail beyond the social frontiers, that is, in the free space between mutually independent societies. (p. 27)

Jung recognized the limits of the law, which does not replace morality outside the boundaries of society; according to Neumann's later formulations this implies individual morality.

Returning to group morality, Neumann explained this idea from another angle and claimed that the original group-man of the primal unity was in fact unconscious but also in the process of development, and in that sense he was a "psychic whole." On the other hand, modern man's regression to group identity is different—he has already gained some strength of consciousness and thus belongs to the ethical developmental stage of the old ethic, entailing the repression of the shadow as the leading method through which the old ethic is employed. The mass-man therefore is in danger of an outburst of his shadow, the primitive or instinctual, corresponding to the ape-man in Neumann's fantasy. In the process of recollectivization, Neumann asserted that the mass and majority are "below the cultural standard of the elite and are violated by the demands of the old ethic." The danger is the consequence of repression and suppression that activate "the negative unconscious side in both the individual and the group" (1949/1990, p. 70). Neumann explained that the psychic method of repression in the old ethic, the consequential regression is highly charged and thus the primitive outbursts are dangerous. These writings echo Jung's (1943/1972) assertion, originally written in 1917 with the note "still true today":

At the present time, too, we are once more experiencing this upspring of the unconscious distractive forces of the collective psyche. The result has been mass-murder on an unparalleled scale. (p. 94)

Although Jung's words were directed at the events of the First World War, revised and annotated as they were in 1943, they acknowledged the horrors of the Second World War. Neumann (1949/1990) closely followed these words of Jung when he summed up the old ethic and directly referred to the Second World War:

Psychologically speaking, the old ethic is a partial ethic. It is an ethic of the conscious attitude, and it fails to take into consideration or to evaluate the tendencies and effects of the unconscious . . . it leads to negative compensatory phenomena in which the repressed and suppressed shadow side breaks through. Within the life of the community, this takes the shape of the psychology of the scapegoat; in international relations it appears in the form of those epidemic outbreaks of atavistic mass reactions known to us as wars . . . this whole situation requires for its solution a new development of conscious and a new ethic. (p. 74)

This may explain the mass madness and sadism of the Nazi regime. Nevertheless, the last sentence may also be seen as Neumann's plea to humanity and evidence of his social activism, encouraging man to develop and humanity to turn to the next step from the old ethic, that is, toward a new ethic.

New Ethic

When Neumann first released his manuscript to German readers in 1948, it was poorly received— a criticism of the situation in Europe and blame pointed at educated Jungians. In 1959, in the preface to the Spanish edition, Neumann (1949/1990) admitted his militant style; nevertheless, he clarified that the book was in the first place meant to be "a declaration of war against an ethic whose practical impotence has brought modern man to the brink of despair" (p. 22). In saying this Neumann expressed his activism and his intention to awaken modern man toward a change that he recognized as needed, a change in ethic. In the foreword, Jung described this call for a change as "conflicts of duty" (p. 14), explaining how such a conflict that cannot be solved by collective morality will become a question of ethics. Neumann (1949/1990) described the conflict of duty in a broader way:

> We are, in fact, witnessing the emergence of an ethic which no longer considers the ethical attitude and decisions of the individual in isolation, and which does not simply evaluate that individual's conscious alignment, but which also takes into account the effect of this alignment on the collective, and includes the situation of the unconscious in the overall moral assessment. (p. 73)

That is, the anticipated ethical development of the individual will take into account its effect on the collective. This is the most advanced phase of ethics, in which Neumann proposed. Instead of the collective's responsibility, the mature individual's responsibility is to the collective and to his fellow man, who may be at times less developed than he is. Not much imagination is needed here to recognize Neumann's plea to the people, individuals, his friends, and Jung to admit their responsibility in not preventing the horrors in Europe.

In Kohlberg's (1976) theory, the third moral level is the postconventional, which he titled "Universal Ethical Principles" (p. 35). Kohlberg wrote that principles such as human rights prevail over social rules: "each person has an obligation to make moral choices that uphold these rights, even when they conflict with society's laws or codes" (1986, p. 495). In this aspect Kohlberg clearly echoed Neumann, indicating that moral conflicts are an outcome of the recognition of ethical principles. I suggest that, as one's ethic progresses or, in Kohlberg's terms, one advances to a higher moral level, he steps away from logical reasoning, that is, the ego-conscious judgment, and becomes more attentive to the inner voice, a call from an unconscious core within, the Self.

Carol Gilligan's criticism (that Kohlberg's *justice* is short of the relational perspective of *care*) becomes more significant at this stage. From the Jungian perspective, reasoning by justice would represent consciousness, and reasoning by care would consider unconscious aspects such as instincts and intuition as well. In addition, as seen from the archetypal perspective, care belongs to the elementary feminine, and following the reasoning of care would call for matriarchal consciousness, entailing an advanced psychological stage, as will be discussed in Part II. Although Gilligan added the relational perspective to Kohlberg's logic, they both referred to moral reasoning. Nevertheless, as mentioned earlier, Kohlberg suggested that the different moral levels should be understood through the way that they represent the relationship between the Self and society. In the postconventional level, he claimed, one has already differentiated himself from the group and therefore the Self turns inward and "follows self-chosen ethical principles" (1958, p. 35). This description almost completely parallels Neumann's formulation of *New Ethic*, in which the individual has integrated the collective moral codes well enough to separate himself from the collective and attend to the call of the inner voice as an inner orientation toward the ethical choice.

As Neumann's perspective was developmental throughout his writings, the differentiation between individuals' psychological developmental stages served as an ontology for his theory. Regarding ethical development, he posited that at the lower level stands the majority, the mass, who are less developed and thus follow the elite, who set the collective values. The elite are the minority of the group, who have developed far enough to recognize the Founder as such and to adopt his ethic by following him. At the most developed stage stands the Great Individual as the Founder of the ethic according to the calling of the Voice: "The revelation of the Voice to a single person presupposes an individual whose individuality is so strong that he can make himself independent of the collective and its values" (Neumann, 1949/1990, p. 67). At this high stage of psychological development stands an individual whose ego is strong and firm enough to no longer rely on the refuge of the collective and who separates himself to become an individual omnipotent psychic unity while still in service to the collective through following an inner voice. As the inner voice is a call from the Self, it is a collective core, rather than personal. In terms of Neumann's latter formulations of the ego-Self axis, in his article "The Psyche and the Transformation of the Reality Plans" (1952/1989), the Great Individual would be one whose personality is centered around the axis and whose consciousness has developed toward the Self, experiencing a unitary world. Therefore, Neumann posited that human ethical development depends on the Great Individual, who time and again, due to his further perspective, appears to be a sinner in light of collective values, although in fact he sees beyond and pulls the collective situated behind him.

Neumann emphasized that the new ethic he suggests is a prerequisite for development toward an integrated personality, entailing "a severe disturbance of the ego and the world of conscious" (1949/1990, p. 77) as it is confronted with the shadow and called to assimilate it as a part of the personality, as did Jacob. It is an advanced phase of the individuation process, not necessarily for all, and relevant only to those people "whose adaptation to the collective has already been made" (p. 77, note 1). This becomes relevant to his critics, mentioned earlier, whom Neumann felt misunderstood his idea, or as he described them, "critics who have not taken the trouble to give the book a careful reading" (p. 20). This note makes clear that the new ethic presupposes the old ethic and is not meant to replace it but to add to it and at times even to challenge it.

The idea of preceding beyond the old ethic may find roots in Jung's description (1933/1965) of what he termed "modern man": one who "emphasizes the past in order to hold the scales against his break with tradition and that effect of guilt" (p. 199). Although Jung was not referring to ethics, he did recognize the progressive nature of the act of moving forward from "tradition" when it is well assimilated. Indeed, here, as was previously shown, in theorizing about ethical developmental stages, Neumann drew from Jung's writings. Therefore, he was granted support for his formulations, although Jung suggested changes that were aimed at softening Neumann's deterministic style.

Neumann (1949/1990) described the act of accepting one's evil as a mature move, as one needs to differentiate personal evil from evil as a collective phenomenon: "'MY' evil may not be an evil at all in my neighbor's eyes, and vice versa; it is precisely this that constitutes the moral difficulty of the situation" (p. 80). He emphasized that the differentiation of "my" evil from the general evil is a crucial element of individuation. Once the ego acknowledges and recognizes the evil "out there" as its own, the inflation of a self-satisfied ego, the "good conscience" of the old ethic, falls apart. The ego must accept its imperfection and reaches a "deeper moral level" (p. 81). Kohlberg and Ryncarz (1990) described the seventh and last stage as one in which the issue of meaning arises, and man is called to reflect on the question "why live?" (p. 192). Although this is not the same as Neumann's assertion, it does belong to the same depth of existence.

Neumann (1949/1990) analyzed the situation of modern man as a "collective disorientation" in which the conflict between one's inflated self-assured ego on the one side and the forces of the dark unconscious—which threaten from below—on the other side leads to a split in personality of both the individual and the collective to which he belongs. Neumann theorized two reactions to this situation to avoid the conflict and noted that both may be true of one individual: "The first reaction is deflationary and collectivist and devalues both individual and ego. The second is inflationary and individualistic" (p. 85) (that is, in the sense that it overvalues the individual and his ego). Neumann continued to theorize about modern man's attempt to avoid the conflict and the split he faces. He described two solutions; one is nihilistic, materialistic, deflationary, and pessimistic, whereas the other is inflationary, and as he termed it, a "pleromatic mysticism" (p. 87). The pleromatic solution has a regressive nature as it involves a perspective of wholeness that precedes the division of the worlds as opposed to the mature achievement of wholeness that manifests a reintegration of the divided worlds. This is one of Jung's important remarks in his "corrections and amendments" (Jung & Neumann, 2015, Appendix II, pp. 361–369) that Neumann did accept and repeated in his foreword: "No-one stands beyond good and evil, otherwise he would be out of this world" (Neumann, 1949/1990, p. 16). He then went on to demonstrate both Nietzsche's madness and the yogi's non-conscious non-acting as their way to avoid the conflict of acknowledging the equation between good and evil, avoidance of which is an impossible solution for modern man.

Neumann accepted Jung's remark, and in the appendix, he added to the book in 1950, "Reflections on the Shadow," he clarified:

> The change of attitude towards the shadow which is essential for the healing of the sick person, who is the representative of modern man in all splitness and disintegration, has nothing in common with any megalomaniac condition of being "beyond good and evil." (1949/1990, p. 143)

He thus makes it clear that his call to assimilate the shadow should not be confused with overcoming the shadow, which is impossible if evil is accepted as an equal existential reality with goodness. The assimilation of the shadow will lead to psychic equilibrium and thus an experience of wholeness; nevertheless, it is essentially different from the modern spirituality, which does not encourage confrontation with the shadow but rather bypasses it, or in current terms, it is the spiritual bypass.

Interestingly, these ideas are echoed in Kohlberg's and Ryncarz's (1990) seventh stage, which as they theorized, "involves experience of a nonegoistic or nondualistic variety" (p. 192), referring to cosmic and existential contemplations. Unlike Jung and Neumann, Kohlberg did not mean to warn of the megalomaniac state; rather he recognized the high level of wholeness involved, citing Spinoza's description of the union of mind and nature. Nevertheless, Jorgensen (2006b), who had access to Kohlberg's unpublished lectures, described a student in this megalomaniac state in which his ego was so inflated that he believed himself to be beyond ego (p. 1). It is clear therefore that Kohlberg arrived at essentially the same understanding as did Neumann, implying that the assimilation of the shadow is a humbling experience that deflates the ego and acknowledges its relativity and limitation.

Neumann (1949/1990) wrote, "The new ethic rejects the hegemony of a partial structure of the personality, and postulates the total personality as the basis of ethical conduct" (p. 92). The personality is total in the sense that it aims toward wholeness in that it takes into account the effect of the individual's attitude upon the collective and upon the unconscious, which means that the responsibility is now carried by the totality of personality, rather than partly by the ego. Here, Neumann arrived at the heart of his argument, and like his final analysis of *Jacob and Esau*, he posited that from the external collective perspective the new ethical responsibility must include mass-man. At the same time, from the individual perspective, the new ethical responsibility must include the mass-man within. Echoing *Jacob and Esau*, he wrote, "The individual must work through his own basic moral problem before he is in position to play a responsible part in the collective" (Neumann, 1949/1990, p. 93); thus, the personal shadow and the adversary figure become one. In 1917 Jung (1943/1972) wrote, "If people can be educated to see the shadow-side of their nature clearly, it may be hoped that they will also learn to understand and love their fellow men better" (p. 26). It seems that here again, in a deeper sense, Neumann's formulation rearticulated, amplified, and suggested a further application of Jung's original thought. It is only when one accepts his own shadow as an inner brother that he can accept the dark side of another human being, and this implies an expansion of personality and growth into the depth. Neumann then concluded his analysis of the individuation process and described it as the incorporation of the unconscious shadowed contents into a greater totality of personality. The next and last phase therefore is the discussion of what is a total personality and what it means to accept evil.

Final Stage: Integrating Evil

In *Jacob and Esau* Neumann's analysis was oriented to the process Jacob went through as a representation of the individuation process, which entails facing the shadow and accepting it as a face of the divine. In *New Ethic*, Neumann theorized about the implications—personal and collective—of this advanced stage. In the aftermath of the events in Europe, its immediate application was to one's ethical stance, one's perception of evil, and most importantly, one's action when facing evil.

Neumann (1949/1990) theorized that, from a new ethic perspective, a unitary structure of personality is established in which pairs of opposites are held together in "the firm embrace of a supra-ordinated unity" (p. 101). In terms of the individuation process, he wrote, "In fact, the central happening in the process of individuation is precisely the way in which the ego takes part in this transformation of the personality, by acting, *suffering*, shaping and being overwhelmed at the same time" [emphasis added] (p. 102). It is important to consider the use of the word "suffering" as it stood at the center of Neumann's and Jung's disagreement.

As Neumann described, another important aspect of the new ethic is its reliance on the creative process that enables the "birth to new values" (p. 103). Here Neumann's formulations strongly rely on Jung's (1933/1965) assertions of the exceptional "unhistorical" individual he described as "modern man," who is proficient in his past and thus can use his creativity to break the tradition rather than dispose of it. This break of tradition is the Promethean sin, which involves a higher stage of consciousness (p. 198). Indeed, like Jung, Neumann asserted that a basic conflict the hero confronts on the path of development involves doing evil: committing a sin or a crime such as stealing fire as Prometheus did or primogeniture as Jacob did. The wrongful deed is essential for the liberation of the ego and its independence to fulfill its own needs, even when this act contradicts collective values and entails doing evil. In such a case, the Voice as the "individual expression of psychic truth" (Neumann, 1949/1990, p. 35) often stands in contradiction to conscience, and this conflict demands to be dealt with consciously. Neumann emphasized that this does not mean being "unconsciously carried away," rather it means "consciously enduring the conflict involved in the 'acceptance of evil'" (p. 106). Neumann clarified that the acceptance of evil does not always involve doing evil as an external action, as it may as well be the realization of an inner image. Nevertheless, five years later, when he wrote the appendix about the shadow for the purpose of clarification, he specifically mentioned that the disobedience he referred to is not to be understood in terms of disobedience to society but rather as existential and primary.

The significant challenge the individual faces when he arrives at a new ethic is the call to create his own scale of values, which is an act of independence and separation from the possibility of refuge in the protection of the collective values. It may well be that by following the Voice one enters a conflicting zone in which no "good" solution is possible. Therefore, the new ethic and the totality of personality do not mean that one feels at peace, as one must consciously and actively live through this negative side. Therefore, Neumann argued, the task of depth psychology is to enable one to be morally courageous enough to live to be himself, no worse and no better.

There are different levels of ethical maturity, and therefore "the conventional collective ethic" would be appropriate for those whose ego is still "primitive or infantile" (Neumann, 1949/1990, p. 112). For others whose personality is more developed and thus more whole, the Voice is the authority. Interestingly, Neumann used the word "conventional" in describing the old ethic, and Kohlberg later termed the second level of moral development "the conventional." Whether or not this is accidental is less important than the fact that it demonstrates the essential similarity of the theories of Neumann and Kohlberg, who both perceived the nonconventional (which is postconventional) as the more progressed stage, in which one have a strong footing in the conventional so that he can proceed beyond it.

As the courageous creative innovator he was, Neumann went farther with this idea of variety of ethical maturity to suggest the radical idea that "the new ethic, based as it is on depth psychology, is not interested in punishment" (Neumann, 1949/1990, p. 112). In saying this, Neumann did not blame and furthermore he did not emphasize revenge; rather, he recognized that a change of attitude is called for. I suggest that at the time of publication, when Neumann's personal relation to the subject is well understood, these words could have been seen as the expression of his mature personality and sincere activism on behalf of a better world.

At this point, Neumann arrived at one of his most challenging formulations, and misunderstood by many of his critics:

> The acknowledgment of one's own evil is "good." To be too good . . . is "evil." Evil done by anybody in a conscious way (and that always also implies full awareness of his responsibility)—evil, in fact, from which the agent does not try to escape—is ethically "good." (Neumann, 1949/1990, p. 114)

These words seem to stand in opposition to what we are accustomed to, and the direction Neumann believed we should go. Based on the understanding that, in the new ethic we are challenged with "good" and "evil" as internal concepts, the responsibility to distinguish between the two, and to bear the consequences, is ours alone. In the final analysis, based on the consideration that individuation aims at psychic wholeness, Neumann concluded that "whatever leads to wholeness is 'good'; whatever leads to splitting is 'evil.' Integration is good, disintegration is evil" (p. 126). What Neumann wrote about good and evil is radical in the way it contradicts and challenges our conventional perceptions. Nevertheless, it encourages civil responsibility and thus manifests social political and ecological activism.

When we accept evil, we accept the world—earth and earthly— and thus we accept ourselves. This is acceptance in the deepest sense of the human totality, embracing consciousness and unconsciousness, and accepting whose center is not the ego but rather the Self. Neumann pointed out that the Self is the center of the psyche as it is of body, and he continued to describe the new relationship between the ego that had grown and the Self that was now "installed" as an expression of "the newly-won ethical autonomy of personality" (1949/1990, p. 123). Neumann explained the use of the term "installation" to signify the affinity to the "proclamation of a god" as known from the history of religion. This means that the ego consciously appoints and recognizes the divinity, that is, the Self, as an authoritative control center. Neumann emphasized that the "installation" implies a change in the experience of the ego rather than something that "happened" to the Self. This means that the ego now can no longer perform its duty to the Self by following collective values and established rules; rather, self-questioning, self-doubting, and self-control are required, and this is an obligation the ego consciously takes upon itself. In the lecture "Religious Experience" delivered the same year he concluded writing *New Ethic*, Neumann (1970/1988) said,

> The ego's new central experience of being guided does not mean that the ego and consciousness are required to renounce their right of self-determination or to yield to the intentions of the unconscious or the editor. The opposite is the case; only insofar as the ego makes use of its right of self-determination is the unconscious structured in such way that the religious phenomena of guidance appear. (p. 24)

The religious phenomena Neumann referred to here is of a mystical nature and manifest a revelation of the Voice to an individual. Neumann's main point is that it is only when the ego is consciously and actively participating can an individual hear the Voice. This is the decisive element that Neumann kept returning to, that the ego at this stage realizes its relativity to the Self and must act in free will in the service of the Self. In his first Eranos lecture, Neumann (1948/1989) wrote, "we have to do with an enlarged, not dissolved consciousness; nevertheless, the ego has to a large extent renounced its autonomy in favor of the Self, which now becomes the directing center" (p. 404). The mature ego must take responsibility by submitting to its origin.

In a letter to Jung (Jung & Neumann, 2015) regarding the ape-man fantasy that Neumann admitted to be the source of *New Ethic*, he wrote that when standing at the abyss of evil, "I do not fall, but jump." He continued, "I know that the danger exists that I will die, but my prayer goes that 'wings of the heart' may hold me . . . it is not about an action of the ego, but about a happening that I must hand myself over to" (p. 332). Neumann was writing about a full, active, free-will submission of the ego to that which surrounds it. In "Religious Experience" (1970/1988), which he wrote at the same time, Neumann clarified that "the ego is forced repeatedly to take part, control, contradict, and give in" (p. 21). It is the culmination of the union of the opposites, when the ego consciously holds the paradox of being fully active in being passive.

The mature ego's responsibility goes beyond itself, as the new ethic implies an individual's collective responsibility. In that sense, an individual whose personality has achieved ethical autonomy becomes an anchor and a still point for the collective. Interestingly, Neumann cited Jung in support of those lines, and it is impossible not to think of Jung as an individual who could have been an anchor in the European storm, even though he was not.

Lastly, Neumann (1949/1990) arrived at the moral problem of the whole human race, about which he wrote that it "is at the same time the moral problem of the Godhead" (p. 132), that is, the moral problem of evil in God. Neumann followed the Jewish perception of God with two faces, good and evil. He asserted that a "man of God," such as Abraham, Jacob, or Moses, was not at all ethically superior. On the contrary, he wrote "their personalities cast a long shadow, but it was precisely for this reason that the center of their being remained in contact with the Godhead, in whose image they had been created" (p. 132). The forefathers were human in that they had shadow, and they were superior in that they maintained their connection with the inner source, with the divine within. This divine, God, was both good and evil, and the inner Voice they followed was of the divine in man. Returning to humanity, Neumann concluded his book *New Ethic* (1949/1990) with the words,

And yet, out of the midst of the circle of humanity, which is beginning to take shape from the coming-together of every part of the human species—nations and races, continents and cultures—the same creative Godhead, unformed and manifold, is emerging within the human mind, who previously filled the heavens and spheres of the universe around us. (p. 135)

Although Neumann was realistic and courageous enough to gaze at reality as is, he was, as all activists are, also essentially optimistic and believed in man.

Conclusion: Jung's and Neumann's Different Approach to Evil

Before approaching Jung and Neumann's different approach to evil, it is important to emphasize they were in deep agreement about the existential reality of evil. It is only in the way one encounter evil that they differed.

Neumann's active approach to evil as expressed in *New Ethic* is at the heart of the new ethic as he formulated it, and it is the core of his theoretical disagreement with Jung, who, unlike Neumann, believed that one can only come to terms with evil and suffer it. The disagreement was essential. For Jung it was presumably a matter of justification and cleansing of the guilt, appropriate to his passive approach toward Nazism and anti-Semitism, whereas for Neumann, the activist, it was a matter of responsibility to act. As noted earlier, Neumann asked Jung to write a foreword to the book. Jung wrote in response, "I will gladly fulfill your wish for a foreword to the planned English edition of your *Ethic*, albeit with the condition that you make a few more revisions to the current text" (Jung & Neumann, 2015, p. 246). Indeed, Jung sent his suggestions as "corrections and amendments" (2015, appendix 2, pp. 361–69).

Nevertheless, as Neumann was an activist by nature, his main motive was an ideological one and he was not intimidated by the conditions Jung posed nor did he feel subject to any approval from Jung.

Lammers (2017) followed Jung's corrections [English translation, published as an appendix of the correspondence (Jung & Neumann, 2015, pp. 361-369)] and Neumann's acceptances and rejections, and pointed to a few of Neumann's responses to Jung's corrections, which indeed indicate the essential difference in approach between the two men. At the beginning of the amended paper, Jung (Jung & Neumann, 2015) wrote,

> Please understand the propositions that follow only as supplementary suggestions. They do not seek to *replace* your text but only to supplement it. This, particularly, where you express yourself in a rather activist way. I do not wish to discourage the activism, but simply to emphasize that the shadow or the unconscious absolutely cannot be eliminated and subject to conscious. We can only learn how a grain of corn must behave between a hammer and anvil. (Appendix II, p. 361)

On the one hand Jung was very supportive. He presented the corrections as suggestions while both recognizing and encouraging Neumann's activism. On the other hand, he concluded with the main point of disagreement, to which Neumann did not submit. Only a few days later in his letter to Jung, Neumann replied, "The ethical behavior of the personality cannot *only* experience itself as the grain of corn between the hammer and anvil" (p. 254).

This essential difference is presumably a reflection of the bigger difference between the two men. Jung would rather repress his guilt feelings for not doing much against the Nazi regime and the horrors that occurred. Neumann would rather feel that he has the power to act in confronting evil. In 1917, many years prior to the horrors of the Second World War and prior to Neumann's formulation on the old and a new ethic, the preface to an article in which Jung's (1943/1972) writings about morality manifest the foundation of Neumann's further theorizing about *New Ethic*, Jung wrote,

> What the nation does is done also by each individual, and so long as the individual continues to do it, the nation will do likewise. Only a change in the attitude of the individual can initiate a change in the psychology of the nation. The great problems of humanity were never yet solved by general law, but only through regeneration of the attitude of individuals. (p. 4)

Neumann read these words around 1933 when he first came to know Jung and his theory, and he referred to them in the manuscript of *Jacob and Esau* (Neumann, 1934/2015, p. 30, note 44). Close reading of this paragraph interestingly reveals that in it, Jung encapsulated the ideas Neumann (1949/1990, 1934/2015) later amplified, broadened, and formulated in both *Jacob and Esau* and *New Ethic*: the shadowed ape-man awaiting within, the projection on the "other," collective progression beginning with individuals, the inadequacy of the old moral code, the call for a new ethic, and self-reflection all as humanity's way out of catastrophes. There is no doubt that Neumann saw Jung as a Great Individual who wrote those things. Presumably, it takes one to know one, and Jung recognized that Neumann had attained the same stature; he recognized that Erich Neumann was a Great Individual.

PART II

EARLY LIFE DEVELOPMENTAL RELATIONAL THEORY

Introduction

Aimed at portraying Erich Neumann as an important and relevant Jungian developmental and relational theoretician, Part II presents Neumann's significant oblation and supplement to Jung's theory, that is, a theory about the psychological development of the child.

Neumann's theory of early life's psychological development entails the development of the conscious from its embryonic state prior to or at birth to its maturity as a unified ego in early childhood. In addition, while attempting to differentiate the development from boy to man from that of girl to woman, it describes psychological development from childhood to its culmination in later life's individuation process. It is at this peak point of individuation that Neumann's theory completes the full circle, as presented in Part I, from the primal unity, symbolized by the paradisiacal uroboros, through the separation of the systems, and back to their mature synthesis symbolized by the mandala as heavenly Jerusalem (1949/2014, p. 37).

As Neumann was a male theoretician, by nature his perspective was masculine, even though he was undoubtedly writing primarily about the feminine aspect of the masculine psyche. He did so by utilizing his psychic femininity, creativity, and intuition. Nevertheless, his masculinity resulted in some bias that needs to be considered regarding his theorizing about the primal relationship, in which Neumann took the baby's perspective as he described the baby's development. I, the feminine author of this book, was immersed in a primal relationship with my four biological children and therefore I carry the embodied psychological experience of these relationships. To some extent, this fact will be woven into this chapter, both unconsciously, and consciously. Unconsciously, by the bias of my inherent feminine perspective. Consciously, by a terminological addition suggesting labeling the time from physical birth and separation from the womb to the psychological birth with the establishment of a unified ego and unified Self as a *psychological pregnancy*.

As early life developmental theory naturally extends from early infancy to a few years of age, some clarification of the terminology is needed. Unlike Neumann who mostly used the "child," the author of this manuscript is utilizing Neumann's theory in working with infants as well. Therefore, in the following, the word *infant* will refer to the initial stage of the uroboric phase, between birth and about 6 weeks of age. *Baby* will refer to the whole duration of the primal relationship whereas *child* will refer to the entirety of childhood preceding primal relationship and prior to puberty.

Chapter 5
Neumann's Conceptualization and Terminology

Background of Child Analysis in Jungian Theory

Jung theorized about the second half of life and the process of individuation characterizing this phase. He did not theorize about early life; he saw children as unconscious beings, an extension of their parents, and thus maintained that a child should be treated through his parents. Moreover, as Fordham (1980) described the early days of Jungian analytical practice, the Jungian perspective held that, due to their unconscious state, children are exposed to the archetypal forces threatening them from within, and it is the role of their parents to protect them. This perspective was espoused by Frances G. Wickes, whose book *The Inner World of Childhood* (1927/1988) was the only Jungian publication about children for many years. This book represents a Jungian approach to child therapy; however, it does not present a Jungian theory about childhood, a fact that Jung himself noted in the introduction he (Jung, 1927/1988) wrote. On the other hand, psychoanalytic theories in England continued to follow Freud's ideas and theorized further about childhood, to the point where practitioners split into groups. Anna Freud theorized about children's defenses, and her followers became the Freudians; Melanie Klein theorized about infancy, and her followers became the Kleinians. Donald W. Winnicott, who is the psychoanalytical source of this chapter, as a central figure in current psychoanalytical theories, was a member of the middle group, later known as the independent group. His theory about infancy still dominates the relational field, and as it complements Neumann's theory and vice versa, it supports the relevancy of Neumann's work.

Fordham and Neumann, Cain and Abel

The gap between the richness of early life theories in psychoanalysis on the one hand and the lack in analytical psychology's early life theory on the other created a need that was addressed by two Jungian theoreticians, Erich Neumann and Michael Fordham. They are perceived as rivals to this day, mainly due to a deprecatory article about Neumann's formulations published by Fordham more than twenty years after Neumann's death and after his book, *The Child* (1963/1990), was posthumously published.

As followers of Jung, both Neumann and Fordham came to Zurich in 1933 to be analyzed and certified by him. Neumann was accepted and analyzed by Jung for a short while before he was sent to Toni Wolff. Fordham's request, on the other hand, was rejected, and he was never analyzed by Jung. Presumably, this was Neumann's first point of advantage. Neumann was close to and favored by Jung, who fostered him and, in many ways, cultivated his work as a theoretician while he worked and wrote in isolation in Israel. On the other hand, Fordham went back to England where he was analyzed in an unconventional way by Helton Godwin Baynes (B. Feldman, personal communication). In London, Fordham was heavily influenced by Anna Freud, Melanie Klein, Donald Winnicott, and Alfred Bion. Although Fordham was English and his natural connection was to the British empirical school of thought, he was nevertheless a passionate Jungian.

Although Jung repeatedly made clear references to Neumann's work, appreciating it as an elaboration of his own Fordham never received such appreciation and clearly expressed his disappointment

(Fordham, 1975, p. 108) at Jung's "making no reference" to (i.e., ignoring) what Fordham wrote about childhood. Symbolically, the rivalry between Fordham and Neumann had characteristics of the biblical story of Cain and Abel (B. Lahav, personal communication). As described, both Neumann and Fordham brought an oblation to Jung. Although Neumann's, like Abel's, was accepted, Fordham's, like Cain's, was denied. Therefore, Fordham "murdered" Neumann in his deprecating and almost disreputable article (Fordham, 1981) that seemed to aim at the annihilation of Neumann the theoretician and his early life theory.

Close reading of the harshly critical article Fordham wrote indicates that he misread Neumann, or rather, Neumann failed to clearly articulate. The following will aim at indicating that there are no essential theoretical differences between Fordham and Neumann. Furthermore, Fordham's misreading may also be partly attributed to the editorial decision by Neumann's wife to publish the *The Child* in unedited form. Therefore, Part II presents Neumann's comprehensive theory of infancy and psychological development of early life to offer a correction to any misunderstandings or misreading of Neumann (When such correction is made, there will be no quotation of Fordham's criticism; instead, only the page number in his controversial article will be noted). Furthermore, the corrections aim to identify and indicate the essential and important points of agreement and similarities between Neumann's and Fordham's postulations. Hence, the following offers a unified Jungian perspective of infant's psychological development that directly addresses a critical need in the field of Jungian psychology.

One of Fordham's repeated criticisms of Neumann was that he did not work with children; therefore, his theory was not rooted in practice. To answer this, first, there is Meier-Seethaler's (1982) comment: "The lack of empirical data, compared to the wealth of symbolical-mythological interpretation is a shortcoming that is more relative than substantial" (p. 3). Second, I suggest that there are three points of reference. The first being that this criticism does not hold enough relevance to fully dismiss Neumann's theory; his major contribution to child analysis relates to the first year of life and especially to the significance of the primal relationship; because this stage of life is nonverbal and unrememberable, any theory about it would require a kind of imagining into the reality of the infant. Secondly, although Fordham analyzed children, he did not see any infants in his first years of theorizing. In later years (starting in 1976), he utilized infant observations that he supervised to approve or adjust his formulations (Astor, 1990, p. 269). Given that he himself never conducted infant observation (B. Feldman, personal communication), therefore he had no advantage over Neumann in theorizing about infancy.

The last point of reference is the way in which one's theory is formulated. Interestingly, Neumann's best advocate is Winnicott (1945), who described the process through which he arrived at his formulations:

> I shall not first give an historical survey and show the development of my ideas from the theories of others, because my mind does not work that way. What happens is that I gather this and that, here and there, settle down to clinical experience, form my own theories and then, last of all, interest myself in looking to see where I stole what. Perhaps this is a good a method as any." (p. 145)

This is an honest description of the creative process, as Neumann would say. This is a process in which one becomes a kind of vessel through which the various components of theoretical ideas come together to give birth to an altogether new theory. It seems that Winnicott has provided an archetypal description of the work of a theoretician that provides insight into the truth of Neumann's approach.

Indeed, Neumann never saw a child patient in his clinic, and this is a shortcoming and disadvantage of the environment from which he delivered a new theory. Nevertheless, the following pages will indicate how, in many ways, his early life theory emerged independently from his initial writings. His single book on childhood, *The Child* (1963/1990), along with the theory, is based, on clinical material presented to him by Jungian analysts working with children whom he met weekly as his supervenes. In addition to this material, Neumann had another inner source. As his old friend Gerhard Adler (1960/1979) wrote in his eulogy of Neumann, "his work did not spring from his intellect but from a deep and living contact with the unconscious sources of creativity" (p. xv). Therefore, I suggest that Neumann had a deep intuitive understanding of the human psyche and a unique ability to imagine the existential reality of a baby.

Neumann, as his biography indicates, was first and foremost a philosopher. On the one hand this assessment implies that his interest was with the "big picture" from which he constructed a theory, according to his collective and archetypal perspective. On the other hand, as Jung (1954/1990c) described, the philosopher, as opposed to the empiricist, "takes it for granted that his own disposition and attitudes are universal" (p. 75). Therefore, arguably Neumann was not as interested in proving the validity of his theory as he was in theorizing per se. In addition, as is widely agreed, Neumann's style of writing was poetic and, in that sense, somewhat feminine, round, and repetitive. He did not strive to be accurate in isolating any given point; rather he took a descriptive and phenomenological stance when theorizing a lived experience. Presumably, this singular aspect of the differences in writing style between Neumann, first and foremost a philosopher, and Fordham, first and foremost an empiricist, became the source of Fordham's criticism of Neumann's writing.

An Overview of Neumann's Contribution

A perspective gained over time indicates that Neumann's early life psychological development theory has proved itself valuable and contributed an important central term to the analytical developmental dialogue—that is, the *ego-Self axis*. Moreover, Neumann's greatest contribution is that he drew attention to the centrality of the relationship between the ego and the Self and its significance in psychological development. Although the term *ego-Self axis* is commonly perceived as originating in his early life theory, it is a central term in Neumann's theory regarding early and later life. Part I pointed to its origin as a germ of perception in Neumann's thought, whereas Part II and this chapter explore the concept in depth to present its origin in the theory and its importance to early life developmental theory. Another one of Neumann's significant contributions is that of indicating and describing the importance of the primal relationship to later psychic health by presenting its archetypal role in the psychological development of the child and the establishment of the ego-Self axis.

The following chapters present Neumann's formulation as the theoretical "skeleton" for the "flesh and blood" of Fordham's and Winnicott's formulations, as representation of other relational theoreticians as well. Hence, Neumann's theory is presented as the archetypal framework of a unified early life developmental theory. Supporting this claim, Carola Meier-Seethaler's article (1982), "The Child: Erich Neumann's Contribution to the Psychopathology of Child Development," provides a comparative and complementary analysis of Neumann and relational theoreticians regarding pathologies. Her article indicates that Neumann's theory contributed to opening an important pathway of therapeutically valuable future research. Joel Cappiello McCurdy (1987) used Neumann's formulation of the ego-Self axis in discussing manic-depressive psychosis rooted in disturbances of the primal relationship, resulting in a damaged ego-Self axis. In addition, Alon and Shany (2022) elaborated on Neumann's concept of ego-Self axis in Trauma to describe the possible damage, and further, the possible repair through analysis.

Neumann spent his fruitful years in Israel, where he taught, qualified, and certified the first generation of Jungian analysts, whom he also supervised. Neumann's theory is to this day alive and central to both the studies and the theoretical framework of Jungian analysis in Israel for analysts working with both adults and children. Moreover, his early life theory found its way not only into child analysis there, but it also (to some extent) informally permeated institutional work, at least as a framework. Sadly, and surprisingly, none of this important work done in Israel was communicated to the world, and not much is known about the two channels through which Neumann's theory remains alive there. One is in the personal settings of Jungian child analysts (private and public services) who strongly endorse Neumann's formulation as a structure, and the second is within the boarding school Hamaon of Neve-Ze'elim, described toward the end of the next chapter.

Neumann died suddenly and at an early age, so much of the anticipated application of his theory was hampered—in particular, his theory about early life psychological development. The clearest unfortunate result was the posthumous publication of *The Child* (1963/1990) by Neumann's wife, Julie, in unedited draft form. Louis H. Stewart (1990), an experienced child analyst and one of the founders of the San Francisco Jung Institute, wrote a foreword to the 1990 edition of the book, in which he said,

> Sad to say, due to Neumann's untimely death in 1960, this book is unfinished. The editors decided, wisely I believe, to leave it in its first-draft state with all the virtues and faults inherent in such a manuscript. On the one hand, we have the rare opportunity to experience the enthusiasm and driving energy that often characterize a

first, unedited draft. On the other hand, we are left with
the inevitable repetitions and incomplete treatment of
certain issues. (p. x)

Although Stewart believed the decision to publish the unedited
manuscript was wise, he nevertheless admitted the disadvantages.
Not only was Stuart right, further, the additional 30 years since
indicate that indeed, the repetitions and confusing articulations were
a major disadvantage that prevented many potential readers from
reading the book. Instead, they relied on opponents' reviews, which
were clearly articulated and widely published. To revive the theory
emerging from *The Child* and to rearticulate it as a comprehensive
yet simple to read theory about the psychological development
of infants, babies, and young children, it is presented in Part II,
supported by relevant articles written by Neumann that further
elaborate the ideas.

Lastly, since Neumann wrote this theory in the late 1950's,
the field of child analysis had developed significantly, mainly
in psychoanalytical circles. Infant observations had become an
important tool in learning about infancy and its psychological
experience, and a central component in the training programs. The
observer is exposed to strong transference and countertransference
experiences that significantly enrich the training. One possible
implication of reviving Neumann's theory, and particularly his
early life development theory, will be to add his perspective and
with it some more theoretical clarity and understanding to the
phenomenological nature of the observations.

The Archetypal Perspective

The ontology of Neumann's theory about the baby's psychological
development is that it is an autonomous archetypal unfolding of the
psychic structure throughout the primal relationship, enabled by a

human mother figure unconsciously manifesting the archetypal role of Mother. Clearly the theory is Jungian, in that it is situated within the realm of the archetypes and the Mother archetype in particular; however, at the same time it grants great importance to the personal mother because only in her presence can the primal relationship take place. Therefore, Neumann's early life theory has the potential of strengthening the bridge between Jungian psychology and psychoanalysis as it is situated in the liminal space between personal and archetypal, reality and inner images.

Neumann's formulations significantly amplify Jung's antecedent writings about children, not only in the sense mentioned earlier— that children are not mere extensions of their parents and treated through them— but also in the perception of the early life relationship. In his early writings, originally published in 1926, Jung (1946/1991) described both parents as equally important, not only to the psychology of the child and to the diagnosis, but also in terms of nourishment and warmth (p. 70). On the other hand, although he fully acknowledged the role of the father in a child's psychological development, Neumann singled out the mother in emphasizing the importance of the primal relationship—between mother and baby— to psychic health. In this case Neumann was referring to whoever takes the role of the mother, implying that a male could do so only from the feminine aspect of his psyche, with all its limitations and with the restriction that he could not successfully assume the role of both father and mother for the child, as one of the two roles would be diminished.

The work that symbolizes Jung's departure from Freud, originally published in 1912 (under a different title), was revised in 1952 as *Symbols of Transformation* (Jung, 1952/1990), in which Jung admitted that his aim was to turn away from the subjective and personalistic perspective that characterized "medical psychology" (p. xxiv) in favor of accepting the existence of an objective and collective psyche in the unconscious. In the introduction Jung edited in 1952, he was more specific, stating that Freud and his followers were dealing with analysis of individual problems whereas his attention was moving toward comparative study of the historical in the hope of broadening the foundations of psychology. Also in this introduction, he mentioned Neumann's work, describing it as the broadening of his own work: "Here the research of Erich Neumann has made a massive contribution towards solving the countless difficult problems that crop up everywhere in this hitherto little explored territory" (p. 6). The "territory" that Jung referred to comprises the historical, mythological, and ethnological parallels to psychology, and with this remark he granted full validity to Neumann's use of mythology in theorizing about human psychological development. Jung wrote this remark in a general sense but referred specifically to *Origins*, in which Neumann made extensive use of mythological material; Jung described it as carrying forward his own ideas.

In his Eranos lecture, "Reality Planes," Neumann (1952/1989) clearly stated that "the development of human conscious is directed by archetypes . . . [that] are characterized . . . by being directive and orientative. . . . And they behave as well as if they had knowledge, or as if knowledge were incorporated in them" (p. 11). Although Neumann referred to the development of human consciousness, obviously his words hold true when discussing psychological development, which first and foremost entails the development of consciousness.

Five years later, in response to an invitation to elaborate on the symbolism of the Great Mother, Neumann published his second major work, *The Great Mother* (1955/1991). In this work, alongside his exploration of the symbolism of the Great Mother using ethnological material, he theorized in detail about the psychological developmental aspects of the archetypal Feminine. To this day this book is considered the deepest analysis ever done about the Great

Mother, and it is commonly cited by scholars. The relevance of his writings about the archetypal Feminine to his developmental theory, stems from the fact that the personal mother is the initial and most significant influence of an individual image (imago) and perception of the Feminine.

One year before his untimely death, Neumann published the essay "The Significance of the Genetic Aspect for Analytic Psychology" (1959), in which he addressed the tension between personal and collective. He recognized a theoretical and a therapeutic need to synthesize the two factors, which means recognizing that the conjunction of personal history with archetypal precondition takes place within the human psyche. Therefore, although he valued the Freudian personalistic perspective, he effectively advocated for a Jungian theory that would suggest an archetypal perspective that complements the personalistic one. Neumann (1959) explained what he was suggesting as "revealing a general plan in which the personalistic events acquire their *position and their value*" (p. 125; emphasis added). The concepts of position and value are at the core of the importance of Neumann's theory to current developmental relational theories, as "position" belongs to the personal timely and historical whereas "value" belongs to the collective timeless and archetypal. Neumann's theory describes the archetypal path of development, and thus any deviation from the path needs to be explored in relation to its position, referring to time as age and the correlating value as the archetypal meaning.

The Self: Early Life Aspects

Before considering the way Neumann theorized about the Self at infancy, and to be faithful and loyal to the overall greatness of his theory, it is important to note that in theorizing about the Self, Neumann took the bravest, far-reaching step in advancing Jung's theory to the realm of metapsychology. This he did mainly in his

Eranos essay "Reality Planes" (Neumann, 1952/1989), in which he postulated the Self as being both the centering archetype, as theorized by Jung, and a reality field encompassing extraneous knowledge as he elaborated Jung's thought. The seed of this thought is found already in *Origins* (1949/2014), where Neumann discussed conscious ego perception, which "has inklings of another and, so he thinks, deeper 'extraworldly' knowledge" (p. 23). There he related it to the borderline experience before birth and after death; in his Eranos article he elaborated it further to describe a mature personality that has gained access to the Self-field. As a deeper layer than the archetypal field, the Self-field encompasses inner and outer, as "a deep regulating or ordering field" (p. 49), which unlike the formative archetypal field, is a formless, creative and spontaneous ordering plane. Neumann wrote, "And the central Self-form, the godhead within us, appears the same as the godhead who is the creator of the world" (p. 59); thus, he described the Self as most within and none the less without. In Neumann's later theorizing about early life development, this idea is echoed in the description of the infant's perception of the Self as both his own and the other.

At the beginning of his posthumous book, *The Child*, Neumann (1963/1990) explains the need to create terminology that would differentiate analytical psychology from psychoanalysis. He argued that "borrowing terms created by Freud and his school tends to blur the profound difference between our thinking and theirs" (p. 8). Here Neumann referred to Freud's personalistic perspective as opposed to Jung's archetypal perspective, as mentioned earlier. As Jung's terminology distinguished his theoretical perspective from that of Freud, Neumann used new terminology, not previously used elsewhere, when he theorized in terms of the archetypal process. Therefore, the criticism of creating new terminology as a shortcoming of Neumann's theory (Fordham, 1981, pp. 107–108) becomes irrelevant.

Some of the new terms Neumann suggested were imprinted in the analytical dialogue. For the most part they referred to and amplified Jung's notion of the Self in ways that had not previously been described by Jung. The most well-known and widely accepted and used term is the *ego-Self axis*, which is an amplification of the notion of the Self and its relation to the ego and a recognition of the importance of the affinity between them. No less important, although less understood, are the terms *centroversion* and *automorphism*, which are functional aspects of the Self, as is the term *body-Self*.

Before proceeding to Neumann's formulations, it is relevant to mention that Fordham's most well-known concepts, *deintegration* and *reintegration*, which will be discussed later, both manifest an amplification of the notion of the Self as well, and they are also a new terminology. Nevertheless, unlike Neumann's formulations, which describe archetypal psychic elements and structure, Fordham's formulations are functional and describe the process through which the structure is created. In that sense, clearly, Neumann's and Fordham's formulations are complementary to one another.

Throughout his writings, Neumann emphasized that, when theorizing about the unconscious, one uses consciousness to describe that which is beyond it; therefore, any attempt is limited to what is perceivable by the conscious. This becomes an obstacle when describing paradoxical psychic elements. Such a paradox clearly exists in Jung's theory, in which the Self is described as both the center and the totality of psyche. Astor (1990) suggested that Fordham solved the paradox by using the terms *deintegrate* and *reintegrate*, which manifest partial aspects of the Self and its dynamism (p. 265). Neumann (1963/1990), on the other hand, not only did not attempt to solve the paradoxical nature of the Self, but he furthered it by adding another paradoxical aspect, indicating that "the Self is that which is most our own, but at the same time it takes the form of 'thou'" (p. 13). As he explained, for the conscious as "I," the Self as unconscious is "thou," represented both inwardly and outwardly—as archetypal projections on the outside world objects—and therefore the Self has an Eros character, that is, relatedness.

This is a very important aspect of Neumann's theory and a source of major misunderstandings of his formulations that were intensified by a sentence he wrote allegedly claiming that the mother *is* the child Self (Neumann, 1963/1990, p. 13). It is more than clear that Neumann wrote this sentence from the infant's perspective to describe how the not-yet-ego-conscious—therefore having no perception yet—experiences the Self. Therefore, Neumann wrote from his phenomenological perspective about the lived experience of the infant, whereas Fordham read Neumann's writings from his empiricist perspective. I suggest that at least some of Fordham's criticism (1981, p. 111) is due to this essential difference in perspective between them. It is worth mentioning that Fordham's empiricism was also at the center of a disagreement he had with Jung about the heredity of the archetypes (cited in Jung & Neumann, 2015, pp. 338–339, and note 579, p. 338). The fact Fordham was in a strong theoretical disagreement with Jung, which Jung discussed with Neumann, is relevant to strengthen the claim of difference in perspectives.

Neumann's formulation of the infant's experience of his Self through the mother is supported and refined by Winnicott's (1964/1987a) clarification:

> In the very early stage of emotional development . . . there is a very simple idea of the self. In fact, with good enough mothering, there need be only the very beginning of an idea of the self, or should I say, *none at all*. (p. 43; emphasis added)

Careful in articulating, Winnicott arrived at the same infantile experience as Neumann described. Nevertheless, although Neumann theorized that, for the infant, the mother is the Self, there is no doubt that at the depth of this statement he saw the Self as a priori. He wrote explicitly that "analytical psychology attributes to the Self, as the totality of the individual, the quality of a datum given *a-priori* and unfolding in the course of life" (p. 19). When he wrote that this is the perception of analytical psychology, he was standing firmly on the grounds that Jung (1954/1969a) had established when he described the relationship between the ego and the Self:

> The ego stands to the self as the moved to the mover, or as object to subject, because the determining factors which radiate out from the self surround the ego on all sides and are therefore supraordinate to it. The self, like the unconscious, is an *a priori* existent out of which the ego evolves. It is, so to speak, an unconscious prefiguration of the ego. (p. 259)

This formulation of Jung may be seen as the firm grounds on which Neumann stood when he was further theorizing about the relations between the ego and the Self. He thus theorized that, although the Self preexists in the psyche, it cannot initially be experienced as a totality by the infant. Although Fordham (1981) described Neumann's formulation of the Self (pp. 104, 114) as another point of disagreement between them, as shown here they were essentially in agreement, both holding Jung's perception of the self as given *a priori* (Fordham, 1980, p. 314).

Neumann (1955/1989) theorized that in the initial state, that of unitary reality (to be discussed later), in which there is yet no ego, there is a "diffusion of the body image in relation to the world" (p. 74). As the mother represents the world, and there is no differentiation between the infant and its mother and accordingly no differentiation between outside and inside, this diffusion implies what Neumann referred to as a *body-Self*.

Body-Self

At birth, while yet absent of consciousness, the only experience available to the infant is sensory; therefore, the body becomes the center of his being. When differentiation begins, the body is the initial source of imagery that will later develop into the conscious. Accordingly, Neumann formulated the body-Self as the first manifestation of the person of the infant and its individuality. In his posthumous manuscript, *The Child* (1963/1990), he wrote,

> To the earliest biological grounded manifestation of the Self we have given the name: body-Self. It is the delimited and unique totality of the individual, now freed from its embeddedness in the maternal body; it comes into being with the biopsychic unity of the body. (p. 11)

Thus, Neumann presented the first important fact about the body-Self; that is, it is a biopsychic unity. Specifically, the infant psychological being is not yet born; as with the physical birth, the psyche is an embryo, and therefore the Self at that stage is experienced exclusively through the body. Accordingly, and significant to elucidating this formulation, he stated emphatically that the body-Self also has the character of a totality and should not be taken as a mere physiological entity, for bodily disposition and psychic disposition, hereditary constellation and individuality, are already present in the biopsychic unity of the body-Self (p. 13).

Here Neumann emphasizes that the biopsychic unity of the body-Self is far beyond mere body as it already contains all the germs of what will later become a unitary Self. Astor (1990) described Fordham's formulation as "a primary or an original self present at birth which then of necessity divided into parts" (p. 262). Clearly Neumann and Fordham formulated essentially the same idea: the Self is at origin an integrated unity, which, with birth, becomes partial or deintegrates and is then motivated to reintegrate.

Neumann furthered this idea and presented his radical point, which was widely overlooked or deeply misunderstood (Fordham, 1980, p. 99; 114–115), when he wrote, "In the earliest stage . . . the mother as externalized Self, as relatedness-Self, *complements* the child's body-Self" (1963/1990, pp. 27–28; emphasis added). It becomes clear that Neumann described the infant's Self as an *a priori* psychic fact that, together with the infant, separates from the maternal womb at birth. Nevertheless, because the infant is not yet psychologically born, and the psychological pregnancy of about one more year begins only with the physical birth, the Self as biopsychic unity becomes a body-Self whereas the psychological aspect of the Self remains in the maternal psychological womb, that is, the mother's psyche. This is a radical idea, and completely unlike the reduction and fragmentation of the Self into a body-Self, as Neumann's critics had unjustly interpreted his formulation. Neumann critically theorized that it is the psychological aspect of the Self that is not yet born at the physical birth. Accordingly, the challenging developmental process awaiting the baby's psyche during the first year of life will culminate in the migration of the relatedness aspect of the Self into the child's psyche and consequently the establishment of a unified independent ego.

When the concept of body-Self is understood as the sensory perceivable partial Self located in the body, the Eros character of the Self—the relatedness aspect—is, from the adult perspective, left deposited within the mother's psyche. Due to her immersion in the unitary reality with the infant, she psychically and critically functions as the infant's psychological Self—as Neumann (1963/1990) wrote, "the functional sphere of the Self incarnated in the mother" (p. 18). Clearly, this is not to say that she is in essence the infant's Self, but rather to say that, as she functions as the Self, *from the infant's perspective* she *is* the Self. This formulation holds truth when thinking of the liminal zone, that which is not within and not without psyche, that which both mother and infant share, there, they relate with unified Self.

Interestingly, Fordham (1980) described a very similar perception—theoretically quite the same—although he used different terminology. For him this initial process involved the process of *deintegration*:

> The idea that the self was primary meant that the state of *participation mystique* would have to be developed and require activity on the part of the infant. Adhering to the language of integration, the self must therefore become active; it must deintegrate. (p. 315)

Critically Fordham expressed the same idea as did Neumann; they both agreed that, as early as the initial state of the primal relationship, the infant's Self is in a sense breaking the integration to leave a part with the mother (Neumann) or send a part to the mother (Fordham). Hence, the remaining disagreement is the question of whether the baby is active or passive in the process, and as at this stage as there is yet no conscious, any activity or passivity is inherent; therefore, the disagreement becomes almost irrelevant.

Once the Self as an *a priori* psychic unity is theoretically established, and as it is clear that the ego is not *a priori*, there arises the question of the relation between these two psychic authorities. Neumann (1963/1990) first described this relation as follows:

> The total personality and its directing center, the Self, exist before the ego takes form and develops into the center of consciousness; the laws governing the development of the ego and consciousness are dependent on the unconscious and the total personality, which is represented by the Self. (p. 9)

Neumann leaves no doubt that he perceives the Self as exists prior to the ego and governing its development. For the structural psychic organ enabling this process of ego development, Neumann coined the term *ego-Self axis.*

Ego-Self Axis

As was previously suggested, the seed of Neumann's formulation of an ego-Self axis is found in his first manuscript, where he cited Jung's assertion from their correspondence: "The inner is invisible and always seems to be powerless. In reality, however, it rules secretly and pervasively and its power is as great as the sun's" (Jung & Neumann, 2015, p. 58). Jung is referring to the moon and the sun which Neumann mentioned in the draft manuscript of his analysis of the Jacob and Esau story. In the final text, Neumann (1934/2015) incorporated Jung's assertion into his first description of the relationship between the ego and the Self, which he then described as inner and outer. He there wrote, "the extent to which the outer stems from the inner, and who see through the outer to the inner standing behind it" (p. 9). Further into this initial manuscript, Neumann anchored the archetypal idea in the psychological manifestation when he referred to "consciousness, this small and late child of the unconscious" (p. 50).

Neumann used this analog of the ego as the child of the Self again in his first Eranos lecture, "Mystical Man" (1948/1989), in which he described the Self releasing the ego so that the ego learns to "walk" (p. 401) and in a later lecture (1952/1989) where he described the ego as an "offspring" (p. 11). Therefore, it is evident that the relationship between the ego and the Self was central to Neumann's thinking long before he theorized about early life development, and presumably the term ego-Self axis emerged naturally from within the theory. Evidently Neumann (1970/1988) first used the term *ego-Self* to represent a psychic structural element in his 1943 lecture, "Religious Experience," where he wrote that "the Self is experienced as an ego-Self, which is superior to the ego alone, or as a singular element in the psychic structure of man manifested in the individual" (p. 23). Here Neumann first pointed to the strong affinity between ego and Self, which implies that structurally their affinity is more significant than independence from one another.

The incubation of this formulation in Neumann's mind took about ten more years, as the first clear mention of the ego-Self axis is in his Eranos lecture, "Reality Planes (1952/1989)." In this first formulation, Neumann defines the ego-Self axis with reference to external knowledge that is not rooted in the ego-conscious and thus must be linked to some other and deeper layers of psyche, the archetypal field and the self-field, which are planes of reality incorporated with knowledge. As Neumann theorizes,

> The ego-Self axis makes the process of image-emergence possible, i.e., it makes possible the emerging visibility of the formed [*gestaltenten*] field and thus the development of luminosity . . . the ego-Self axis brings about the conceiving of archetypal images and thus the beginning of the process-of-becoming-conscious itself. (p. 58)

In this early definition, Neumann established the foundation for his later work on early life development, where he describes the axis as a decisive structural element, enabling the creation of forms and thus images that are crucial to the development of conscious and thus the ego and to psychic health.

In this lecture, as mentioned earlier, Neumann (1952/1989) suggests a significant elaboration of Jung's original notion of the Self as an archetype when he presented the Self as a field deeper than the archetypal field. This is another and extremely important point of agreement between Fordham and Neumann regarding the perception of the notion of the Self. Fordham wrote, "It followed that descriptions of the self involving the idea of its being an archetype are inappropriate, and I found it better to think of the self as beyond archetypes and ego" (1980, p. 315). It is clear therefore that, like Neumann, Fordham saw beyond Jung's initial definition; moreover, Jung never contradicted either of them on this issue. Therefore, they both arrived at a conclusion that elaborated and amplified Jung's theory.

In addition, in this formulation, not only did Neumann's theory go a step beyond Jung's, but he also surpassed psychology to become metapsychology, as his title reflects: "The Psyche and the Transformation of the Reality Planes: A Metapsychological Essay." The essay effectively presented a revolutionary perception of psychic life, which extends psychology toward existentialism. Accordingly, Neumann theorizes that the external knowledge that awaits the psyche in the archetypal field stems from this deeper layer of the Self-field. This he saw as the regulating field, from which human creativity and freedom originate. This fact is important as creativity is central to Neumann's theory, as he claimed that creativity is that which is human. He theorized that the connection and relation of these layers, the archetypal-field and the Self-field, with consciousness is via the axis, the ego-Self axis: "The connection between the Self-field and ego-consciousness is brought about, as I see it, by the *Self-ego and ego-Self axis*; namely, the central axis which constellates the regulating phenomenon of form, and thereby the possibility of cognition per se" (p. 20; emphasis added). Contained in this very initial formulation are the decisive elements of the axis, representing a significant amplification of Jung's original perception of the relation between the ego and the Self as purely hierarchical, beyond which Neumann saw that they are reciprocal personality centers revolving around the axis.

There is no doubt that the concept of the ego-Self axis is Neumann's greatest recognized contribution to the analytical dialogue. Nevertheless, his formulation of their reciprocal nature is commonly overlooked, especially by his critics who presumably confused *stable* with *stagnated* in Neumann's theory. It can never be emphasized enough that this was not Neumann's perception or postulation. In *The Child* (1963/1990), he wrote,

> The ego-Self axis is always in motion, for it is affected by every change in conscious. Not only in sleep and in dreams, but in every psychic process the relation between conscious and the unconscious and between the ego and the Self, are modified. (p. 47)

Neumann indicated here the multiple situations in which the axis is affected and in motion. When he mentioned sleep, he implied that a change occurs in the axis every night while the ego is suspended. Nevertheless, the change is not structural; rather it is functional and is the move toward and away from each other.

He later added another important aspect when he wrote that "the ego-Self axis is normally in flux" (1955/1966, p. 85); presumably this may be described as the change in direction of psychic energy. This assumption is supported by Neumann's initial remarks (1952/1989) about the term *ego-Self axis*: "All changes, expansions, and transformations of the personality, not merely the development of the ego and the conscious mind, take place by way of this axis" (p. 57). This is highly significant and relevant as it points to the importance of the axis beyond early life—to the flow of psychic energy, to the developmental process, and to therapy. Indeed, Edward F. Edinger elaborated on Neumann's original formulation and described the relationship between ego and Self as "two processes occurring simultaneously, namely, progressive ego-Self separation, and also increasing emergence of the ego-Self axis into consciousness" (1972/1992, p. 6). He used this description to theorize about possible therapeutic application, relying on different possible positions of the ego on the axis and in relating to the Self as they manifest in explicit psychic situations.

The second important aspect of the axis, beyond its structural importance, is functional. The axis has a regulatory function, which

Neumann theorized originates in the creative and spontaneous ordering and regulating nature of the Self-field. In the archetypal developmental process, during the primal relationship, the mother holds and manifests the psychological functional relatedness aspect of the Self, and therefore she is the regulating factor in terms of compensation. Hence, once the primal relationship is concluded, the ego becomes the center of the conscious, and the Self the center of personality and the inclusive totality of the Self field. The ego-Self axis is thus established as manifesting the relationship between the ego and the Self and therefore as the psychic regulating factor. Both aspects of the axis—the reciprocal and the regulatory—became pivotal to Neumann's early life developmental theory. The first was mostly overlooked, and the second became a decisive function in the primal relationship, as will be described subsequently.

Apparently, Neumann's original formulation of an ego-Self axis was not necessarily specific to early life development; it also had relevancy to later life developmental processes such as individuation. In this respect, the term has significant therapeutic relevance not only to child analysis but also to adult analysis. The centrality of the axis to the functioning of the total personality, as it connects between the different systems, implies that any therapy will aim to ensure the stability and strength of the axis.

Jung (1951/1978) described the importance of the relation between ego and Self for adult psychology in "*Aion: Research into the Phenomenology of the Self*":

> The ego is, by definition, subordinate to the Self and is related to it like a part to the whole. Inside the field of consciousness it has, as we say, free will . . . the subjective feeling of freedom. But just as our free will clashes with necessity in the outside world, so also it finds its limits outside the field of consciousness in the subjective inner world, where it comes into conflict with the facts of the

> Self . . . the ego is sometimes actually assimilated by
> unconscious components of the personality that are in the
> process of development and is greatly altered by them.
> (p. 5)

In this passage, although Jung was describing the ego, he nevertheless pointed to the fact that the ego is the executor of the Self, and even when it allegedly acts in free will, the will is subordinated to the Self as the total personality, often to the point of conflict. In the previous chapter it was shown that in Neumann's theory the conscious subordination of the ego to the Self (as a free choice made by the ego) is an advanced achievement of individuation.

In the Eranos lecture, "Reality Planes (1952/1989)," in which Neumann first used and imprinted the term *ego-Self axis* with relation to the connection between reality planes, he also created a clear connection of the axis to early life and to psychological and conscious development:

> We call the connection between the ego and the Self an
> axis because the whole development and shaping of the
> personality circles around it. It is, as reality, inherent in
> the psyche from the beginning. . . .This axis, however, is
> also the mainstay for the formation and development of
> the conscious mind. (p. 57)

Here Neumann clearly situated the ego-Self axis in the realm of early life. Nevertheless, he did not further the discussion about the establishment of the axis during the primal relationship.

Indeed, in 1955, the significance of the establishment of the ego-Self axis during the primal relationship was already well rooted in Neumann's thinking as it appeared in two articles he wrote that year: "Unitary Reality" (1955/1989), presented at Eranos, and "Narcissism and Self-formation (1955/1966)," which was published in Zurich. At the latter, Neumann delivered the clear definition and decisive importance of his newly imprinted term *ego-Self axis*: "That means that the ego-Self relationship, the ego-Self axis, *the backbone of psychic development*, is here constellated in a paradoxical inner-outer situation between the person of the child and that of the mother" (p. 86; emphasis added). Here Neumann identified two aspects of the importance of the axis in early life. The first is its significance and centrality to psychic development and health, which is Neumann's important contribution to the depth psychological understanding of early life development. That is, the importance of the primal relationship and the mother to the establishment of the axis and the significance of the axis to psychic health. Indeed, this contribution was acknowledged by Meier-Seethaler (1982), who wrote, "Neumann has been the only investigator, who saw with such clarity how the ego-Self axis depended on the primal relationship" (p. 371). As mentioned, her article elaborates on the pathologies of negative primal relationship in synthesis with other psychoanalysis theories.

The second important aspect Neumann identified is the paradox that, in the psychological embryonic phase, during which the axis comes to be, the baby is not yet a person. However, because his relatedness Self, previously presented as the psychological aspect of the Self, is externalized with the mother, the establishment of the axis between the awakening ego and the directing Self becomes a process taking place in the liminal space between mother and baby, pointing to the pivotal importance of the mother in creating a positive primal relationship and the potential disturbances that may result from negative relationships.

In concluding the role of the ego-Self axis for psyche and for psychic health, Neumann (1955/1966) said,

> The ego-Self axis is the center of a complicated network
> of two-way processes connecting the unconscious and
> the directing center of the totality on the one hand, with
> consciousness and the ego center on the other. (p. 89)

In these words, Neumann encapsulated the importance of a well-established axis between ego and Self, which will be discussed later as the purpose and achievement of psychological development through the primal relationship. Therefore, not only was the ego-Self axis central to Neumann's theory, but it was also imprinted deeply into analytical thought and terminology as the central psychic structural organ that is crucial for psychic health. To describe the psychic function of the axis, Neumann used the terms *centroversion* and *Self-formation*, which he later defined as *automorphism*.

Centroversion and Automorphism: Functions in Service of the Self

The two terms *centroversion* and *automorphism* are both well known as Neumann's contributions and are often misunderstood and confused. Neumann did not provide a comprehensible definition of each or a clear distinction between the essential function of the two terms. It is only by combining his descriptions of the two terms throughout his later writings that the difference is clarified. The following is an attempt to explain the differences between the two terms, which both apply to functions of the Self and the ego-Self axis.

In his first and early description of these terms in *Origins* (1949/2014), Neumann used one to describe the other when he wrote of *centroversion* as a trend of development in which "center of gravity . . . lies . . . in self-formation; that is to say, in the building up and filling out of a personality" (p. 35). This description indicates that in Neumann's thinking there is a strong affinity between the two from the outset. It is only in his later writings that it becomes clear that for Neumann not only are the two terms inherently and essentially connected to one another, but they both also relate to early life psychological development and to the ego-Self axis as much as they do to later life developmental processes and individuation. Nevertheless, the origins of these terms in Neumann's thinking are separated. He originally coined the term *centroversion* in *Origins* (1949/2014) to describe a function of the Self and therefore as an amplification of Jung's theory. Automorphism, on the other hand, was presented in *Origins* as Self-formation. The term *automorphism* was not used by Neumann before 1955, when he used it to describe the psychic tendency toward totality and fulfilment, which he wrote is "Self-formation." Indeed, as translated from Greek, automorphism is Self-formation.

He later defined the term in *The Child* (1963/1990): "the automorphism of the individual, his need to fulfill his constitutional and particular nature within the collectivity and if necessary independent of, or in opposition to it" (p. 8). He also added that automorphism is initial and apparent from the very outset, although in the first half of life the challenge is the adaptation to the collective. As Kutzinski (personal communication) said, "Neumann used automorphism to distinguish what he saw as the innate psychic tendency to fulfill one's blueprint, from what the 'Freudians saw as primary narcissism'" (author's translation). That is, for Neumann, narcissism in infancy is crucial to automorphic development, which means becoming oneself.

On the other hand, *centroversion*, a term coined by Neumann as early as *Origins* (1949/2014), is "the innate tendency of a whole to create a unity within its parts and to synthesize their differences in unified system" (p. 286). Based on this initial definition and the understanding that this term is used to describe psychic processes, it is evident that centroversion works in the direction of centering the psychic systems and their integration. In analyzing the symbol of the uroboros, Neumann, drew on Plato (*Timaeus*) and described the importance of the autarchy of this stage as symbolized by the serpent "eating its own waste" (p. 33) as its self-sufficiency. He thus theorized that in normal development autarchy is not to be seen negatively but rather as developmental necessity, and that self-development, self-differentiation, and self-formation are legitimate trends of libido, as does the extraverted relation to the object and the introverted to the subject. Regarding extraversion and introversion he wrote,

> But besides this trend of development there is another, equally legitimate, which is self-related or "centroverted," and which makes for the development of personality and for individual realization. . . . Its center of gravity, however, lies . . . in self-formation; that is to say, in the building up and filling out of a personality which . . . uses the objects of the inner and outer worlds as building material for its own wholeness. (p. 35)

Here, in his first formulation of centroversion as an important trend of libido, aiming at creating the centers of the personality, Neumann arrived at an important conclusion that was commonly overlooked or minimized by his critics (Fordham, 1981, p. 102, 109). He posited that centroversion and self-formation, which in the second half of life manifests as individuation, govern the growth of conscious and the development of the ego during infancy and childhood. Therefore, in this sense, like Fordham, Neumann recognized at least an aspect of individuation, as early as in childhood even if he did not explicitly state it in his writing.

This is a point of agreement between Neumann and Fordham, even though Fordham presented his idea about individuation in childhood as if it were opposed to Neumann's. Fordham's first publication about childhood, dated 1944, was *The Life of Childhood* (1944). He revised it to produce the current edition, first published in1969, *Children as Individuals* (1969/1994). Therefore, in the time between the two publications, Fordham's view emphasized that children are individuals. On the other hand, Neumann, in his article dated 1955, wrote,

> In the course of child's gradual development from a stage
> of life antecedent to the ego, we find that a being without
> psychic or physical boundaries between itself and a Thou
> or an outside world. . . becomes an individual with clearly
> defined boundaries whom we are able to recognize as a
> human person. (1955/1989, p. 84)

Hence, Neumann emphasized that a baby becomes a child and a person, a human individual, with the emergence of his ego, which according to Neumann, takes place at about one year of age. Therefore, it seems that essentially Neumann and Fordham agreed; when we speak of a child, he is already an individual human person who will further individuate throughout his life. Fordham's effort to present this agreement as a point of disagreement is presumably due to his overall objection to Neumann, leading to his devaluation of Neumann's use of the new term *centroversion* and consequently overlooking the essential idea it represented. In the case of centroversion, he never contradicted Neumann, although he also did not approve. Astor (1990) said that "Fordham linked deintegration with ego development" (p. 262), and interestingly, in an appendix to his book, Neumann (1949/2014) included a lengthy description of centroversion as the function motivating and putting in motion the psychological development of the ego in its relation to the Self throughout life (pp. 397–418). Once again, it seems that, despite the way Fordham (1981) presented the differences between himself and Neumann, these differences are more terminological than essential.

Later, in *The Child*, Neumann (1963/1990) said, "we give the name centroversion to the psychic function of the totality" (p. 9); that is, it is the function of the Self. Therefore, during the first half of life, centroversion motivates the development of the ego and the adaptation to the outer world, whereas during the second half of life, it manifests the very function of the individuation process.

In his article "Narcissism and Self-formation (1955/1966)," Neumann presented a definition that clearly indicates the connection and relation between the three important terms he imprinted in the analytical dialogue—ego-Self axis, centroversion, and automorphism:

> Because the ego-Self axis—that is, the relation between the two personality centers—plays an essential part in the development of the personality, we have subsumed the process of its inception and the processes of differentiation and integration associated with it under the concept of centroversion. It has proved necessary, however, to exclude from this concept the concept of automorphism, or Self formation, and reserve the centroversion concept for the specific relation of the personality centers to each other. The term Self formation [i.e. automorphism] is more inclusive. It concerns not only the centers but also the development of the conscious and unconscious systems and their relation with each other . . . and those processes which further the development of the total personality. (pp. 82–83)

It seems that Neumann described centroversion as a psychic function, just as Jung described the typological introversion and extraversion. Although introversion is subject oriented and extraversion is object oriented, centroversion is the function that is center oriented. Automorphism, on the other hand, is more inclusive and is the function of self-formation. Here there is another point of essential agreement with Fordham (1980), who wrote, "Thus the self seemed to introduce an *organizing process that centralised the personality*. It could be defined as a totality, a system which combined in itself both the conscious and unconscious *structure and processes*" (p. 315; emphasis added). The italicized words indicate the essential agreement. Specifically, in addition to the Self being a priori, its psychic role is structural, and most importantly it functions as the origin of the processes toward centralizing personality (i.e., centroversion) and totality (i.e., automorphism).

The General Plan

Relying on Jung's assertions that the timeless and transpersonal factors are as important as the personalistic historical ones, Neumann (1959) pointed out that, by shifting its focus "from childhood and the temporal and personal, to the transpersonal and timeless as the fate-determining factor" (p. 125), analytical psychology may offer healing beyond what was possible through psychoanalysis. This shift of focus is based on what was described earlier as Neumann's ontology, according to which there is "an archetypal structure of psyche, that unfolds by itself" manifesting a General Plan, which is "the autonomous unfolding of the archetypal structure of psyche within which, and through which the development of the ego and of the conscious proceeds" (p. 126). This means, that for an individual child, the transpersonal and timeless Mother archetype incarnates in the temporal and timely personal mother and thus acquires a genetic and historical dimension, implying that the role of the personal mother is to "imprint" the human. In doing so, the mother facilitates the infant's psychological development in terms of structure and of emotions. From his Jungian archetypal perspective, Neumann theorized structurally and described the mother's role in the establishment of a strong and heathy ego-Self axis. Winnicott (1945), on the other hand, held a personalistic perspective and thus described, with the same emphasis on the importance of the mother's role, the way she facilitates the infant's emotional health.

Neumann (1963/1990) emphasized that, by following her instincts, the mother manifests her archetypal role as Mother in the archetypal constellation of the primal relationship, and most importantly in doing so she "activates" the archetypal development

of her baby's psyche, in accordance with the "General Plan."
This process was described by Neumann (1959) as the "personal
evocation of the archetype" (p. 128); that is, the personal mother
evokes the Mother archetype in the baby's psyche and accordingly
also the expectation to be mothered:

> The mother constellates the archetypal field and evokes the
> archetypal image of the mother in the child psyche, where
> it rests, ready to be evoked and to function. This archetypal
> image evoked in the psyche then sets in motion a complex
> interplay of psychic functions in the child, which is the
> starting point for essential psychic developments between
> the ego and the unconscious. These developments, like
> those embedded in the organism, remain relatively
> independent of the mother's individual behavior, provided
> that the mother lives with her child in accordance with her
> archetypal role. (Neumann, 1963/1990, p. 24)

Therefore, the General Plan of child psychological development
implies that the personal mother is, on the one hand, a representation
of an archetype, yet, on the other hand, her role is crucial in
enabling the psyche to join the path of normal psychic structure
development. Clearly, although Neumann wrote from the Jungian
archetypal perspective, he most certainly recognized the crucial role
of the personal mother in providing the conditions for archetypal
development. In that, he is found to be in absolute agreement with
Winnicott, who wrote from the psychoanalytical perspective, but
nevertheless recognized the archetypal even if he did not name it as
such. According to Winnicott (1956/1984), "The mother . . . provides
a setting for the infant's constitution to begin to make itself
evident, for the development tendencies to start to unfold" (p.
303). In a later article, Winnicott (1968/1987) delved even farther
into the archetypal perspective of psychic growth when he wrote,
"these inherent tendencies on the psychic side include those that

lead towards integration or the attainment of wholeness" (p. 90). Therefore, like Neumann, Winnicott emphasized the importance of the mother's fulfillment of her role in that she thus enables the inherent development of human psyche to unfold.

In order to indicate the importance of the evocation of the Mother archetype by the personal mother, Neumann used the analogy of a door's lock and key, which must ultimately fit one another. He further theorized that, as the key releases the lock that opens the door, it also grants entrance to a room. Therefore, for the human, the evocation of the archetype, Neumann (1959) wrote, "discloses a whole world and activates a unitary layer in psychic structure" (p. 128). The unitary layer Neumann referred to is the archetypal, which begins with the uroboros and continues to the matriarchate, followed by the patriarchate. Neumann (1963/1990) regarded these archetypal layers as "world related" (p. 84) in the sense that they comprise a field of relatedness, that is, the perspective through which the world is experienced and in which the archetypal image is the representation of the relationship. Notably, however, Neumann (1959) wrote that "this sequence cannot be reversed" (p. 127), implying that regardless of life circumstances—even when the mother is missing—when conscious develops and proceeds from the uroboric layer, the archetypal layer of the matriarchate will be the first to be encountered, implying the infant's world-related layer, that is, the lens through which he perceives his relatedness to the world. This is an important aspect of Neumann's theory, as it identifies a twofold consequence for the primal relationship that begins with the uroboric layer and continues to the matriarchate layer and culminates there. On the one hand, the expectation to be mothered becomes a need, which the personal mother in normal circumstances will meet and fulfill. On the other hand, this implies that pathology is imprinted within the expectation because failure to meet this need, whether due to the mother or because of her absence, will be a deprivation that results in a disturbance of development.

Winnicott arrived at a similar formulation, leading him to coin his most well-known phrase, "good enough mother," based on the description of the mother who can sense and fulfill her infant's needs, and although not perfect, manifests a holding environment. The mother's failure to meet all her infant's needs to fulfilment is inherent in Winnicott's designation "good enough," and in Neumann's theory in the concept of compensation and regulation, which will be further discussed in the next pages.

Indeed, Neumann (1959) described the General Plan as one "with which the individual lives in harmony when he fulfills it, or with which he does not live in harmony so that he becomes ill" (p. 127). Therefore, pathologies are embedded in the idea of a General Plan as Neumann theorized it; they are an organic part of the plan, and as mentioned, this is one of his most important contributions to child analysis.

The General Plan Neumann argued for is therefore situated in the liminal space between the personalistic genetic and the archetypal transpersonal and implies the successive biopsychic process of development in a human baby, cared for by a human mother within the primal relationship through which the mother archetype is evoked, the psychic structure is established, and the psychic organs develop. Similar to Winnicott's (1960) formulation of "good enough," referring to the mother, her holding, her care, or the environment, Neumann theorized that according to the General Plan, when a normal mother takes care of a normal child in a normal environment and under normal conditions and circumstances, she successfully assumes her archetypal role, and the child is apt to develop a positive attitude toward himself, others, and the world:

> [The mother's] unconsciously directed behavior, which
> enables her to coincide with the mother archetype, is

vitally necessary to the normal development of the child. For this reason excessive individual deviations from the norm, either in a good or in a bad sense, are harmful. (1963/1990, p. 21)

Neumann also referred to this normality with the term *average human* and explained that the average human mother functions in a real world, a personalistic one, and therefore some deviation from the norm is unavoidable. As he explained, "In a positive, successful, primal relationship the negative experiences inseparable from child development are compensated by the mother who represents the world and the Self" (p. 72). Therefore, for Neumann, not only are the negative experiences a part of the General Plan, but also their compensation and remedies by the loving comforting container of the mother that therefore manifests the archetypal Great Mother both as world and Self. What Neumann's theory suggests is that, although archetypal autonomous development defines and manifests normality, it is the personalistic aspect that creates an individual mother's variations from the norm and their consequent pathologies. Although arriving at the formulation from their different theoretical perspectives, Neumann and Winnicott were in complete agreement as to the developmental damage caused by unmet needs, described by Winnicott (1956/1984) as a "distortion of development at an early phase" (p. 301). At the same time, as the General Plan is archetypal, the remedies of a personal negative experience are embedded within its nature; these will be discussed in the next chapters. Nevertheless, the crucial element for the fulfillment of the archetypal General Plan is the existence of a positive primal relationship.

Chapter 6
Primal Relationship

Primal Relationship in General

When viewed from the Jungian archetypal perspective, the relationship between mother and baby is archetypal in the sense that it is typically human. As Jung (1931/1972) wrote, "There is inherent in the archetype, in the collectively inherited mother-image, the same extraordinary intensity of relationship which instinctively impels the child to cling to its mother" (p. 373).

Neumann followed Jung and further amplified the understanding of the importance of the relationship between mother and baby, which he described in *The Great Mother* (1955/1991) from the perspective of the elementary character of the Feminine, as ensuring the mother's devotion to her newborn, motivated by his dependency. At this initial stage of theorizing about this unique relationship, Neumann was describing their phenomenology. A few years later, he was already theorizing about the mother/baby situation, and he coined the term *primal relationship,* of which he wrote, "The primal relationship, as a specifically archetypal constellation, embraces both individuals in its transpersonal reality, each pole—mother and child—appearing to the other and acting upon it as an archetype" (1963/1990, p. 22). The amplification of Jung's perspective that Neumann suggested here, beyond the use of the term, is the mutuality of the relationship, implying that once giving birth, both mother and infant enter an archetypal realm within which both hold the tendency and the expectation to fulfill the relationship. Accordingly, he also wrote, "The primal relationship is a relationship between two living beings whose instinctive tendency impels them to seek fulfillment in each other and who . . . are oriented toward one another" (p. 83). The mutuality is important to the understanding of the lived experience of both mother and baby, who are immersed in a shared and encapsulated archetypal reality for the duration of the primal relationship. As the relationship is archetypal, the baby's psyche needs it to develop as a human, and it is a crucial perquisite to a baby's normal psychological development.

As suggested earlier, although Neumann did not elaborate on the mother's perspective, the primal relationship refers to the mother as it does the baby, implying that it has implications for the mother's psyche and psychology as well. Winnicott (1956/1984) recognized this unique psychological state of the mother and referred to it when he coined the term *maternal preoccupation.*

In writing about the primal relationship, Neumann used a few terms interchangeably to describe its unitary nature. Each of these terms has a different antecedent, which calls for clarification and differentiation between them so that their use will not appear accidental.

The term *unitary reality* was introduced by Neumann (1955/1989) in his later years, and it represented his theoretical elaboration of the earlier idea of the *participation mystique,* introduced by philosopher and anthropologist Lucien Levy-Bruhl (D. Kutzinski, personal communication). As theorized by Neumann (1955/1989), the unitary reality is the reality that is both before and beyond the original separation of the systems from which conscious develops, and it is "the primordial divine world" (p. 90). Existence in the unitary reality is the borderline experience of the beginning of all things, and therefore every human has the instinctive knowledge of it and a nostalgic longing for it as the inner and outer, Self and world, are all united. As a borderline concept, it encompasses psyche and world; "it is the starting-point of all the experience of the individual, because it is the initial, crucial, formative experience of childhood" (p. 77).

Highly relevant to this chapter, another aspect of the unitary reality that Neumann pointed to is that in it the Eros principle is the determining factor. Therefore, the immersion of mother and infant at this level of existence is implied by the archetypal nature of the primal relationship in which, Neumann (1963/1990) wrote, "every mother is *the* mother, every child is *the* child, and the relationship between them is *the* primal relationship" (p. 23). Neumann stated that originally the term *participation mystique* referred to the deep identity of man with nature, beyond mere projection, a situation in which the boundary between subject and object is blurred to the point of suspension. Nevertheless, in "Unitary Reality (1955/1989)," he credited his use of the term in theorizing about the primal relationship to Jung, who used it to describe the unconscious identity between children and their parents. In this 1926 article, relying on the participation mystique between parent and child, Jung (1946/1991) said, "I analyzed the father through the dreams of his eight-year-old son" (p. 53). Therefore, Neumann (1955/1989) wrote,

> If something of this kind can happen in an eight-year-old child, whose ego and conscious mind are already comparatively well developed, we can readily understand how far reaching the identity between child and mother must be at the time of the original primal relationship, when there is nothing in the child's mind but an infantile, nuclear ego and some points of consciousness emerging like islands. (p. 79)

Not only did Neumann indicate how he arrived at the use of the term through Jung, but he also noted how deeply the participation mystique is rooted in the nature of the experience of primal relationships by both mother and baby, central to any analysis of them. Moreover, in discussing the Mother archetype, in "Psychological Aspect of the Mother Archetype," Jung (1954/1990c) clearly referred to the identity with the mother in the primal relationship and to her role in evoking the Mother archetype:

> The carrier of the archetype is in the first place the personal mother, because the child lives at first in complete participation with her, in a state of unconscious identity. She is the psychic as well as the physical precondition of the child. (p. 102)

This is the foundation on which Neumann stood when he developed his theory, as here Jung provided in a nutshell all that later was formulated and described in detail by Neumann under the term *primal relationship*. It is important to note that, following Jung, Neumann used the word *identity* and emphasized that it is essentially different from i*dentification* in that identity is unconscious whereas identification is rooted in recognition of the object and is thus conscious. The identity Neumann referred to is "primary identity, that is, an identity which is simply present as such," and he further emphasized that "this 'being-present-as-such' is, precisely, characteristic both of the unitary reality and of existence in a non-subjective cosmic state" (1963/1990, p. 16). This is a fine distinction that Neumann was attempting to present to avoid confusion with *identity* in its simple sense as obviously the situation he referred to is archetypal.

This distinction becomes even more important when considering Winnicott's assertion of the "very great psychological difference between . . . the mother's identification with the infant and . . . the infant's dependence on the mother" (1956/1984, p. 301). Winnicott added that this difference is due to the infant's inability to identify in the early stages, which means that, like Neumann, he saw the essential identity between mother and infant. Hence, although the term *unitary reality* implies the level of existence and the nature of the reality for the mother and her infant in the primal relationship, the participation mystique in this context refers to their deep immersion in the psychological identity within this deep level of reality. Although Neumann pointed to the deep identity between mother and infant while theorizing about the psychological development of the infant, this identity must have far-reaching implications for the mother's psychology as well, and these will be discussed separately, as an amplification of Neumann's theory.

Lastly, Neumann (1963/1990) used the term *dual union,* which he borrowed from Leopold Szondi. Neumann explained that this term does indeed describe the precise primary situation of the infant and the union with the mother; nevertheless, it is not as universal as participation mystique.

Although emphasized that psychological development is fluid, Neumann nevertheless referred to the whole of the relationship between mother and baby at the genesis of life while placing the chronological boundaries of the primal relationship from birth to about one year of age. He described a dynamic relationship that evolves in accordance with the baby's psychological development and in two phases. The first, while in the maternal uroboros, is the uroboric world-related layer and is characterized by its unitary nature. The second is the phase of the uroboric Great Mother, which is on the transition to and in the matriarchate world-related layer, in which the dual union begins to differentiate into "I" and "thou." The dissolution of the primal relationship occurs with the psychological transition of the child to the third world-related layer, that of the patriarchate.

Interestingly, Fordham stated that he had no concrete dis-agreement with the description of the primal relationship that is so essential to Neumann's early life theory. Moreover, he wrote that "My account is shorter compared with Neumann's lengthy discussion. Nevertheless, I believe that it represents the essential of what he says with the contradictions which I have included in my account and have not attempted to resolve" (1981, p. 111). This is highly significant to the synthesis between Fordham and Neumann, in aim at presenting analytical psychology's theory of early life development.

In his magnum opus, *The Great Mother* (1955/1991), Neumann analyzed the Feminine archetype and described two characters of the Feminine, the elementary and the transformative, which represent the way women experience themselves and men experience them. The two characters of the archetypal Feminine manifest "ordering principles of consciousness" (p. 38) differing from the archetypes and the other structural authorities of the psyche. Although the transformative character belongs to later stages of conscious development, the elementary character is active during the primal relationship and early childhood and manifests the decisive element in the mother's psyche in the initial stages. Surely this is a strong conjunction point for Neumann and Winnicott, as Winnicott's "good enough mother" will not fit this description unless she acts from the elementary positive character, that is, containing, holding, caring, and compensating.

The baby's psychological development throughout the primal relationship manifests in the development of the ego, which initially is only an *ego-nucleus* and gradually becomes a *unified child ego*. Important to Neumann's theory, and unfortunately a source of significant misunderstanding, is his postulation about the way the baby's psychological development is reflected in the psychic authority of the Self. Neumann theorized that the Self becomes a unified-Self throughout what I suggest terming a *psychological pregnancy* of the primal relationship until its resolution by the psychological birth of the baby. The fact that the evolution of the primal relationship is determined by the baby's psychological development, which is facilitated by the mother, indicates the difference between mother and baby.

Although the baby is entirely dependent on the mother and her presence in the primal relationship, the mother is present only to the extent that her baby needs her to be. That is, although the mother is immersed in the participation mystique of the primal relationship with her baby, and she lives in the dual union with him, she may at the same time hold other relationships with her other children, husband, and relatives, for example. Therefore, the mother's reality comprises more than just the primal relationship, whereas the primal relationship with his mother *is* the whole world for the baby. This notion of the mother's differing immersion in the primal relationship is similar to Winnicott's (1956/1984) *maternal preoccupation*, in which he described the mother's slow withdrawal from her participation in the dual union according to the infant's differing need. Although Winnicott arrived at his formulation from the phenomenological perspective, as he observed mothers and babies, Neumann arrived at his formulation from the philosophical theoretical hermeneutic point of view. Therefore, the two formulations potentially complement one another and strengthen the theoretical idea about the mother's differing immersion in the primal relationship.

Neumann (1955/1966) described the psychological relational nature of early relationship, beyond primal relationship, as one in which the element of dependency is central: "dependance upon an "other" occupies the foreground" (p. 89). It is important to remember that Neumann described the primal relationship as the relationship between a mother and her newborn from birth to about one year of age. Nevertheless, in his theory about ego development, which will be presented in chapter 7, the bond between a baby and his mother is significant and stronger than other relationships beyond the first year of life and in a declining way to about 4 or 5 years of age (to the patriarchate).

Biopsychic Importance: A Psychological Pregnancy

To signify the tremendous importance of the mother's role to the psychological development of the infant during the first year of life through the primal relationship, I suggest the term *psychological pregnancy*.

As early as *The Great Mother* (1955/1991), in following the research and theories of zoologist Adolph Portman, Neumann wrote, "the infant, during the first year of life, may be regarded as an 'embryo outside the womb'" (p. 32). In his later formulations in *The Child* (Neumann, 1963/1990) he described this as a "post-uterine, post-natal embryonic phase" (p. 7). This postnatal phase "is in fact an embryonic year" (Neumann, 1955/1989, p. 83), as unlike other mammals, humans need another year to mature into an individual being. Neumann theorized that this biological fact implies a psychological meaning. Accordingly, he described the baby: "already as an embryo, he is not just physically enclosed within his mother, but . . . the vital final stages of his maturation are completed within his primal relationship to her, i.e., . . . he is enclosed within her psyche" (p. 83). Neumann here recognized that the physical birth of the infant is not the final stage of his maturation and furthermore that the birth signifies the beginning of the last stage, which is psychological.

Interestingly, these conceptions that Neumann formulated from the theoretical perspective are supported by Winnicott's description based on his phenomenological perspective. Winnicott (1945) first recognized a significant psychic development at around 5 to 6 months (to be discussed later in this chapter as the second phase of the primal relationship), which he described as discernable by observing the baby. Relying on this observable stage, he concluded that birth signifies a prior important stage and explained that "my reason for saying this is the great difference that can be noticed if the baby is premature or post-mature" (p. 148). Based on this formulation he presented his thesis accordingly: "The early emotional development of the infant, before the infant knows himself (and therefore others) as the whole person that he is (and that they are), is vitally important" (p. 149). Winnicott here referred to the emotional development of the infant because, unlike Neumann, he was not theorizing about psychic structure, and in this sense, their theories are complementary.

Therefore, I suggest that the concept of a psychological pregnancy can be discerned from what Winnicott wrote about the early stage of emotional development beginning at birth and what Neumann wrote about the first extra-uterine embryonic phase. The analog of pregnancy clarifies some important aspects of this time in a baby's life in which the psyche comes into being, similar to the way the embryo's body comes into being throughout pregnancy. What was in the physical pregnancy the pre-ego state, only an ego-germ, will become at the end of the psychological pregnancy an independent ego. The baby's Self also undergoes a process of maturation, and its culmination in a unified child Self signifies the termination of the psychological pregnancy. Like physical pregnancy, psychological pregnancy is instinctual and autonomous, and any disturbances in the inherent sequence will disrupt health, in the sense of psychological development. The psyche, like the embryo in the womb, is contained and safe while the psychic organs gradually develop from being initially very fragile to later being independent and finally detaching themselves from the mother when the child psychologically comes into being.

The term *psychological pregnancy* acknowledges the importance of the mother as the psyche-containing womb, facilitating the development of the psychic structure and organs, and acknowledges the time limitation for this process, which like physical pregnancy, comes to an end with the birth of a person, when an infant becomes a baby who then grows to be a small child able to say "I."

The Uroboric Psychological Experience

It is at this point that the three books at the core of Part II become intertwined. In *Origins* Neumann (1949/2014) described the development of the ego beginning in the uroboros, and in *The Great Mother* (1955/1991) he gave a comprehensive analysis of the archetypal Feminine as the Great Mother. In *The Child* (1963/1990) he theorized about the two phases of the primal relationship; in the first phase the psyche remains psychologically in the uroboros, and in the second phase the Great Mother is the dominant archetype.

As previously mentioned in his metapsychological essay, "Reality Planes" (1952/1989), Neumann expanded and elaborated on Jung's perception of Self as an archetype of the totality to theorize the Self-field as a reality plane that is deeper than the archetypal one. On the one hand, this does not mean that the Self is only a reality plane, as in its paradoxical nature it is also a psychic organ. On the other hand, if the Self is the deepest reality plane, the implication is that human psychological existence originates in a reality that is prior to that of the collective unconscious and the differentiation to archetypes. It seems that, like his early life psychological development theory, this innovative aspect of Neumann's theory, psychological existence prior to the collective archetypal layer never received the attention it deserved.

As described earlier, defining archetypes as patterns of behavior was an important transition in Jung's thinking about the primordial image. This transition is significant as it marks the understanding that, first and foremost, the archetype originates in an instinct. Jung (1954/1972) wrote that "we may say that the image represents the meaning of the instinct" (p. 201); therefore, the archetype is an instinct that manifests as an image, and in accordance with the growth of consciousness, the image becomes better perceived and differentiated. This is a fundamental connection between psyche and soma in Jungian psychology, and it supports the understanding of

Neumann's concept of the body-Self, which relies on the priority of the body in the infant's perception.

In *The Great Mother* (1955/1991), Neumann expanded this explanation when he divided the archetype into its components: "In order to explain what analytical psychology means by an 'archetype,' we must distinguish its emotional-dynamic components, its symbolism, its material component, and its structure" (p. 3). This analysis of the archetype simplifies the conscious understanding of the borderline concept and its two poles—in the body and in the mind. The emotional-dynamic component that Neumann referred to is the energetic effect of the archetype—the emotional charge, positive or negative—that is the embodied effect. The symbolism refers to the different psychic manifestations in images, the material component is the component of meaning and relates to a spiritual element, and the structure component binds these former three together (D. Kutzinski, personal communication). As an instinctual pattern of behavior, archetype does not require consciousness. This is the origin of Neumann's description of the archetypal primal relationship, which implies that, for both mother and baby, the bond is instinctual, and the Eros character—which is manifested in the bond as relationship—is secondary.

In Jung's (1954/1972) description of the instinctual aspect of the archetype, he wrote, "Psychologically, however, the archetype as an image of instinct is a spiritual goal towards which the whole nature of man strives" (p. 212). Thus, he added the spiritual aspect, the numinosity of the archetype, which Neumann later referred to as the material component. In describing these two poles of the archetype, the instinctual and the spiritual, Jung referred to the alchemists who, in their attempt to express the natural affinity between spirit and matter, used the symbol of "the Uroboros, or tail-eating serpent" (p. 213). The uroboros became a central symbol in Neumann's theory as described here.

Describing these poles of the archetype led Jung to the important distinction between the archetype as-such and the archetypal image, a distinction that is highly relevant to this part of Neumann's theory. According to Jung (1954/1972), whereas the archetypal image is a representation of a meaning mediated by the unconscious and "approximately" perceivable (p. 213), the archetype as-such is "irrepresentable" and thus not perceivable by the conscious. It is at this point exactly, the not-perceivable, irrepresentable, prior-to-image layer of archetype, where Neumann theorized that psychological life begins.

In the previous chapter, the uroboros was presented by Neumann from the phylogenetic perspective to describe the initial psychological state of humanity prior to the rise of consciousness. In theorizing about the primal relationship in his later writings, Neumann elaborated on the symbol of the uroboros when theorizing about the ontogenetic development of the conscious. Neumann was criticized (Fordham, 1981, p. 106; Giegerich, 1975) for using the parallelism between ontogenetic and phylogenetic development. His formulations were misinterpreted as a concrete reduction of primitive man to a childlike conscious state, overlooking the fact that, according to Neumann's (1963/1990) theory, primitive man's ego should have developed in accordance with the General Plan. Neumann wrote that "early man's functions were just as highly developed as those of modern man and, though different from ours, the state of his psyche must not be regarded as primitive" (p. 145). Hence, what Neumann suggested is that the patriarchal layer of the primitive man is uroboric in terms of the patriarchal layer of modern man because human consciousness has developed significantly from the primitive days to the current day. Neumann was theorizing that in psychological development the General Plan applies to both primitive and modern child, who both follow the same archetypal stages and phases—that is, from the uroboric layer and an embryonic ego to the patriarchal layer and a unified ego. Nevertheless, what was for the primitive the most developed stage of the patriarchate layer, in terms of human consciousness, was yet uroboric.

Turning back to ontogenetic psychological development, and following Jung, Neumann used the symbol of the uroboros to describe the original unitary state from which human existence begins. Importantly, the uroboros is a very rich symbol, and Neumann used the full scope of its symbolism in a somewhat hierarchal order. That is, the uroboros is the first psychological archetypal world-related layer of the three layers through which the human psyche develops. At the same time, the uroboros symbolizes a psychological developmental stage. As such, it is fluid, and what initially is all uroboric later becomes a maternal uroboros and then a paternal uroboros, which may allow the image of the Great Mother to emerge. Therefore, when Neumann referred to the uroboric phase, he described different subphases. In addition, he referred to the uroboros as a symbol of the uroboric experience, which is relevant to any human at any age under certain psychological conditions. Therefore, to follow Neumann's description, one needs to consider the full scope of symbolism related to the uroboros and interpret Neumann's use of the symbolism according to the text. A similar explanation applies to the mother archetype, although Neumann used Feminine, Great Mother, Good Mother, and Terrible Mother; for these archetypes, the hierarchy is easier to understand.

Neumann (1949/2014) wrote, "This round and this existence in the round, existence in the uroboros, is the symbolic Self-representation of the dawn state, showing the infancy both of mankind and of the child" (p. 11). As the representation of the Self, the uroboros is the initial perfect paradisiacal state, prior to all differentiation, in which inner and outer, above and below, are still one and the same, and the unitary reality prevails. As Neumann (1963/1990) described, this initial paradisiacal uroboric experience is fundamental to psychic existence: "The primary unitary reality is not merely something that precedes our experience; it remains the foundation of our existence even after our consciousness, grown independent" (p. 33). Thus, Neumann's theory of early life development originates with the paradisiacal heavenly bliss of the complete unity, when the mother manifests the elementary character of the Feminine, which is passive and holds fast in its all-embracing form, representing the initial unity and that which is the goal of the later life individuation process as well.

In *The Great Mother* Neumann (1955/1991) theorizes about the different archetypal layers, beginning with the uroboric, which represents the development of the ego in terms of the ability to differentiate the inner figures. The pre-ego-germ lies in the uroboros, the irrepresentable and undifferentiated layer of the archetype from which psychological life originates, and the embryonic ego, which just begins to experience buds of differentiation and perception of images, is in the maternal uroboros. As the infantile ego develops, which implies the emergence of conscious along with initial differentiation and perception, the maternal uroboros becomes the uroboric Great Mother, which soon after becomes the Great Mother image (good or bad), perceived by the adolescent ego at the end of the uroboric phase of the primal relationship. These archetypal layers represent the transition between the initial uroboric state of no differentiation at all, and thus no ability to perceive an image, to the last stage of the Great Mother, when the baby's conscious is developed enough to hold a clear differentiation between the image of the Good or the Terrible Mother.

In a personal communication, Kutzinski (October 12, 2017) offered an analogy to simplify Neumann's descriptions of unconscious and growing ability to perceive an image. She suggested imagining a formless, undifferentiated, mashed mixture of cookie dough that is first made into one big flat cake and then is rolled out and cut into cookies of various forms and shapes.

As a clarification of the formulation of these layers, and specifically to explain that his perspective was not dogmatic, Neumann (1955/1991) described the transition from one layer to the other:

> But the transition between the uroboros and the primordial archetype of the Feminine, and between the latter and the archetype of the Great Mother, are fluid. For the degree of mixture between the archetypes and the difficulty of distinguishing the still almost formless figures from one another increase as we penetrate more deeply into the collective unconscious. (p. 19)

Here Neumann explained the difficulty of describing psychological development in terms of exact symbolic positions and layers. Therefore, it is important to note that the description of archetypal phases is subject to this limitation and that it is much easier to describe development in terms of what the conscious has already achieved and is capable of than to describe where exactly the development of consciousness is situated in terms of its position in a defined layer. Clearly, although Neumann formulated fluidity between the layers, he described an original uroboric situation of no conscious from which development begins. This psychological stage is not a developmental stage as the first stage is maternal (even from the perspective of biological survival), and Neumann referred to it as the maternal uroboros.

The uroboros, the maternal uroboros, the uroboric Great Mother, and the Great Mother comprise the archetypal layer of the infant's psychological development throughout the first year of life during the primal relationship. Thus, these layers are maternal, and the elementary character of the Feminine prevails in them. Nevertheless, because the initial uroboros already contains all the potential of later psychological development, both the masculine and the feminine elements are contained in it. Neumann theorized that the very symbol of the uroboros as a closed round symbolizes the elementary feminine roundness, stillness, passivity, and containment. Whereas the serpent, as a symbol of transformation, manifests the transformative feminine, the masculine linear fertile creativity and activity are embedded within the serpent consuming its own tail, as both the begetter and the conceiver.

The original pair of feminine and masculine were discussed by Jung (1954/1990b) as the "divine syzygies, the male-female pair of deities," of which he wrote, "We can safely assert that these syzygies are as universal as the existence of man and woman" (p. 59). Indeed, Neumann (1949/2014) theorized that it is crucial for the psychology of infancy to understand the psychological meaning of experiencing this uroboric containment both as womb and as parents. The World Parents, the syzygies, symbolize the unity and wholeness of the initial situation prior to any differentiation that is embedded as a potential, and thus the paternal side of the uroboros, whereas the womb symbolizes the psychological pregnancy, in which psyche as an embryonic pre-ego is contained, held, and nourished, and thus the maternal side of the uroboros. Here Neumann described a *psychic mother-fluid* in which the embryonic ego rests in the stillness, prior to the rise of any tension between opposites. Psychologically these opposites are the systems of conscious and unconscious.

As a psychological developmental phase, the uroboric is initial; nevertheless, it evolves. Therefore, the psychological experience develops and changes from the uroboric bliss at the birth of an ego-germ, through the minimal discomforts of an embryonic ego in the maternal uroboros, to the infantile ego's transition to the next phase, that of the uroboric Great Mother, in which discomforts are regulated by the mother. These stages will be described in subsequent paragraphs.

It is important to note that, although it is clearly the intention of the General Plan that the biological mother will be the mother, it is nevertheless clearly emphasized by Neumann and other theoreticians as well that the mother can be a nonbiological mother if she is the infant's mother in all other aspects.

First Phase of the Primal Relationship: Uroboric, Maternal Paradise

Neumann (1963/1990) provided an explicit and decisive description of the first phase of the primal relationship and the infant's psychological development, the uroboric:

> Because the early, uroboric phase of child development is characterized by a minimum of discomfort and tension, and a maximum of well-being and security, as well as by the unity of I and thou, Self and world, it is known to myth as paradisiacal. (p. 14)

Although Neumann referred to the mythological paradise, he was nevertheless theorizing about the real experience of a real infant. In writing this, Neumann encapsulated the decisive elements of this very short time of approximately one month in an infant's life. The newborn infant is not yet a person; he is mostly asleep while in the psychological womb of the maternal uroboros with his mother, who manifests the elementary character of the Feminine. The first phase of the primal relationship, as a psychological pregnancy of the infant's embryonic psyche within the mother's psyche, is thus characterized by the deep identity between the mother and the infant, in which they form a dual union and live in a participation mystique in a unitary reality.

Meier-Seethaler (1982) pointed to the essential innovation of Neumann's perspective when she compared his view with those of Freud and others, who posited that the infant perceives the nourishing breast as a part of his body, whereas Neumann theorized a unitary reality in which the infant does not differentiate inner from outer, and the mother's body is within as much as without. Here it is also relevant to mention Winnicott's (1964/1987b) well-known claim that "there is no such thing as a baby" (p. 88), thus recognizing the total dependency of the baby on the mother's care in a broad sense. (Although he originally referred to "someone," not necessarily the mother, and to a later stage that was clearly relevant to the earlier stage, nevertheless, he was referring to the nature of the dependency.)

Neumann (1963/1990) wrote, "at this point, the fusion of mother and child, Self and ego, is dominated by the constellation of mutual relatedness and dependency on Eros" (p. 17). The Eros nature of the relationship implies that, as the infant at this stage cannot yet relate, the mother holds the relatedness of them both. Neumann formulated that the infant's totality resides in his body, which is thus yet only the *body-Self* as the "functional sphere of the Self incarnates in the mother" (p. 18). As Neumann explained (1955/1966), the word *incarnates* is here used to describe the paradox he was trying to postulate: "constellated in a paradoxical inner-outer situation between the person of the child and that of the mother" (p. 86). Neumann described the paradoxical nature of what will be established as the *ego-Self axis* through and throughout the primal relationship in a liminal zone of the unitary reality shared by mother and child in their dual union. Thus, his formulation was clearly not suggesting a split or disintegrated *a priori* Self; instead, he suggested that at birth the infant, who is yet unable to relate, "leaves" within his mother's psyche the relatedness aspect of the Self.

Here, on the surface, Fordham (1980) theorized differently and claimed that "An infant is, in the first place, a separate self from his mother and maintains a degree of that separation through his development" (p. 315). Considering his empirical perspective, he is right, and I believe Neumann would have agreed, as he theorized that the germ of Self-formation, that is, the automorphic tendency, is inborn and from this perspective the infant is an individual from the outset. As Neumann was not an empiricist, and he held a phenomenological approach and, theorizing about the infant's lived experience, he described an infant whose experience is paradisiacal, uroboric, and unified in the sense of a complete absence of boundaries and containment within the mother. Winnicott (1945), who observed the infant from another angle, arrived at the same conclusion: "We postulate a primary unintegration" (p. 149). Hence, in Neumann's theory, as the infant and the mother are in a psychological uroboros forming a unitary reality, the relatedness aspect of the Self incarnates within this liminal space in which the infant's psyche is incubated within the psychic womb of the mother's psyche.

From the developmental perspective, what is at birth an ego-germ develops through this very initial short phase to be an embryonic ego, that is, an embryo in the psychological pregnancy. Once the infant is first held by his mother, the all-embracing experience of the ego-germ manifests in minimal intervals of tension followed by relief. As Neumann (1963/1990) stated,

> Normally, the child rests secure in this unitary reality. When a tension arises, it signals by screaming; the need is more or less quickly satisfied and the tension relieved, whereupon the child sinks back into sleep. (p. 12)

In this description is embedded the paradisiacal experience in which the infant is not yet exposed to discomforts, and his needs are almost instantly and fully met. Winnicott (1951/1984) described the same immediate and fully satisfying response of the mother, who "starts off with an almost complete adaptation to her infant's need." Later on the same page he wrote that the adaptation "needs to be almost exact" (p. 238). Therefore, both Neumann from his theoretical perspective and Winnicott from his phenomenological perspective described the first few weeks of an infant's life as paradise.

The fact that there is no conscious implies no configuration of images; thus, the uroboros is anonymous, and the personal mother who nourishes the baby is not yet perceived as Mother, let alone as "my mother." At this point she is the world for him. Neumann (1963/1990) explained that at this stage "the primal relationship stands at once for the child's relationship to its own body, to its Self, to the thou, and to the world" (p. 26). He described the crucial role of the mother, who constantly assures the restoration of the paradisiacal experience and by compensating, grants the infant the initial sense of safety and security in the nourishing containing mother/world and thus Self and thou as well. Clearly, as the mother is the world for the infant, her emotional reality determines the infant's existence in terms of his immediate and future life. Winnicott (1945) theorized similarly: "An infant who has no one person to gather his bits together starts with a handicap in his own self-integration task, and perhaps he cannot succeed, or at any rate cannot maintain integration with confidence" (p. 140). Like Neumann, he saw the crucial importance of the mother as the regulating factor, manifesting the restoration of integration for future psychic health.

Neumann (1949/2014) described this paradisiacal uroboric situation as the initial and "perfect form of autarchy" (pp. 33–34), which is highly important for later Self-development formation and differentiation. He emphasized that this is not to be confused with primary narcissism, as at this stage there is no object and no relationship but rather the Eros of the relatedness character of the primal relationship. In a very similar way, Winnicott (1951/1984) described this state as one in which "omnipotence is nearly a fact of experience" (p. 238) enabled by the "good enough mother," who at this stage has so fully adapted to her infant's need that the infant holds the "illusion" that her breasts, ensuring survival, are a part of him. This autarchy is enabled by the deep identity of mother and infant, as both Neumann and Winnicott theorized.

The uroboros, as the initial whole, contains both feminine and masculine elements; nevertheless, Neumann (1963/1990) theorized that in the initial stages the opposition is experienced as between "active and passive, stimulating and stimulated" (p. 103). In the dual union of mother and infant, the infant experiences these opposites through the mother. As it is a maternal uroboros, the masculinity is embedded in the mother's unconscious. Her stimulating actions along with the infant's spontaneous body stimulations are the disruptions of the paradisiacal experience and thus represent the masculinity in the maternal uroboros. In describing how the masculine and feminine elements of the uroboros are experienced by the infant, Neumann referred to the body and the alimentary urge, which is the determining factor of waking and sleep preceding that of day and night, dark and light. The fine elements of archetypal experiences Neumann described here are supported by Fordham (1980), who seemed to theorize similarly and posited that psychic archetypal processes take place "without having resource to ego functioning" (p. 315).

The upper oral and lower anal are "concentration points"; therefore, as Neumann (1963/1990) explained, pleasure at this stage is "alimentary orgasm," an inner pleasure of the whole alimentary path, spanning from mouth to anus (p. 36). At this stage, the infant's whole world is his body and senses, and the initial buds of differentiating between inner and outer arise from the skin. As Neumann wrote, "In the unitary reality phase the infant already begins to distinguish between itself and what is outside, and to take elements of the cosmos back into itself" (p. 38). For Neumann, in this early phase the mother is the world and thus the cosmos, and the idea of the infant taking parts of the cosmos into itself seems very similar to Fordham's (1969/1994) formulation of the deintegrate sent out to the world to "collect" experience and reintegrate (pp. 84–88).

The initial biopsychic utmost balance will forever be the subject of the psyche's longing, the constant wish to take refuge in the all-embracing comforting love of mother, a state of optimal equilibrium that is archetypally imprinted in the human psyche. In addition, Neumann (1963/1990) explained that the oceanic diffusion of mother and infant in the boundaryless state becomes "the prototype of love experience as such" (p. 46). Here he pointed to a highly important aspect of the positive experience of the primal relationship as the psychic imprint of the sense of love toward oneself, thou, and the world. As there is no conscious, no psychological experiences are recorded in this phase. If there is a disturbance in the paradisiacal experience, the very fundamental perception of oneself and the world as trustworthy will be damaged, and it will be extremely difficult, if not impossible, to access and process to heal in later life.

Second Phase of the Primal Relationship: Uroboric Great Mother

As psychological development progresses in the psychological pregnancy carried by the mother's psyche, the all-embracing experience of the embryonic ego in the oceanic mother-fluid of the maternal uroboros develops to become the infantile ego's initial differentiation. Following Jung, Neumann described the development of the ego as "[emerging] like an island out of the ocean of the unconscious for occasional moments only, and then [sinking] back again" (p. 15). He theorized that these initial unavoidable "ego-arousing disturbances" (1963/1990, p. 26) are necessary for psyche to proceed in its development toward the uroboric Great Mother, the second phase of the primal relationship.

Whereas at the first uroboric phase the accent is on the Uroboros, and the mother is anonymous, in the second phase, the accent shifts to the Great Mother, who will gradually become an individual human figure of mother. As Neumann (1963/1990) wrote,

> The functions that were previously performed by the anonymous, formless world in which the still undelineated child "floated"—the function of containing, nourishing, warming and protecting—are now humanized. That is, they are experienced in the person of the mother who, at first in isolated moments, then continuously, is experienced and known as an individual human being. (pp. 24–25)

Thus, Neumann described the significant achievement of the embryo's ego-germ that developed into the infant's embryonic ego and will then proceed to become the baby's infantile ego when the primal relationship is close to dissolution. At this transitional stage of the uroboric phase, the ego-germ, which has already budded out and is an embryonic ego, is still only a small psychological embryo and is thus very fragile, receptive, and exposed and needs the loving, close, and attentive instinctual care of a mother who performs as Mother manifesting the elementary maternal character of the archetypal Feminine. In the normal archetypal path the mother, by following her instincts, attempts to attend to her infant's needs, which she mostly does successfully, or, she successfully compensates. Thus, she performs as what Winnicott (1960) termed a "good enough mother," who provides good enough holding and care in the overall good enough environment. For Winnicott (1951/1984), the decisive characteristic of the good enough mother is her ability to actively adapt to the infant's needs as they lessen, in accordance with the infant's ability to cope and metabolize her failures and the consequent frustration. That is, both Neumann and Winnicott, acknowledged the importance of the mother's ability to correct and compensate for her failures. Fordham (1969/1994) also recognized the importance of the disruption and repair intervals, and thus arrived at his formulation of deintegration and reintegration as the motivating force behind cycles of disruption and repair. That is, the infant's self is not steadily integrated, but rather a disruption causes deintegration, which "collects" information from the outside to reintegrate with the repair.

As described previously, in this initial stage, the infant's experiences are embodied; thus, by having his physical needs met, the infant feels secure and restful, and his conscious is not called to "awake" prematurely. Nevertheless, the short instances of physical discomfort are the significant elements in enhancing the infant's psychological development as they initiate the first buds of consciousness through exposure to an experience other than and opposite to the bliss of paradise. On the one hand, when the mother, experienced as world and Self, successfully regulates discomfort, her instinctual act imprints the experience of the Self as the regulating authority that will later become the decisive function of the ego-Self axis. On the other hand, in repeated exposure to discomfort, the negative experiences are the first perception of "opposite." Thus, they enhance the beginning of differentiation in what Neumann (1963/1990) referred to as the "separation of World Parents" (p. 110), manifesting psychologically as the differentiation of the Great Mother into the images of the Good Mother and the Terrible Mother. The unavoidable first exposure to the Terrible Mother results from disturbances of the well-being, which first represent the masculine element of the uroboros as the unconscious masculine (animus) of the mother's psyche.

Hence, Neumann formulated that the baby's inner psychic axis between ego and Self is created with the support of the mother's ability to hold the Eros and the relatedness aspect of the Self in the liminal space of the shared unitary reality with her baby, which is both in and out of the psyche. The mother does so until the baby is able to integrate this part within his biopsyche; until he does so, she is for him the Self, the world, and thou. This formulation is very similar to Winnicott's (1951/1984) formulation of the *transitional object* as an object not of the outer world but as a "not-me" (p. 231).

The transitional object, Winnicott explained, is a representation within an "intermediate area of experience . . . not part of the infant's body yet . . . not fully recognized as belonging to external reality" (p. 230). Both theoreticians recognized that during early psychological development the baby's experiences are located within a liminal zone, which is not in him and not out of him but is rather within his shared reality with his mother.

Although initially the ego is only a germ, it develops in a process that progresses in three dimensions: frequency, length, and intensity; in other words, what initially is no ego at all starts to appear rarely, briefly, and weakly, but gradually more frequently, for longer periods of time, and with more intensity. The ego-germ rests, asleep within the uroboros, the containing womb of the mother/world; yet on rare occasions the baby's ego emerges from the unity to be on one side of the axis, with the Mother/Self on the other side. This movement, which Neumann theorized as bursts of libidinal force initially triggered by hunger, has an autonomous rhythm and is highly important for psychic life. In this movement of emergence and immersion is embedded the sense of acceptance and security. As described by Neumann (1963/1990), "the ego has perfect confidence in the Self" (p. 39). Moreover, the infant exists in a rhythmic sheltered world, including the rhythms of hunger and satiety, as well as wake and sleep, day and night, and cold and warm. Neumann theorized it is the matriarchal order, ensures the infant's sense of belonging and worthiness and of being loved, accepted, and a part of a greater order. Accordingly, Neumann wrote, "But this fundamental Self-confidence . . . has its source . . . in primary relationship to the mother" (p. 88). Clearly, here he tied a positive and successful primal relationship to later life's self-confidence and self-esteem. In addition, Neumann (1963/1990) claimed that at its depths the sense of belonging to the matriarchal order means an ordered world capable of integrating negative experience; therefore, it is the essence of morality as it is the deepest "order of things," and importantly it is determined by feelings.

Another consequence of this movement, manifests in the "normally tensionless and fearless" (p. 39) transition between wake and sleep that Neumann (1963/1990) saw as "vital":

> The ego, with the natural confidence which is the foundation of the ego-Self axis in child and adult alike, suspends itself and entrusts itself to the Self. Even in the states of not-being-an-ego, the ego must be suspended in the sheltering wholeness of the Self, and . . . this is one of the essential conditions for its existence. (p. 39)

That is, the transition from being awake to being asleep implies confidence of the ego in the Self; this is a possible theoretical explanation of the difficulties around falling asleep, especially when the child is young, and the ego is still weak. In addition, at this point, Neumann's early life theory and later life development theory become intertwined. In both, the ego finds shelter in the Self, suspends itself in front of the Self, and submits itself to the Self. Although in early life this process is due to the ego's weakness, in later life it implies ego strength, described in Part I as an advanced achievement of the ego conscious. Importantly, Neumann (1955/1966) emphasized that he was referring to a suspension of the ego rather than a dissolution, as the ego "disappears as the object of its own experience. The experience is now the Self, the total personality, and no longer the affiliated ego" (p. 85). Thus, he emphasized the essential oneness and unity of the two psychic authorities related to one another by the axis.

As development proceeds, the movement reaches the point of transition between the uroboric layer and the matriarchate. The ego has become stronger, and although not independent yet, it is now capable of differentiation and configuring an image. This implies that the baby has gained initial perception of "I" and "thou" within the mother dyad. Winnicott's (1945) description is similar and thus he supported Neumann's formulation when he pointed, as mentioned earlier, to the age of 5 to 6 months as the point of transition from which he could refer to the infant's emotional development (p. 147). Clearly Winnicott recognized and referred to a point in which a significant change has occurred. Thus, the anonymous uroboric container now becomes the archetypal Great Mother in a process that Neumann (1959) referred to as a "personal evocation of the archetype" (p. 4). This process, which Neumann theorized is a critical conjunction point between the archetypal and the personal, was described earlier as the activation of the archetypal field and then the evocation of the archetypal image of the Great Mother by the personal mother.

In this phase of ego development, according to Neumann (1963/1990) the ego is no longer embryonic but is instead an infantile ego. Not only does the mother becomes the personification of the Great Mother archetype, but the baby is also able to differentiate, to some extent, between pleasure and pain and accordingly the Good Mother from the Terrible Mother. In a normal primal relationship, at this stage the shelter of the positive Good Mother is the primary state of being for the baby, and the pain of bad and negative experiences, which are still sensory and thus mainly hunger, are attributed to the Terrible Mother. Each time the mother comforts and consolidates bad experience, thus regulating stress, she effectively supports the development of her baby's ego and his ability to regulate and integrate bad experiences as well as the strengthening of the axis between ego and Self as the regulating function.

As the baby develops and gains some ego strength, the disruptions in the psychic balance are not only embodied; the migration of the Self into his biopsyche has begun. At this stage, frustration is a disruption, and the mother is still mitigating the Self as the regulating factor when she compensates. Additionally, there seems to be some motion between ego and Self and thus in the axis. As Neumann (1963/1990) stated, "The two centers and systems sometimes move away from, and sometimes towards each other . . . the ego-Self axis is always in motion, for it is affected by every change in consciousness" (p. 47). If Neumann's formulation here is seen as a dynamic process of disruption and repair, or disturbance and regulation, then there is a very significant similarity to Fordham's formulation. As Astor (1990) wrote, Fordham "considers deintegration and reintegration to be the dynamic processes of normal development" (p. 270). In addition, Astor pointed out that Fordham, like Neumann, followed Jung's formulation of the ego emerging like an island from the sea (1954/1990b, p. 66), which led him to arrive at his hypothesis. According to Astor (1990), Fordham conceived that

> there was a primary or original self present at birth which
> then of necessity divided into parts as its relation to the
> world developed, thus enabling consciousness to arise.
> . . . He proposed the term deintegration for this process.
> . . . In this way Fordham linked deintegration with ego
> development. (p. 262)

Therefore, in the most essential formulation of their theories (Neumann's ego-Self axis and Fordham's deintegration and reintegration), they recognized the same psychic process, and they were in agreement.

The progression of the ego, whereby the baby achieves continuity and thus becomes integrated, advances the process of migrating the functional aspect of the Self, initially deposited in the mother, gradually back into the baby's psyche to become a unitary Self. Support to Neumann's formulation is found in Winnicott (1988), who also recognized this as a significant developmental milestone: "A subsidiary task in infant development is that of psycho-somatic indwelling" (p. 29). Therefore, the successful primal relationship enables a unitary Self and an integral ego. Accordingly, Neumann (1963/1990) stated that,

> The normal child development, guaranteed by a secure primal relationship, culminates in the formation of an integral ego which emerges while the child is living in a situation of identity with the Good Mother and has the power to assimilate negative experience up to a certain point, or to abreact it. This gradually becomes the ego-pole of the Self-ego axis, the Self being the ground in which the psyche is rooted. (p. 56)

In terms of ego development, Neumann described the dissolution of the positive primal relationship with an integral ego, which is now ready to further develop, as will be discussed in the next chapter. In addition, Neumann created a clear and one-sided connection between a positive primal relationship and healthy psychological development, resulting in an integral and strong ego able to sustain the tension of life's conflicts and a well-established axis to the Self as the unitary psychic source. Additionally, he presented the outcome of a positive primal relationship and the emergence of an integral ego as the ability to accept the world as well as to accept oneself, an outcome of the embodied continual experience of acceptance and tolerance by the mother. Hence, once the child's ego is consistent and independent of the mother, the child's Self becomes integrated, and the child is ready to be psychologically born.

Importantly, Neumann also added that, as during the primal relationship, the mother/Self also stands for thou, a positive primal relationship will lead to a positive relation between ego and Self and between one and thou. That means that, for a person with a healthy ego-Self axis, the relationship with others will be healthy as well. Neumann (1963/1990) wrote that "integral ego . . . enables man to love himself, as well as his neighbor, with both his good and his bad qualities" (p. 69). Thus, in his posthumous book *The Child*

(1963/1990), Neumann presented (although not for the first time) the closure to the circle he created with his very first writings in both *Jacob and Esau* (1934/2015) and *New Ethic* (1949/1990).

It is the healthy personality emerging out of a positive primal relationship who has a solid axis between ego and Self; can love himself, others, and the world; and has achieved psychic integration, consciousness of his evil shadow, and synthesis of the systems of the conscious and the unconscious.

Disturbed Primal Relationship

According to Neumann (1963/1990), "The primal relationship is the ontogenetic basis for being-in-one's-own-body, being-with-one Self, being-together, and being-in-the-world" (p. 26). It is therefore unavoidable that a disturbed primal relationship will affect, in various ways, these four realms of relation: to the body, to the Self, to the other, and to the world. Naturally the body realm is the most vulnerable, as the infant at the early stage and during the psychological pregnancy has only embodied experiences and, if any memory is possible, it is embodied as well, an idea encapsulated in Neumann's term *body-Self.* Therefore, Meier-Seethaler (1982) posited that Neumann's formulation implies the importance of the kind of body care given to the infant by the mother during the post-uterine time of psychological pregnancy, as "the child's psyche may suffer a crucial trauma . . . traumatization occurs in the experiential field of the elementary body function and the way they [the traumatizations] are dealt with by the mother" (p. 361). This statement has far-reaching implications on the understanding of the possible psychological damage done to infants and babies whose caregivers failed to tenderly care for their bodies. It is also supported by Donald Kalsched's (2017) emphasis on the importance of the body as the host of emotions and thus as the door to emotional work and his description of "traumatic experience [as]. . . often encoded in the body" (p. 489).

Accordingly, Neumann assigned the primal relationship a crucial role in ensuring healthy psychic development. He stated that, unless organic illness is involved, a positive primal relationship will generally lead to a healthy personality that is able to surmount life's disturbances and disorders. He added that "this healthy personality is synonymous with a normal ego-Self axis" (1963/1990, p. 62). This statement represents Neumann's Jungian archetypal perspective of a General Plan of normal psychological development as the prerequisite for the establishment of the ego-Self axis as the route of psychic information flow between ego and Self, conscious and unconscious. Therefore, a disturbed and negative primal relationship will harm the fluency of the information in the axis and consequently the relationship between the psychic systems. Nevertheless, as described earlier, the archetypal General Plan inherently includes unavoidable disturbances and disruptions for which the mother can compensate and thus ensures the cycle of disruption and repair as a part of the matriarchal world order. Therefore, when describing the disturbed primal relationship, Neumann referred to the kind of disturbances that are not well compensated and thus result in a negative charge that is not well integrated within the overall secure safe and nourishing mother/world. In the primal relationship the mother manifests the world, the thou, and the Self for the baby; her emotional state becomes the emotional tone of the baby's world and is thus highly influential. Here another important aspect of Neumann's transpersonal perspective becomes relevant, as he pointed out that, in addition to the personal factors in disturbances, which may be seen as inadequacies of the mother, there also exist transpersonal factors, meaning outer world circumstances such as dangers, war, sickness, and other tragedies. These transpersonal factors must be considered in psychological anamnesis because they render the child's archetypal experience through the mother and beyond the objective data.

Neumann (1963/1990) described the positive experience of the primal relationship as paradisiacal; likewise he equated the negative experience to hell. He wrote a very moving description of the baby's psyche cast out of paradise:

> A reversal of the paradise situation is characterized by the partial or total reversal of the natural situation of the primal relationship. It is attended by hunger, pain, emptiness, cold, helplessness, utter loneliness, loss of all security and shelteredness; it is a headlong fall into the forsakenness and fear of the bottomless void. (p. 74)

This is a very strong and emotional description of the experience of a baby who is deprived of what he is entitled to by nature's General Plan. Disturbances at the initial stage are extremely harmful as they fundamentally impact the infant's initial world, causing damage to his sense of Self, to the ego-Self axis, and most importantly, to his future ability to relate to and love others and accordingly to his social adaptation. Kalsched (2017) described the traumatized child, like Neumann's deprived child, as the archetypal orphan, who is wounded, abandoned, exiled, rejected, and lonely. Also, like Neumann, he saw the traumatized child's suffering and agony at being expelled and falling from paradise (p. 481).

In the positive primal relationship, the Good Mother is activated and constellated; the bad primal relationship is ruled by the image of the Terrible Mother, and the ego is threatened by her. If the deprivation in the primal relationship takes place too early, as Neumann (1963/1990) wrote, "it leads to egoless apathy and decline" (p. 74). The result of such early disturbance and a declined ego is the danger of being flooded by the unconscious. As Neumann described, "displacement of the ego-Self axis in the direction of the Self can lead to disintegration of the personality with all the destructive phenomena characteristic of psychosis" (p. 49). Here Neumann referred to what may possibly be a severe psychic illness in an adult. Indeed, McCurdy (1987), who wrote of manic-depressive psychosis, used this formulation by Neumann to describe the importance of the concept of the axis for understanding interpsychic connections. He therefore described the displacement of the axis as psychic fragmentation and suggested that the severe disturbance in the connection between conscious and unconscious is manifested as the loss of ability to symbolize in manic-depressive states. This indeed is a suggestion made by Neumann in a note that he added to an earlier article (1955/1966). Moreover, McCurdy (1987) explained the manic-depressive oscillation as the ego's suspension between the two opposites, "between its dark and luminous sides, oscillating between the two poles of depression and elation" (p. 320).

Neumann explained the creation of a weak ego as the lack of libidinal "charge" during the first emergences of the ego, when the mother should have positively responded to allow the assimilation of the charge through the erogenous zones and thereby strengthen the ego. Meier-Seethaler (1982) suggested that, in his view of the erogenous zones as charged in both pleasure and discomfort (thus as tension zones), Neumann significantly differed from Freud, who perceived the erogenous zone as one-sided, a source of pleasure only.

If the deprivation in the primal relationship takes place later in the child's development, when the ego has already "achieved a certain stability," then the negative charge will lead to "*a distressed and negativized ego*" (1963/1990, p. 74; emphasis added). Meier-Seethaler (1982) justly pointed out that, when Neumann discussed the distressed ego, created when the disturbance of the primal relationship takes place after the ego has gained some strength, he referred to its manifestations when confronting the world, not as a baby but rather as a child in the second or third year of life. These manifestations will be discussed separately as ego disturbances.

Neumann's term *distressed ego* is based on the understanding that the compensation and dissolution of tension, which arises constantly throughout infancy, is enacted by the mother/Self as the regulatory function. When the baby has a consistent experience of undissolved tension and regulation is not experienced, then the tension will be imprinted and what were the healthy ego's legitimate needs will become the demands of a distressed ego. Meier-Seethaler (1982) wrote that this tendency to demand is due to the pathology of "a very low threshold of tolerance to frustration" (p. 366). Today, this is a very common disruption, perceived as a behavioral issue and treated as such. Here, Neumann's archetypal perspective may add significantly to the understanding of the roots of the disturbance, which is of great therapeutic value.

Chapter 7
Ego Development Throughout the Primal Relationship

The Stages of Ego Development

In describing Neumann's theory, it is important to emphasize that, although he was knowledgeable of other psychological developmental theories and at times he referred to them, his perspective was Jungian and thus archetypal. This implies that his formulations are essentially different from those of psychoanalysis in that they describe a General Plan that is relevant to the primal relationship as much as to further life development. Obviously, the personal element is as important for development as the archetypal one, and Neumann constantly mentioned it as a determining factor for health or morbidity. Neumann's relevancy is therefore rooted in the fact that he provided the framework for the path of ego development after which, if there are no interruptions, psyche follows. Naturally and clearly, the archetypal path begins with birth and ends with death; nevertheless, in between life and death are life circumstances that are crucial to the anticipated outcome.

In ego development theory, Neumann employs unique terminology, usually relating to the relevant mythological amplifications as a point of reference. Some readers find the terminology clear, and others find it highly confusing. As this book is intended to make his theory accessible to more readers, it follows his description of the stages and phases of ego development in terms of the theory and wording in *Origins*. Nevertheless, it is important to present Neumann's notes (1963/1990) about the notion and limitations of describing development of the ego conscious in terms of stages: "The phases of ego development that we distinguish are structural phase of the personality and not distinct successive stages in time" (p. 212, note 1). He also noted that "we must stress time and time again, all the stages we have mentioned merge and overlap and can be clearly distinguished only in the abstract" (p. 212, note 3). These two notes help prevent misunderstanding of Neumann's formulations, as he described what might be considered milestones of ego-conscious development in the sense of achievements and gained capabilities. Therefore, the following description will characterize the ego at each stage as it becomes stronger and more powerful.

As described earlier, Neumann theorized that the layers of psychological development proceed in an irreversible order from the uroboros to the matriarchate and then the patriarchate; and the ego becomes an integral ego only at the second transition to the patriarchate. Here, the concepts of centroversion and automorphism become relevant as the psychic automorphic tendency to become oneself manifests by the centroversion that activates and motivates psychic and ego development. Neumann referred to the concept of body-Self, relying on the idea that the body is born out of the mother's body immediately at birth and becomes independent once the umbilical cord ceases to pulse. At that point, the body-Self functions as the regulating and balancing function of the body; therefore, centroversion, as the function of the Self, "has a biological and organic prototype" (1949/2014, p. 286). At a later stage, centroversion manifests as the motivation of ego development and the directing center.

Neumann theorized the development of the ego from the germ to the integral ego, following the stages of embryonic ego, infantile ego, adolescent, and hero. It is highly important to emphasize that, as he was theorizing about archetypal development, it is inherent in the idea that this development belongs to different stages in life. Accordingly, the hero belongs to early life development as much as it does to later life processes. Therefore, in the following description the integral ego refers to the achievement of a successful primal relationship and belongs first to early childhood.

Embryonic Ego

The genesis of the ego occurs during the first phase of primal relationship, the maternal uroboric, the paradisiacal experience of participation mystique in the unitary reality, and the psychological dual union between mother and infant. There, the pre-ego-germ rests asleep, an embryo in the womb of the psychological pregnancy. There is no tension yet. Thus, Neumann (1949/2014) wrote, "The waking ego is easily tired . . . because poor of libido . . . passive . . . receptive, though even this receptivity is exhausting and leads to loss of consciousness through fatigue" (p. 277), referring to the fact that the infant in this early stage of the first few weeks is mostly asleep. Naturally, at this stage, as the mother represents the world—the uroboric world—she represents both the feminine and masculine elements embedded within the uroboric situation. In relation to Neumann's description in *The Child* (1963/1990), this stage correlates to the phallic-chthonian vegetative stage.

Infantile/Childish Ego

During the second phase of the primal relationship, that is the uroboric Great Mother, the embryonic infantile ego has already gained some minimal strength, although not continuity, and it progresses toward differentiation. At this stage, the ego from time to time emerges from the unconscious, gradually more frequently and for longer periods of time while "charged" by libido and gains strength. This period of ego development within the primal relationship is characterized by the dominance of the unconscious and the body, "ego activities that depend largely on the totality of the body, on the accentuation and experience of the body" (Neumann, 1963/1990, p. 137). Neumann referred to this stage as an infantile non-ego and emphasized that this not-yet-ego is essentially different from the psychologically advanced adult, who can suspend his ego to the state of non-ego in favor of the Self, as described earlier. At this early stage, the automorphism tendency becomes evident in the baby's wakening ego and gradual attempt to become an "I." As it progresses throughout this stage, the infantile ego initially becomes aware of the opposites through the body, with the experience of pleasure and pain, tension and release. Interestingly, Neumann posited that milk at this stage is experienced as "his own" due to the uroboric sense of autarchy and self-sufficiency. Nevertheless, as the uroboros contains both the masculine and the feminine elements, the milk is also experienced as fertilizing and masculine compared to the feminine receptiveness of the baby, leading to the initial separation of the World Parents. The first buds of differentiation between feminine and masculine are the precursor of consciousness, which at this stage is manifested with the patriarchal uroboros as the door of transition to the next stage. As the baby is still in unconscious identity with the mother, the fertilizing milk is coming from within and thus, as noted, this is an autarchy at this stage. Neumann stated that autarchy should not be confused with omnipotence, which is irrelevant when there is yet no ego to experience power. Nevertheless, although not yet differentiated, the infantile ego is gradually able to experience small signs of its dependency in the uroboros, which therefore configures the image of the Great Mother and the end of the participation mystique experience. In a positive primal relationship, the uroboric Great Mother is experienced as the Good Mother.

According to Neumann's description in *The Child* (1963/1990), this stage correlates to the phallic-chthonian animal stage (p. 137). I would say this stage begins at about 10 weeks (2 to 3 months) and lasts to about one year of age.

Adolescent Ego

The last stage of ego development within the primal relationship is a long and developmentally significant stage in which the ego has already budded out and gradually progresses toward consolidation. The adolescent ego is still under the maternal care of the matriarchate, has gained enough strength to perceive an image and continuity of experience, and it is only beginning to differentiate "I" and Mother. Nevertheless, the mother, as he perceives her, is still not his personal mother and represents the Great Mother as the residue of the uroboric situation and the yet relative weakness of the ego. The formless uroboros has now become the figure of the Mother as Good or Terrible, although for a long time she is still androgynous in the sense that her masculinity at this stage still manifests in her negative aspect, appearing as the Terrible Mother.

This stage was discerned by Neumann (1949/2014) as the first stage of ego consciousness. Due to his new ability to perceive the uroboric Great Mother as much larger than himself, the baby begins to experience her as dangerous and threatening at some times and fascinating at others. This is the first sign of clear differentiation between the ego and the maternal, "I" and "thou," the baby and the mother, and eventually feminine and masculine. Therefore, at this stage the milk is no longer "his own"; rather, it comes from outside and thus represents masculine invasion. The ambivalence toward the mother is manifested in the baby's attempts to separate by briefly releasing himself from her embrace and crawling away from her and then returning to her hands. From the psychological perspective, the ego gradually manifests its strength for short periods of time and then sinks back into the unconscious maternal embrace.

In agreement with Winnicott's (1956/1984) concept of maternal preoccupation, implying the mother's gradual withdrawal, Neumann (1949/2014) pointed to the importance of the mother's consent to release the baby: "The uroboric unconscious symbolized by the Great Mother is a system which has to relax its hold upon the ego and consciousness" (p. 305). He continued to explain that without this release and subsequent separation, development is disturbed. Therefore, in the adolescent stage, which lasts a few years, the ego is gradually springing out, gaining strength and continuity, and beginning to differentiate itself from identity with the mother. Neumann (1963/1990) described the ego at this stage as in need of experiencing itself as the center of an ordered world. Thus, ordered rituals of time, people, and activities are necessary for its consolidation. This sense of ordered world gradually becomes an omnipotence of "power over the body" (p. 148). In addition, the ego tends to concentrate on itself, a fact that Neumann claimed is not pathological secondary narcissism, but rather the centroversion tendency motivating the centering of the ego in relation to the Self, that is, the migration of the Self to the biopsychic unity and the establishment of the ego-Self axis. Specifically, he wrote, "But by this same token the ego-Self axis is established as the axis of the personality which in achieving its independence sets itself apart from the unitary reality" (p. 148). That is, the ego progresses toward the end of the primal relation to the mother and toward independence, which is the precursor of the next stage, that of the hero ego.

In relation to Neumann's description in *The Child* (1963/1990), this stage correlates to the magic-phallic and magic-warlike stages (p. 137). This is the last stage of the primal relationship, and I suggest that in current days it last to about the age of 4 or 5.

Hero Ego

Gaining more and more strength, and having sustained a positive primal relationship, the ego now struggles to free itself from the unconscious Great Mother. Neumann (1963/1990) theorized that for both boys and girls this stage is symbolized by the Hero archetype, and with reference to this stage, he wrote,

> Not omnipotence but power . . . is now the necessary goal of an ego development in which, after formation of the ego-Self axis, the conscious ego rather than the Self becomes the executor of the vital will of the personality. (p. 154)

This statement explains one of the fundamental aspects of the relation between the ego and the Self in Neumann's theory; that is, whereas during the first half of life the overall direction of the ego is away from the Self, in the second half of life the ego turns to face the Self and move toward the Self. As consciousness is masculine for both sexes, its strengthening manifests in its resistance to the feminine, that is, at this stage the Great Mother. Therefore, the symbol of the hero is applied to both boys and girls. Nevertheless, the significant difference between their development begins at this stage, in which the World Parents are already divided. Neumann (1951/1994) wrote, "Following a decisive point in his development, the male child experiences the mother as a 'dissimilar thou' different from himself while the girl child experiences mother as a 'similar thou' and not different" (p. 5). In writing this Neumann followed Jung (1954/1990c) when he pointed to the different significance of the "mother-image" in man's and woman's psychology. For the woman "the mother typifies her own conscious life as conditioned by her sex. But for a man the mother typifies something alien" (p. 105). Although this stage describes the ego development of both boys and girls, their psychological development differs from this stage on.

In terms of the libido, Neumann (1949/2014) wrote, "There are retentions and blockages of libido which have to be breached by a new phase of development. Always the 'old system' hangs on until the opposing forces are strong enough to overcome it" (p. 305). This description emphasizes that this stage entails struggle and difficulty, which means that it is attainable only when the ego's will to break free from the unconscious and the Great Mother's "shelter and clinging embrace" (Neumann, 1963/1990, p. 181) is strong enough. Therefore, at this stage, the feminine maternal is manifested as the Terrible Mother, which evokes anxiety. Neumann pointed out that this anxiety does not spring solely from the superiority of the archetypal world over the developing ego; rather it also arises at the point of transition from one archetypal phase to the other and is "set in motion by the Self" (p. 182). As centroversion is in service of the Self, Neumann theorized that anxiety in the transitional phases is a necessary symptom of centroversion, which ensures the process of development:

> For the . . . life of the child, this means that regardless
> of her personal behavior, the mother, the vehicle of the
> archetypal image, becomes, in the transition from the
> matriarchate to the patriarchate world, a negative power
> from which the ego must turn away. (p. 169)

Neumann used this explanation to waive the psychoanalytical formulation of the castration complex (discussed further in Chapter 8) as an outcome of a lived experience. Instead, he claimed that the anxiety and the transition themselves may create the effect of the castration without any concrete event taking place. He then concluded that the normal and necessary anxiety is consequent to an incisive quantity of libido that becomes available to strengthen and consolidate the ego.

It is at this stage—when the ego has gained enough strength and continuity and become integral, the child Self is unified, and both manifest the two poles of the ego-Self axis as an internal psychic structure—that the child is ready to leave the primal bond with the mother. In addition, it is at this stage, when the ego is developed enough to perceive an image and the mother represents the Great Mother in her Good and Terrible manifestations, that the difference arises, and the psychology of boys and girls differs. Nevertheless, before further development is described, disturbances in ego development need to be addressed.

Disturbed Ego Development

Neumann theorized that the late deprivation of the maternal, which results in a negative charge that produces an exaggerated ego and the lack of automorphic development, is compensated by the phenomenon that he suggested is *narcissism*. As noted earlier, he defined the ego resulting from a negative primal relationship as a distressed ego and theorized it as the central pathology. He explained,

> [The ego] becomes prematurely overaccentuated by way of compensation. . . . It is awakened too soon and driven to independence by the situation of anxiety, hunger, and distress. . . . The distress-ego deprived of the experience of security . . . is forced to develop a narcissism that is the expression of an ego reduced to its own resources. (1963/1990, pp. 77–78)

Therefore, from the structural perspective, the consequence of severe disturbance in the primal relationship is damage to the development of the ego and obviously to the ego-Self axis. An earlier disturbance tends to lead to ego weakness. A later disturbance, on the other hand, leads to a negative and distressed ego and a lack of security and confidence. This damage is compensated by exaggeration of the opposite; thus, the ego becomes inflated, stiffened, and rigid. From the emotional perspective, Neumann described the distressed ego as unable to assimilate, subordinate, and integrate its own aggressions, which thus make their appearance. In addition, as the ego lacks support from the world/mother, it is forced to rely on its own resources too early and to be too strong, resulting in narcissism and inability to create and maintain human relationships.

Here, Neumann described what he saw as a "vicious circle" (1963/1990. p. 78) in which the ego, which has already gained enough strength, defends itself at the cost of aggression, rigidity, and stiffness, leading to "feelings of forsakenness, inferiority and unlovedness, each set of feelings intensifying the other" (p. 78). As described earlier, Neumann theorized that the experience of love in the primal relationship becomes the prototype of love-as-such for the infant, and therefore reinforces the ability to maintain loving relationships in the future. In a reductive way, the lack of love creates an unmet need, which in later life will be manifested as a desperate need of love, described by Neumann as "almost inappeasable yearning" (1955/1966, p. 95). Meier-Seethaler (1982) suggested that this is another point of departure between Freud and Neumann. For the latter, the consequence of deprivation of maternal love is indeed and necessarily infantile narcissism. Nevertheless, this is a secondary and pathological phenomenon rather than a primary phenomenon as Freud theorized it.

Another important pathological symptom Neumann (1963/1990) recognized as characterizing the result of a negative and insecure primal relationship is the *"primary feeling of guilt"* (p. 86), which is highly important for clinical use and analysis. Neumann theorized that, when a negative primal relationship creates a lack of love and acceptance in the early stage, the infant, who has an undifferentiated perception of himself and the world, develops a feeling of guilt as if he has been cast out of paradise due to his own fault. He described it as "following the formula: To be good is to be loved by one's own mother; you are bad because your mother does not love you" (p. 87).

The primary feeling of guilt is constellated when the disturbance is at an early stage—a pre-ego phase—and thus Neumann also referred to it as *archaic guilt,* leading to the existential conviction that not being loved means being abnormal (as opposed to the realistic abnormality of the primary circumstances). This is a condemnation by the supreme and higher judgement associated with the guilt of the original sin.

The developmental damage resulting from a negative primal relationship will manifest itself in the morbidity of the *diverted ego,* which, when the ego gains some reflective ability, will intensify and justify the sense of guilt. Even more directly, and as is typical of Neumann (1963/1990), he stated,

> A negative primal relationship in the early phase of childhood causes not merely a partial, but a total disturbance; a child expelled from the primal relationship is expelled from the natural order of the world and comes to doubt the justification for its existence. (p. 87)

This statement by Neumann over half a century ago could be of great therapeutic value in understanding the major depression and suicidal tendency in children and adults. Significantly, Neumann admitted that, although these primary guilt feelings are not easy to transform, the task is easier with children when the analyst may be able to reconstruct the axis than in later life when it can be accomplished only by raising the primary guilt feeling to consciousness, which is obviously not an easy task.

For the distressed and negativized ego created because of a negative primal relationship, which constellated the Terrible Mother image and a damaged axis between ego and Self, the regulatory function of the Self does not function. Therefore, as described, the ego become negativized, narcissistic, aggressive, asocial, and intolerant due to its unmet need for tolerance in the primal relationship. This vicious cycle, which leaves the ego isolated, neglected, and lacking comforting compensation, causes the ego to become intolerant toward itself and thus easily leads to secondary and rational guilt feelings motivated by the ego's self-awareness and reflection. Here Neumann arrived at the definition of the *ego ideal* as the wished-for image of a non-guilty, non-suffering, and independent ego and therefore the ego's ideal image of itself. The most pathological aspect of the ego-ideal is an inner arbiter (which will hereafter be discussed regarding Kalsched's trauma theory) and a negative superego, which mostly replaces the Self as the higher authority. The ego-ideal's independence is clearly due to the negative experience of dependency in the primal relationship. The ego-ideal has already repressed the maternal element of the Self and identifies with the patriarchate and its morality. At this point, the similarity of the terminology used in Neumann's early life developmental theory to that used in his later life theory as presented at Part I indicates the entanglement of the ideas.

Returning to the ideas Neumann expressed years before about the new ethics of the developed adult, he tied his later life theory to his early life development theory:

> The "old" moral code typical to the West. Its goal is not that of automorphism, not the wholeness of a balanced personality directed by the ego-Self axis and creatively related to other people, but rather a split personality determined by the ego-ideal and the superego. (Neumann, 1955/1966, p. 99)

The split personality of the adult, casting its shadow on the other, as Neumann theorized in *New Ethic* (1949/1990), may originate in the split created in the infant or the baby who experienced a negative primal relationship or severe trauma. The harmony of the axis as implied by the General Plan was disturbed, and as Neumann (1963/1990) wrote, "This fundamental experience of harmony with the Self is the foundation of automorphism. It reappears in the second half of life as the moral problem of individuation" (p. 91). Here

Neumann clearly closed the circle of psychological development by linking the initial experience of early life to the later life individuation process, and therefore the uroboric snake consumes its tail.

Edinger (1960; 1972/1992) recognized the importance of Neumann's formulation for the understanding of psychic structure and deficiencies, and he emphasized Neumann's assertion of the "flux" of the axis in describing a continuous process of union and separation between ego and Self. Edinger (1960) differentiated two central disturbances in terms of their therapeutic relevancy. One is ego-Self identification, leading to an inflated position of the ego that will be best treated, he suggested, by reductive interpretation. The other, ego-Self alienation, is the opposite. Edinger suggested that this disturbance is best treated by the transference phenomenon, when the patient uses the therapist as the centering authority of the Self, and the decisive element is the "acceptance" by the analyst as experienced by the patient.

Highly interesting and useful for the purpose of presenting Neumann as a relevant Jungian theoretician, his formulations of disturbances presented here are strongly supported by Kalsched's (2017) trauma theory at the forefront of current Jungian trauma dialogue. In his article, Kalsched revised his earlier formulations of the self-care-system and presented an abbreviated version of his current perceptions.

Kalsched described the weakened and traumatized ego, which cannot defend against a critical violation of "a core of affective vitality" as the "sacred inner core of the phenomenal self" or "soul" (2017, p. 477). Regarding the ego-Self axis and Neumann's formulation of the reciprocity of the flux through it, this description by Kalsched would refer to a severe disruption of the flow between ego and Self, imposing a fragmentation and a split. Indeed, Kalsched described the process as such: the weak ego then uses dissociation and fragmentation by means of archetypal powers to create what he defined as a core complex. The unbearably painful experience of the trauma causes psychic fragmentation in which two archetypal forces are activated; the trauma is associated with the "pure evil or pure hatred or pure violence or pure negation" (p. 478) as an internalization of the abusive parent. The result is the creation of an "internal saboteur" attacking the fragile vulnerable core/soul. Viewed from Neumann's perspective of the negative primal relationship, this is the activation of the Terrible Mother and the creation of a distressed ego, which when it becomes an ego-ideal as mentioned earlier, will act as an inner arbiter.

On the other hand, Kalsched theorized that because of the fragmentation another archetypal force is constellated, representing the Good: "If the dark angel is persecutory, the bright is protective" (2017, p. 479). In Neumann's theory, the protective is the elementary character of the Feminine manifested as a representation of the Good Mother. Not surprisingly, like Neumann, Kalsched described the split as the mythological biblical fall from paradise caused by the original sin and the resulting guilt. Also, like Neumann, who described the aggressiveness and rigidity of the distress ego, Kalsched described the inner persecutor manifested in aggressiveness toward the core/soul and the outer world's objects of its projections.

The close affinity between Kalsched's current formulations and Neumann's long-standing theory points to Neumann as an important Jungian theoretician on infancy and early life. Neumann established and formulated the analytical understanding of the General Plan of archetypal development and the possible consequences of disturbances. Moreover, in articulating the archetypal development, Neumann critically created the foundation for further formulations of pathologies and remedies, as well as therapeutic applications.

Applications and Possible Remedies

A year before his untimely death in 1960 at the age of 55, Neumann (1959) concluded his last essay with the words "It is only the continual broadening of theory that enables us to understand what we do in practice" (p. 11). Hence, he provided an explicit and precise explanation of the value and relevancy of his theory to practical work.

Neumann's assertion of the importance of the conjunction between the personal and the archetypal was mentioned earlier regarding the merger of Jungian archetypal theory with the personalistic perspective that prevailed (and still prevails) in psychotherapy and in child psychotherapy in particular. It becomes relevant to the possible application of Neumann's theory in practice, working with children. The conjunction of the personal and archetypal is contained within the concept of the personal evocation of the archetype, which explains the significance of the personal circumstances—mother, family, community, and overall environment—in the evocation of the transpersonal archetypal constellation. Neumann (1963/1990) described the implications:

> The diagnosis of a damaged primal relationship and of a hungry, forsaken, lonely, and despairing child is never a sufficient basis for a prognosis. It is also necessary to consider the extent of the damage, the time of its inception, its duration, the way in which it has been compensated by the environment, and last but not least the constitutional factors. (p. 80)

This was further explained in his last essay, where he suggested that the conjunction of the archetypal as transpersonal and *timeless* with the personal as a manifestation of the sequence of development in *time* gives significance to the "positional value of symbol in the 'sequence-dating' phase of psychic development" (Neumann, 1959, p. 11). The vertical *time* was referred to by Neumann as psycho-historical, which is the developmental stage of the disruption. It converges with the horizontal *timelessness*, which refers to the different amplification of the symbols. With reference to the symbols of the Great Mother, her appearance as a witch in the early stages may represent the negative experience of the Terrible Mother; in later stages the witch may represent the imminent transition to the patriarchate. As Neumann wrote,

> It is only this positional value, together with amplification, that enables us to undertake the actual interpretation of the symbol, and to find out whether it has a progressive or regressive significance, and what the prognosis of the situation is. . . . None of this can be ascertained by amplification, only by orientation about the position of the individual in the psycho-history of the stages of human development. (p. 11)

The conjunction between position and value confirms the therapeutic importance of Neumann's theory as it manifests a theoretical conceptual framework for other relational theories of practice. Indeed, Batia Brosh, senior Jungian analyst, (personal communication) confirmed the use of Neumann's theory as the conceptual framework for psychologists and social workers in Israel. Brosh described how the first generation of Jungian analysts in Israel came from Europe, as did Neumann, before the Second World War. Also, like Neumann, they had been analyzed and certified by Jung and therefore they worked as psychologists and Jungian analysts in Israel. Jungian thought and Neumann's formulation were a part of their professional perspective. As Neumann was the star among them, his writings were circulated and read by them and their students even before publication. His writings in the German language were therefore unofficially translated into Hebrew by the first generation Jungians who were his friends and colleagues, sometimes before they were published or translated into English. Hence, the third generation Jungians in Israel got their Jungian education through their institutional work, even before Neumann established the Jungian association in 1959. Brosh described how they used various theories in working with children, but Neumann's theory was considered as a framework for understanding the symbolic material and with relation to the conjunction of position and value.

Neumann's archetypal perception of development suggested that the remedies for disturbances in the primal relationship and early childhood are inherent in the perception of the mother as a representation of the archetypal Mother. Accordingly, the representation that activates the archetypal field and images does not necessarily need to be human. Neumann (1963/1990) suggested that "sometimes an older child turns back to the mother archetype as embodied in nature" (pp. 80–81), and he specified natural objects such as trees, sky, and forests as serving this role. This idea holds great hope and therapeutic potential, especially regarding another remedy that Neumann suggested. He asserted that children live in a mythological world, and the archetype of the Good Mother, with her containment and nourishment, may be activated to some extent in the process of play and imagination. In addition, Neumann posited that, because children live on a lower conscious level and their perception is symbolic, in treatment their concrete expression should be listened to on both the concrete and the symbolic level. For example, when a child is excessively hungry and wants to eat more, we hear, along with the concrete need for food, a need to take in more nourishment or to take in the world in the sense of understanding and apprehending it.

In Jungian practice symbolic work is of course central, and with children this symbolic work is achieved by means of different sorts of play, such as painting, sculpting, and Sandplay. In the Jungian world in general, and in Jungian child analysis and in Israel in particular, Sandplay is a central tool in working with children.

Hamaon, Neve Tze'elim

Entering the theme of the Maon (boarding school) of Neve Tze'elim in Israel, is like entering a chamber, a sacred space, in which one needs to walk slowly, carefully, and in awe. The Maon, was for many years the living paradise of emotionally deprived children, those who lived the experience of being expelled to hell.

Among first generation Jungians in Israel was Marion Baderian, who in 1953 was the head of a group of psychologists and educators, some of whom were Jungian oriented, that established the Maon of Neve Tze'elim. Rivka Lahav (2016; personal communication, 2020), a senior child Jungian analyst in Israel, worked in the Maon for many years. She is the only one among the team members who is willing to tell the story of the Maon in Neve Tze'elim. When talking about it, she described an atmosphere that strongly resembles the participation mystique experience, and thus explained the sense of sacredness around the place. She noted that the clearest manifestation of the uniqueness of the shared reality, experienced by both the child tenants and the staff, is the special language that emerged there. Although they used the Hebrew language, they gave special meanings to the words which became embodied.

Maon in Hebrew means home and is commonly used when referring to day care; nevertheless, *Ha* (the) *Maon* was a boarding school that aimed to be the children's physical and psychological home. *Neve Tze'elim* in Hebrew means "an oasis of acacia trees" symbolizing "endurance of the soul and immortality" (Lahav, 2016, p. 347), and it encompasses what Baderian and her colleagues had in mind when they dreamed and created this home in the oasis of the psychic desert of deprived children. In the only short article ever written about the Maon, Lahav (2016) described a treatment center built, designed, and directed in the spirit of Jungian and Neumannian conceptualizations. Baderian was a Jungian analyst "taught and inspired by Erich Neumann" (p. 347), and as she headed the Maon from its establishment in 1960 until 2003, Neumann's formulations found their way into the very spirit of the place.

Lahav (personal communication) described the deep thought that went into all parts of the place, with all small details considered, and in the midst of constant change and innovation, keeping a living relationship with all tenants, both children and adults. The Maon was able to accept up to 75 children, aged 10 to 18, who were of average to high intelligence and enrolled at the Maon as an alternative to psychiatric hospitalization. The staff was chosen to facilitate the orientation to the children's needs. It consisted of educators (with special education training), therapists, and counselors. The decisive element, as described by Lahav (2016), was the tight collaboration and sharing of information and ideas among the staff members, which created a wide net of support for the children, with each seen in terms of his individual needs.

The dominating Neumannian perception was that of "creating a field of unitary reality in which the children's outer world and their inner worlds correspond with each other" (p. 349). This meant that nothing was accidental, and all activities, learning sessions, and therapies were designed according to the individual needs of each child. As Lahav wrote, "Each child who entered the Maon had a personal mentor, who was aware of his or her habits, likes and dislikes, and was involved in guiding and consulting the child" (2016, p. 352). In this way, the Maon was functioning as a real home for children whose initial situation in life could not provide them with what they needed. Lahav concluded that Neumann's "stages of development were conveyed in the philosophy of the Maon. The child's development included movement from the matriarch to the patriarch—from caring and warm treatment to independence and responsibility" (p. 362). The Maon was a home for children who needed a warm nourishing nest to grow up in, support of good teachers so they learn how to fly, and enough inner freedom to fly away.

Conclusion: A Unified Jungian Early Life
Developmental Theory

The Jungian theory of early life development was never articulated in a unified form. Jung was not as interested in early life as in the second half of life and therefore his theory is lacking in the aspect of early life development. Neumann, who held a philosophical perspective, arrived at theorizing about early life from his formulation about the development of consciousness. His central term and significant contribution to the analytical dialogue—the ego-Self axis—originated in his thought when he was theorizing about later life development. He was responding to a need that came from the field, and the term he coined (ego-Self axis) is widely used, as its successful establishment encapsulates the essence of the primal relationship and the psychological development through it. The Jungian analysts that Neumann supervised saw child patients, and he used a reciprocal process of articulating his formulations from what his supervisees described and then refining and reframing them according to the analytic findings. Neumann utilized his intuitive understanding of the human psyche, his wide knowledge of the theories formulated at the time, and his extraordinary mind as the Great Individual that he was to formulate a theory about the preverbal stage of life. Had he not died early, his formulations would have been further refined and elaborated, and—as indicated in his letters to Jung and in notes within his published works—he planned to write a whole volume about the development of the Feminine. When Neumann died suddenly, his writings about children were left in draft form, which was then published in unedited form by his wife.

An unedited work is very vulnerable and easy to criticize as it is personal and originates from and thus touches and exposes the author's soul; yet when it holds deep archetypal truth, it also belongs to the collective. In that sense, Neumann's wife, Julie, made the right decision when she decided to publish the draft as it was, unedited. Nevertheless, such a book calls for a gentle reader, one who can dive into the depth from which the pages were written.

The need for early life theory was also addressed by Fordham, who was not as poetic as Neumann and was aware of his disadvantage in writing (B. Feldman, personal communication). Unlike Neumann, Fordham was an empiricist; he was a psychiatrist, and he worked with children in his clinic. This was to his advantage when he theorized about children as he was able to examine and correct his formulations constantly. Nevertheless, like Neumann, he never saw or observed infant patients and therefore he relied on observations by supervisees. As was shown, Neumann and Fordham agreed on the essential issues and furthermore on most issues, even if their formulations and their terminology were slightly different.

The General Plan of archetypal development as presented in Part II, which includes Neumann's theory with the essential formulation of Fordham, may be seen as the unified Jungian archetypal theory of early life development. Such a unified theory, supported by Winnicott's formulations, can only be confirmed by repeated comparison with lived experiences and therapeutic practice over a prolonged period. Half a century has passed since the articulation and publication of these formulations, and as presented throughout this chapter, other theoreticians have applied and amplified those formulations for therapeutic use in both adult patients with infantile emotional states and child patients. This seems to demonstrate that the Jungian field stands on solid ground in claiming its contribution to early life developmental theory.

Chapter 8
Review of Further Psychological Development

General

In *The Origin* Neumann (1949/2014) described at length the development of consciousness and of the male ego as man's psychological development. He repeatedly declared his intention to publish a similar volume describing the psychological development of the female. His untimely death prevented this publication; nevertheless, the stages of woman's psychological development are described in a volume titled *The Fear of the Feminine* (1950—1959/1994), and in particular in the essay "The Psychological Stages of Woman's Development (1951/1994)" that is included in this volume. In interpreting the myth in *Amor and Psyche* (1952/1971), which Jung described as "brilliant" (Jung & Neumann, 2015, p. 287), Neumann described the psychic development of the Feminine, that is, the man's anima and the woman's psyche. This chapter offers a unified presentation of Neumann's (unfinished) theory about feminine psychology based on a synthesis of his writings about the Feminine and woman's psychology.

The development of the ego, which represents man's psychological development, is central to Neumann's writings and known to the Jungian reader, whereas the psychological development of a woman is only briefly addressed in Neumann's writings and consequently less known. These two lines of development as theorized by Neumann are presented in this chapter in a some-what abbreviated form, which is sufficient for the overall picture of psychological development, as well as for the understanding of the various developmental stages in such a way that may add a theoretical framework and clarity to therapeutic work.

Consistent with Neumann's theory, each stage of psychological development is identified using Neumann's terminology in *Origins* (1949/2014) and in the article "The Psychological Stages of Woman's Development" (1951/1994).

From Boy to Man

Still under the shelter of the Great Mother within the primal relationship, the boy recognizes the mother as a "dissimilar" thou. Therefore, as Neumann (1951/1994) wrote,

> The male child experiences this principle of opposition between Masculine and Feminine within the primal relationship to the mother, a relationship that must be surrendered if the male child is to come into and find his identity as a male. (p. 6)

This is a fundamental fact that becomes a decisive experience for the psychology of man; his Self-discovery and identity stand in opposition to the primal relationship that he must leave during his development and due to automorphism. In addition, it is a disappointing discovery that the mother of the identity and the participation mystique is different and a non-Self, which is imprinted in the male's perspective of close relationship throughout life.

Once the boy perceives the mother as different, she is fascinating as well as threatening. Thus, there begins an ambivalence toward the mother, in which on the one hand the boy still needs her and wants to be close to her, but on the other hand he is afraid of her and of her overwhelming superiority and power.

Son-Lover

Neumann (1949/2014) coined the term *son-lover* to describe the ego of the boy trying to liberate itself from the unconscious, the realm of the mother; finding that he cannot withstand her powers, he thus becomes her lover. The boy surrenders to the power of the Great Mother, but later, as he progresses, he starts to struggle. In these struggles Neumann saw "[the] first sign of centroversion, Self-formation, and ego-stability" (p. 88). The masculinity of the boy when in the stage of son-lover is in its youth and not yet as strong as the ego-conscious will be, and thus it is still centered in the body. It is best represented by the figure of Narcissus, and at this stage the castration complex becomes relevant. Neumann insisted on the symbolic use of the term "castration complex" although Jung disapproved it and believed it may be perceived concretely and thus suggested "sacrifice archetype" as a preferable term (Jung & Neumann, 2015, pp. 195-202). At this stage, Neumann pointed out that it is not the body alone that signifies the son-lover, but also the developing reflecting ability that becomes apparent.

In this stage, when the ego emerges and sinks back, the boy departs from the mother only to shortly seek her again. The concrete manifestation of this stage is the boy's physical clinging to the mother, still seeking her closeness and the warmth of her maternal body. Centroversion is manifested by the fear of growing consciousness, which is at the transitional phase and not strong enough to be independent but no longer helpless in the face of the Great Mother. Therefore, the ego cannot yet be aggressive toward the Great Mother and thus turns against itself. Neumann (1949/2014) drew from his early writings when he described this self-destructive tendency as an inner dichotomy that "can be seen in the motif of the hostile twin brothers" (p. 95), referring, of course, to his writings about Jacob and Esau. He claimed that this initial separation is indicative of the emerging consciousness and thus a forerunner to the separation of World Parents.

Separation of the World Parents

Neumann (1949/2014) theorized that this stage begins when "ego consciousness . . . become[s] truly independent and capable of standing alone" (p. 101). As described in Part I, the separation of World Parents pertains to the first differentiation of the opposites: upper and lower, above and below, sky and earth, masculine and feminine. This new ability to differentiate was seen by Neumann on the one hand as a creative act of the ego, but on the other as leading to loneliness because the maternal embrace is no longer compensating, leading to the experience of the original loss, the deportation from paradise, which evokes the sense of guilt. The separation into opposites also implies the beginning of repression and suppression of the shadow, and accordingly creates an initial sense of morality and the patriarchate guilt feelings, as described in the subsection on disturbances (see p. 220).

By raising the opposites to consciousness, the separation of the World Parents initiates the independence of the ego and therefore calls forth masculinity as opposed to the feminine unconscious. Consciousness means both action and cognition, and as Neumann wrote, "The center common to conscious action through the will and to conscious knowledge through cognition is, however, the ego" (p. 127). It is the separation of the World Parents that places the "son" between them, "thereby establishing his masculinity" (p. 152).

The Hero

The hero represents the boy's ego paving the way to the father and the patriarchate. At this stage, preferably but not necessarily, the father is positively involved and redeems his son from the maternal in the sense of initiating and accepting him into the male group. Neumann (1949/2014) pointed out, nevertheless, that something more than the personal father is needed. It is the patriarchate and therefore the boy's initiation into masculinity that comes from the patriarchal surroundings when he identifies himself as a part of the male group. The manifestation is in the "birthplace not only of consciousness and of the 'higher masculinity,' but of individuality and the hero" (p. 144).

Neumann wrote, "The hero is the archetypal forerunner of mankind in general . . . the stages of the hero myth have become constitutional elements in the personal development of every individual" (1949/2014, p. 131). Importantly, he described the hero who is ready to embark on the journey as representing the bearer of masculinity rather than the paternal or Father. Although the masculine experiences the *participation mystique* as estranged and different, the paternal is associated with the uroboric situation and the matriarchate. It is at this point that the hero's journey begins the long path into adulthood and masculinization through which the male ego overcomes both parents to become an individual, and his rebelliousness against them forces him toward the "dragon fight" (pp. 150–152). Following Jung, Neumann interpreted this fight as one in which the unconscious forces pull the ego down, to be swallowed back in an "insect" act into the realm of the Great Mother, from which the male ego aims to liberate itself.

The Fight for Liberation of the Anima

Here, at the stage of the dragon fight, Neumann's formulations in *The Great Mother* (1955/1991) elucidates the further development of the male psyche. Previously in Part II, there was frequent reference to the elementary character of the Feminine, pertaining to the maternal aspect of the Mother. Here, it is important to note that the Mother archetype is a differentiated fragment of the Feminine archetype that manifest its elementary character through the Mother. Nevertheless, as the feminine figure in an adult man's psyche is the anima, there is, in addition to the elementary character evidenced by the

Mother archetype, another secondary character, the transformative, appearing in the figure of the Anima archetype.

Neumann distinguished the two characters as conservation versus dynamism, but he emphasized that they are interwoven, and it is never one or the other but always a combination of the two in which one dominates. In the initial stages, the elementary character symbolizes conservation (holding and containing) of the growing ego; later development entails dynamism, motion, and transformation, and thus the Feminine appears as transformative. Neumann described the transformative character as first dominated by the elementary and later assuming independence.

Although the two characters of the Feminine are represented in relation to male psychological development, Neumann wrote that he was describing both "woman's experience of herself and . . . man's experience of woman" (1955/1991, p. 24). Nevertheless, he posited that it is important to distinguish between them. Although for both the transformation is a biopsychological process, for the girl, due to menstruation, the change is much earlier and more apparent than for the boy. Therefore, the woman experiences her transformative character regarding childbearing, childbirth, and child rearing and thus in relation to thou. Furthermore, Neumann claimed that once the transformative character ceases to be unconscious and the woman is conscious of herself, she can relate to her mate as an individual; hence, "she has become capable of genuine relationship" (Neumann,1955/1991, p. 36). For the man, the anima is the "soul image" and it is the carrier of the transformative character of his inner femininity, whether it is projected on a woman in the outer world or as an inner figure (soul). Indeed, in describing Psyche as the feminine heroine undergoing transformation, Neumann (1952/1971) repeatedly pointed to the decisive element, Psyche's active inner powers, also manifested in her conscious activity during the last task, which is described in the next subsection: "In the myth Psyche is so active that all actions and transformations start with her" (p. 142). This is the active aspect of the feminine element and thus the masculine power of the feminine, the positive anima in man motivating transformation.

Initially, the transformative character is dominated by the elementary and thus there is no conflict with the ego, which in the early stages has no strength and no independence. Hence, when the ego gains strength and is fighting for its independence, the transformative character, the anima, theorized Neumann (1955/1991), "confronts the ego hero with a 'trial' that he must withstand" (p. 34). Archetypally, the anima is the further differentiation of the Great Mother; therefore, the act of liberating the anima entails ego strength and growth, enabled to withstand the unconscious power of the Great Mother. Freeing the anima is therefore the heroic act, of which Neumann (1949/2014) wrote, "A feminine component is built into the structure of the hero's personality. He is assigned his own feminine counterpart, essentially like himself, whether it be a real woman or his own soul." Importantly he added, "and the ego's capacity to relate to this feminine element is the most valuable part of the capture" (p. 354). He then explained that only when the man releases or redeems the anima does the feminine aspect of his psyche become his partner.

Like any archetype, the anima has both positive and negative aspects. The negative will manifest in *anima possession*, which is a fascination of the man by the anima figure; on the other hand, the positive manifestation is creativity, sensitivity, intuition, eros, and love. Neumann (1949/2014) explained the animatic creativity: "Creativity in all its forms is always the product of a meeting between the masculine world of ego consciousness and the feminine world of the soul" (p. 355). This statement echoes Neumann's interpretation of the Jacob and Esau story where (Neumann, 1934/2015, p. 74) he described creativity as the ascent and descent between sky and earth, upper and lower, conscious and unconscious. For Neumann, creativity is that which is human (1948/1989, p. 375).

From Girl to Woman

As the primal relationship becomes the prototype of relationship, manifesting relatedness itself due to the mother's function as the infant's relatedness aspect of the Self, for the baby girl the emergence of the conscious toward the end of the primal relationship leads to an experience that is completely different from that of the baby boy. Neumann wrote (1951/1994) that, unlike the boy, who must leave the primal relationship in order to further develop, the girl does not need to do so:

> Even when she "comes into her own" as woman, identity with her mother in the primal relationship can continue to exist to a great extent, and her Self-discovery is primary since Self-discovery and primal relationship, in the case of the girl child, can coincide. (p. 9)

This is of the utmost importance, as here Neumann described how it is possible for the girl to physically mature into womanhood and function in the survival reproduction role without ever psychologically leaving the uroboric state. At first, this statement seems inappropriate today; nevertheless, there is an essential truth here, and as shown in Part I, Neumann was a man of truth.

Self-Conservation in the Maternal Uroboros

Neumann (1951/1994) defined the maternal uroboric stage in the psychology of the woman as the *Self-conservation* stage. Psychologically, this stage is uroboric in nature, as the girl maintains a close and primal relationship with the mother as a representation of the Great Mother. It is an important stage, and the survival of the human species is dependent on it as it includes the role of childbearing. Despite the initial and uroboric nature of this stage, and due to its feminine nature, as mentioned earlier, a woman can mature, get married, and bear children—and thus assume her role in the chain of survival—without ever psychologically leaving the maternal uroboros. As Neumann wrote, "In so far as she remains in this realm she is, to be sure, childish and immature from the point of view of conscious development. . . . The woman merely remains fixed, held fast in an immature form of her authentic being" (p. 9). Therefore, from Neuman's theoretical point of view, the boy is forced to leave the primal relationship due to physiological fact that leads to psychological development. The girl has no such encouragement, and she remains in a close bond with her mother. Although most girls develop further, this is not necessary. A girl can remain in the maternal uroboric situation with her mother and yet physiologically mature, get married, and have children while she psychologically remains a daughter and a mother but not yet a wife as she is still in the uroboros of the collective and cannot see her husband as an individual.

Neumann (1951/1994) described this state as one "in which the female ego remains bound to the maternal unconscious and the Self" (p. 11). He further described such women as alienated and even hostile toward masculinity and man, both within the psyche and without. A marriage with such an unconscious woman was presented by Neumann as a *marriage of death*, in which the conscious cannot rise, but rather dies. In his writings about the primal relationship in *The Child* (1963/1990), he described the surrender of the infant to the ordering principles imposed by the mother as a representation of the Great Mother, and the surrender of conscious to the unconscious while falling asleep as "a preliminary form of the 'marriage of death'" (p. 108). In *Amor and Psyche*, Neumann (1952/1971) interpreted Psyche's marriage to Eros as the original paradisiacal bliss of the "ecstasy of darkness" (p. 70) in the marriage of death, in which the woman is still in the matriarchate, an unconscious and collective phase, and thus perceives man as anonymous; she does not yet see him as an individual. To psychologically develop, the woman needs her masculine inner forces that resemble the stage of the invading patriarchate uroboros.

Invasion of the Patriarchal Uroboros

This stage still belongs to the matriarchate and the experience is still a symbiosis between the girl and her mother; hence, it is a transitional stage indicating "a development in the direction of the patriarchy" (Neumann, 1951/1994, p. 15) and thus the patriarchal uroboros. The archetype of the Great Father starts to emerge and differentiate from that of the Great Mother, correlating with the separation of the World Parents in boys' psychological development. The girl experiences the masculine as an invading "overwhelming power" (p. 15) or, as Neumann described it, an "unconscious inner force and transpersonal contents whose energetic charge greatly exceeds that of woman's consciousness break into the personality with the emergence of the parental uroboros" (p. 17). That is, the unconscious forces, the archetypal powers, are experienced as an invading conscious, and as such they manifest as masculinity.

For a woman, these forces would manifest as fascination with an idea or a guru. Kutzinski (personal communication) suggested that today this would explain the phenomenon of cults of women worshipping a man who appears to be highly spiritual. For a girl, these forces would appear as masculine elements in dreams and growing interest in boys her age as objects; this psychological stage is motivated by the physical changes occurring at about 10 to 12 years of age, changes that are transformative. This physical transformation of the young woman's body antecedes and motivates the psychological transformation entailed in this stage, mentioned earlier in describing the way a woman experiences the transformative character of the Feminine, of herself. The psychological experience of the invading masculine as an overwhelming power, typical of archetypal forces, acts in the service of automorphism "since its invasion 'fructifies' and changes the personality it seizes" (Neumann, 1951/1994, p. 17). The experience of invasion is also a psychological kidnapping, as in the situation of cults or as associated with Hades' mythological kidnapping of Kore from her mother, Demeter. Importantly, Neumann suggested that the overwhelming masculinity of this stage evokes a sense of inferiority and inadequacy in the woman compared to the masculine power.

Although a woman can develop further and overcome this sense of inferiority and inadequacy, it is important to mention that not all women develop further. As described earlier, it is possible for a woman to perform as a mother and as a wife without psychologically leaving the uroboric situation, manifested as symbiosis with her mother. In such cases, the inner psychic overwhelming power of masculinity manifests in outer-world inferiority as Western culture's outer world is masculine.

In interpreting the mythological story of Amor and Psyche (1952/1971), which is the story of Psyche's psychological development, Neumann described the stage of invading masculine powers as beginning with Psyche's sister and culminating in the second task, whereas the third and the fourth tasks belong to the patriarchate. Neumann described Psyche's sister as the paradoxical representation of her shadow, as the devouring power of the matriarchate on the one hand and feminine consciousness on the other, and as motivating Psyche to develop. Her development will entail a conscious reunion with Eros, which means development from the sensual instinctual connection with the male (as she does not see or know Eros) to the relationship with Eros (D. Kutzinski, personal communication).

Neumann (1952/1971) distinguished the hero from the heroine, pointing out that whereas in the hero's journey the dragon is killed and dismembered, the heroine's journey is different: "In its feminine variant this need of knowing [conscious] remains bound up with the greater need of loving" (pp. 74–75, note7). Therefore, although Eros is manifested in the dragon, Psyche will not kill it, but rather will "know" it and thus consciously reunite with it in love. Neumann stressed that the invading masculine inner powers of the patriarchal uroboros are the manifestation of the conflict within the sphere of the feminine, the conflict inherently entailed in development, and not between the feminine and the masculine. For Psyche, the conflict manifests in the four labors she must fulfil to reunite with Eros. These tasks comprise a very finely differentiated representation of these masculine inner powers in four levels.

In the first task, Psyche needs to differentiate "the uroboric mixture of the masculine" (Neumann, 1952/1971, p. 95), referring to the uroboric anonymous promiscuity that she needs to transform into selectivity with the help of her instinctual earthly powers. Thus, Neumann indicated that, unlike the male developing conscious, which entails detachment from the unconscious and instincts, the female develops her conscious and at the same time remains bound to her earthly instinctual unconscious nature. It is important to note that here Neumann describes the archetypal normal development. Today females are strongly challenged in this phase of development as the surrounding culture is patriarchal; therefore, it is rather easy to follow the masculine path of development and cut the umbilical cord with earthly instincts and unconscious and thus the feminine nature.

Concluding her first task and moving toward the second, Psyche encounters Pan, representing the old knowledge of nature. He gives her a decisive advice for the remaining three tasks, which at this point seems nothing more than a conflict imposed on her that involves hard labor. Pan's advice is to use "tender submission"; as Neumann wrote, "be feminine and win his love" (Neumann, 1952/1971, p. 97). Not only does Pan direct Psyche to use her inner masculine powers while maintaining the connection to her feminine nature, but he also gives meaning to the labor: winning Eros. Here Neumann interpreted the conflict as a journey; it is the path to winning Eros back by love.

The second task is to gather a hank of wool from the sheep—the rams of the sun, representing the solar male spirit. Neumann described Psyche's psychological task as facing the threatening and burning masculine spiritual powers, that is, the negative side of the patriarchal uroboros. The reed, representing water as opposed to fire (sun), comes to Psyche's aid, and once again she is reminded to maintain and utilize her feminine nature: "Wait, be patient. Things change. Time brings counsel" (1952/1971, p. 100). This is a fundamental feminine aspect relating to pregnancy and bearing children. The reed's advice is that, unlike the masculine way of attacking and taking using force, the feminine waits patiently for the right moment and takes with love (D. Kutzinski, personal communication). The reed helps Psyche to avoid becoming fascinated by the masculine magical power to the extent of cutting herself and her Self off from her feminine nature; thus, the reed reminds Psyche that she herself owns the wisdom of the matriarchal consciousness. Neumann beautifully summarized this task: "The feminine need only consult its instinct in order to enter into a fruitful relation, that is to say, a love relation, with the masculine at nightfall" (Neumann, 1952/1971, p. 101). Being able to be in a fruitful relationship with the masculine, the woman enters the patriarchate.

Self-Surrender in the Patriarchate

This psychological stage, which belongs to the transition between the patriarchal Uroboros and the patriarchate, entails the girl's overcoming her fear and surrendering, which she eventually experiences as empowering. When describing the infant's experience of the mother's masculinity in the primal relationship, Neumann (1963/1990) described the sense of being overpowered by a higher source and surrendering: "This ability to surrender itself to the intervention of a superior power is an essential consequence of a successful primal relationship." Importantly, he added, "it is of even more far-reaching importance for the girl than for a boy" (p. 108). This is true precisely due to the similarity of the girl's psychology to that of the mother. During the primal relationship, the identity between the infant (of either sex) and the mother entails the infant's experience of the mother's unconscious masculinity. Nevertheless, for the girl, this is the initial experience of what she will confront later in her life, when she develops to separate from the mother and leave the uroboric situation. There, her own masculinity invades in the form of the patriarchal uroboros, and she is called to overcome her fear and surrender to the powers as her own.

Neumann described the growing girl as challenged to differentiate her own masculinity, which manifests in the matriarchal consciousness, from the surrounding cultural masculinity that belongs to the patriarchate. This is a very important but nevertheless confusing, and often overlooked distinction that Neumann (1963/1990) described when he wrote, "The unconscious masculine world in woman represents the principle of *logos* and *nomos* (law), spirit and morality, which in analytical psychology is termed the world of the 'animi'" (p. 97). The principles of spirituality and morality Neumann referred to are not the patriarchal ones, but rather they stem from the deep unconscious layer of the Feminine, which is nature, and thus they are rooted in the body. Accordingly, Neumann (1951/1994) wrote that "speaking symbolically, she does not understand with her head but with her entire body" (p. 19). The girl, young woman, or mature woman who stands at this developmental stage is called to surrender to the overwhelming powers emerging from within and to be attuned to her instinctual and intuitive guidance, often in opposition to culturally accepted attitudes. Therefore, this act of surrender is motivated by centroversion in the service of the automorphic tendency to become oneself. Nevertheless, there is always the danger that she will not progress to the state of surrendering, and the woman as much as the girl is often held captive by her fascination with the transpersonal archetypal powers. In this case, she will not come to terms with her own nature; instead, sadly, she will remain fascinated with the masculine as spirit, ideas, and inspiration because the earthly and concrete component of the feminine is lacking. Here Neumann pointed to the fact that, without being strongly rooted in her femininity, a woman loses her connection with the Great Mother, which is a prerequisite to fertility and mothering.

As conscious is masculine, the development of a woman inherently entails Self-alienation and thus her liberation from this exile is the task of the male hero. Now, it is no longer a transpersonal masculine force of the patriarchal uroboros; instead, the masculine hero appears in an individual and personal form, inner and outer liberating masculine, leading her into the patriarchate. Initially, the masculine is projected on a man, and as Neumann (1951/1994) wrote,

> Only in later and higher forms of development can this archetypally masculine force be experienced and known for what it is, as something inner, to the degree that the woman attains her "autonomy," i.e., to a relative independence from her external male partner. (p. 27)

The higher forms of development Neumann referred to here is in *The Great Mother* (1955/1991) where he described a woman becoming conscious of her transformative character, that is here, her animus. Neumann described this stage as one in which the woman collects her projections and becomes independent of her male partner, with whom she is now able to relate as an individual. Nevertheless, there awaits another danger, which is commonly defined today as *animus possessed*. As consciousness is masculine, and as Western culture represents the patriarchate, an independent woman is in danger of "loss of Self" (p. 30). Being aware of this danger, understanding how far away from femininity women may drift, and how deep inside men repress their feminine aspect, Neumann repeatedly advocated redeeming the feminine aspect. Here again the matriarchal consciousness, as the conscious element within the feminine, comes to the fore.

In *Amor and Psyche* (Neumann, 1952/1971), Psyche, while in her second task, needed to encounter the masculine spirit to "take" from it; her third task is to manifest her femininity as the vessel containing it. She is sent to bring water from the Styx, the huge uroboric stream of the water of life, running from above to below and back, and thus "to give form and rest to what is formless and flowing" (p. 103). In this task she must reconcile with the masculine spiritual power that she was overcoming in the previous task. She has been sent to take, contain, encompass, and give form to this masculine power that threatens to shatter her. She is helped by the eagle, the symbol of Zeus and masculinity, whose role Neumann interpreted as the "male-female spirituality of Psyche" (p. 105), who contains like woman and knows like man. In addition, he claimed that Psyche's tasks evidently involve the Eros component in the gradual conscious awareness of the masculine spiritual element and that her development is both toward him and toward herself.

In progressing as she did, Psyche now knows Eros and relates to him with love as she confronts her last task, which is to descend to the underworld with a box to be filled with divine beauty ointment, to come back with the box unopened, and to prohibit pity. The conscious descent to the underworld is indeed a heroic act in which the challenge of not helping the beggars demands that Psyche consciously act in opposition to her feminine nature and thus perform ego stability as a masculine virtue. As Neumann (1952/1971) wrote, "This is the difficult task that confronts every feminine psyche on its way to individuation; it must suspend the claim of what is close at hand for the sake of a distant abstract goal" (p. 113).

Now, as Psyche has already attained her inner masculine powers, she is able to suspend her feminine nature for the purpose of her goal, the loving union with Eros. At this point the box of beauty ointment comes to the fore and becomes the decisive element. It seems that by opening the box Psyche has failed and regressed to her previous weak ego state. Nevertheless, here Neumann recognized a significant shift. He interpreted Psyche's failure as a crucial act of femininity: "The feminine manner of defeating the dragon is to accept it" (p. 121). This is the decisive feminine element that Neumann pointed to as differing from the masculine in its manner of acceptance rather than triumph. With the strong conscious she gained through her journey, Psyche decides to act against the conscious to obtain the immortal beauty that will ensure Eros's love. Psychologically Neumann explained, "By preferring beauty to knowledge, she reunites herself, rather, with the feminine in her nature" (p. 123). That is, at this stage, when she has gained the masculine spiritual knowledge, she is consciously and willingly sacrificing it for love, for Eros, for her true nature. It is at this point of the feminine individuation process that Neumann's theory arrives at the matriarchal consciousness.

Matriarchal Consciousness

Toward the culmination of the primal relationship, the decisive difference between the boy and the girl appears. The boy experiences a non-Self thou and is motivated to leave the primal relationship to attain Self-discovery and develop his consciousness. The girl, on the other hand, has the opposite experience; her Self-discovery is within the primal relationship from which she must alienate herself to further develop her conscious. Therefore, at the stage of redeeming the conscious from the unconscious, both boys and girls are involved in the Hero battle. For the boy it is a step toward Self- discovery whereas for the girl it is a step away and a danger of losing her sense of Self. Therefore, Neumann pointed out that, as the Feminine is the unconscious origin from which conscious develops, for both man and woman, estranging the Feminine is a necessary developmental phase, although the psychic experience of the man is different from that of the woman. Therefore, for both man and woman, the Feminine becomes the repressed psychic element, and its redemption is crucial in proceeding towards psychic wholeness.

As conscious first arises in the matriarchal layer of the maternal uroboros stage and becomes stronger as development proceeds toward the patriarchate, there is a phase belonging to feminine psychology, that he termed the paternal uroboros, in which consciousness is already strong enough to be regarded as consciousness. Nevertheless, this consciousness belongs to the matriarchal layer and is an early consciousness, which is childlike relative to the mature masculine patriarchal consciousness and soon to be repressed by it.

Matriarchal consciousness is a hallmark and a unique and important aspect of Neumann's theory. In some of his articles it is prominent and in others it is concealed. He critically described it as belonging to the matriarchal stage of both men and women. Nevertheless, as it belongs to the psychology of the Feminine; for women it is a natural mentality, and for man it is the anima, prevalent in unconscious states, whether creative or crises. As described, both are compelled to be estranged from it while developing toward the patriarchal consciousness.

In a woman's psychology, the matriarchal consciousness belongs to the patriarchal uroboros, which may be her psychological world-related layer well into adulthood. Here, Neumann's theory is confusing, as our mind is accustomed to think in terms of masculine conscious. Nevertheless, his description in terms of layers clarifies what is deeper in the unconscious and what is closer to the conscious. Neumann (1963/1990) theorized that the woman's conscious "is dominated largely by the Eros principle of relatedness" (p. 97) (that is, her matriarchal consciousness), whereas, as noted earlier, her unconscious is masculine and ruled by the principles of logos and spirit, manifesting her animus as the "upper" or more superficial layer of her unconscious. Therefore, the deeper layer of her unconscious resides in the matriarchal consciousness (in terms of layers, belonging to the patriarchal uroboros), in which awaits the masculine spirit of her own masculinity, rather than that of the patriarchate. As Neumann (1963/1990) clearly stated,

> Here we discern a hierarchical order. Uppermost, at the level closest to consciousness lie the animi pertaining to the largely patriarchal culture stratum. . . .The spiritual forces of the Old Woman, who incarnates the human stage of matriarchally determined existence, are likewise masculine; that is, they are animi of the matriarchal stratum; they belong to the spiritual aspect of the feminine and like it are largely overlaid and repressed by patriarchal animi . . . these matriarchal animi . . . [are] symbols of the feminine wisdom rooted in nature and instincts. (p. 98)

Here Neumann described the feminine wisdom of her own nature. When the woman surrenders to the masculine powers coming from within her, she assimilates the masculine of the patriarchate level of her own consciousness, which is different from the masculinity of the patriarchal culture. By accepting her masculinity instead of logical knowledge, she follows the wisdom of Eros and thus "realize[s] the feminine spirit which is the secret revealed by the patriarchal uroboros" (p. 101). This is what Neumann meant by redeeming the Feminine; it is the return from the alienation from Mother Nature, it means redeeming the spirit of the Earth, it is liberating Sophia.

Concluding with Sophia

The end of Chapter 4 pointed to a difference between Jung and Neumann in their perception of confronting evil. Here, at the end of this manuscript, a strong essential agreement between them is coming to the front: the call for the redemption of Sophia. Owens (2018) wrote that both men recognized that humanity is facing an end point, and a turning point of a new epoch of consciousness. In simple words, Neumann theorized that Western man, with his patriarchy of the Judeo-Christian tradition, became estranged from his own nature, from the Feminine element. In the Jewish Kabbala tradition it is the Shekhinah and in the gnostic myth it is Sophia; in Neumann's psychological language it is the matriarchal consciousness.

Although for Neumann it was a leading theme, woven throughout his writings, in Jung's writing it was concealed. Owens suggested that Neumann recognized it in Jung's writing when he read the manuscript of *Answer to Job*. In a letter he wrote to Jung, Neumann (Jung & Neumann, 2015) wrote, "In reality, you believe in the feminine Sophia as the highest authority without admitting it. Perhaps it only seems to me to be so because this is how it is for me personally" (p. 272). Owens (2018) further suggested that Jung had already dealt with Sophia in the *Red Book,* and he described this suggestion through the gnostic myth of Philemon that Jung undoubtedly dealt with. In a brief outline of the development of the gnostic myth, Owens described Sophia as the twin partner of Logos, both originating in the same cosmic womb, as the first syzygies of World Parents. Whereas Sophia is the conception of thought, Logos is the potential of thought, and one cannot do without the other. In the Jewish tradition with which Neumann was well familiar, it is the Shekhinah who is the Lord's "constant delight" (Proverbs 8:31). In separating from her twin, she fell to the depth, the underworld of chaos; she is exiled in the material world, she is its spirit and in need of redemption.

In theorizing early life, Neumann (1963/1990) indeed arrived at Sophia through the body and food. He described, using body symbolism such as "digest" or "eliminate" how the infant "knows" the world through his relationship with his mother, and thus the affiliation between love and knowledge is established in his psyche. He further wrote,

> Positive Relationship provides an essential foundation—not the only foundation to be sure—for the openness to the world indispensable to the child's subsequent intellectual development. This is one more reason why the "Great Mother" in her positive aspect is not only she who confers life and love, but, in her highest forms, is Sophia, the goddess of knowledge and of wisdom. (p. 31)

Sophia as a higher spiritual aspect of the Feminine, is present in psychic manifestation from the very beginning. In *The Great Mother* (1955/1991), Neumann pointed that at the higher levels Sophia is the vessel in which the matter and the spirit are molded together to achieve the highest spiritual stage, of which he wrote "the heart spring of Sophia" (p. 329). He further described "the heart that sends forth the spirit-nourishing 'central' wisdom of feeling, not the 'upper' wisdom of the head" (p. 330). This was King Solomon's strength, as the highest among judges, who had the "knowing of the heart."

At this point, Neumann arrived at the heart of the matter, and described Sophia differing from the Great Mother. The Great Mother, he wrote, is interested in nourishing the infant, the child, and the immature man who refuses to develop. Sophia, on the other hand, is interested in a whole man; she governs his transformation from the elementary material to the transformative spiritual. At about the same time Neumann wrote his first Eranos essay, "Mystical Man" (1948/1989), in which he described the work of the Great Individual, the Jewish Zaddik, in the Messianic age: "His work consists in reuniting the parts that have been separated from the godhead—the

Shekhinah, God's female immanence, which has been wandering about in exile—with God's transcendence" (p. 409). For Neumann, Sophia is the incarnation of the Feminine Self, both of mankind and of every woman. Therefore, Sophia becomes the goal of individuation, whether she is the liberated anima for man, the Self of the woman, or the redeemed Feminine Earth of mankind.

Epilogue

It has gradually become clear to me what every great philosophy up until now has consisted of—namely, the confession of its originator, and a species of involuntary and unconscious autobiography; and moreover that the moral (or immoral) purpose in every philosophy has constituted the true vital germ out of which the entire plant has always grown. (Nietzsche, 1886/2019, p. 8)

It is evident from this study that Neumann's theory was indeed his confession, and rather an impressive one. He was only 29 when he first met Jung and wrote the deep reflective manuscript of *Jacob and Esau* (1934-2015). He continued to be prolific for twenty-five years until his untimely death at age 55. During those years, Neumann wrote a theory that is authentic and truthful to the lived experience on the one hand and that challenges and transcends conscious mind on the other hand.

When I started my research, I thought I would cover only the part of the theory that describes early life development. Soon I was completely hooked and wanted to read and understand more. The more I researched and realized the extent of Neumann's theory, the more I found myself thinking of therapy in terms of his formulations. I was astonished both by the potential of the theory to promote psychological understanding of therapeutic meaning and by the neglect of his writings in the current Jungian world. Of course, there are many Jungian writers; nevertheless, Neumann had the concrete potential to realize a school of thought of his own, a "Neumannian" branch in Jungian Psychology.

Researching and writing the dissertation that led to this book has been a long and lonely journey. Spending the time in my study with Erich Neumann, I came to know him in a very intimate way, and although I have no idea of him as a person, I have a strong sense of him as a theoretician and a deep appreciation. I hope that this work will be a fresh breeze blowing on his old pages, a spring bloom to his theory, and the feminine spirit he so called for.

References

Adler, G. (1979). On Erich Neumann: 1905–1960. In E. Neumann, *The essays of Erich Neumann: Vol. 2. Creative man* (E. Rolfe, Trans.) (pp. xi–xvii). Princeton, NJ: Princeton University Press. (Original work published 1960)

Adler, G. (1990). Editorial note (R. F. C. Hull, Trans.). In H. Read, M. Fordham, G. Adler, & W. McGuire (Eds.), *The collected works of C. G. Jung: Vol. 9, Pt. 1. The archetypes and the collective unconscious* (2nd ed. pp. v–vi). Princeton, NJ: Princeton University Press. (Original work published 1954)

Astor, J. (1990). The emergence of Fordham's model of development. *Journal of Analytical Psychology, 35*(3), 261–278.

Bernardini, R. (2016). Neumann at Eranos. In E. Shalit & M. Stein (Eds.), *Turbulent times, creative minds: Erich Neumann and C. G. Jung in relationship (1933-1960)* (pp. 199–236). Asheville, NC: Chiron.

Bick, E. (1964). Notes on infant observation in psycho-analytic training. *International Journal of Psycho-Analysis, 45*, p. 558.

Edinger, E. F. (1960). The ego-Self paradox. *Journal of Analytical Psychology, 5*(1), 3–18.

Edinger, E. F. (1992). *Ego and archetype*. Boston, MA: Shambhala. (Original work published 1972)

Ellenberger, H. F. (2019). *The discovery of the unconscious*. New York, NY: Basic Books.

Fordham, M. (1944). *The life of childhood*. London, England: Kegan Paul.

Fordham, M. (1957). *New developments in analytical psychology*. New York, NY: Routledge.

Fordham, M. (1975). Memories and thoughts about C. G. Jung. *Journal of Analytical Psychology, 20*(2), 102–113.

Fordham, M. (1980). The emergence of child analysis. *Journal of Analytical Psychology, 25*(4), 311–324.

Fordham, M. (1981). Neumann and childhood. *Journal of Analytical Psychology, 26*(2), 99–122.

Fordham, M. (1994). *Children as individuals*. London, England: Free Association Books. (Original work published 1969)

Furlotti, N. (2016). Companions on the way: Consciousness in conflict. In Shalit E. & Stein M. (Eds.), *Turbulent times, creative minds: Erich Neumann and C. G. Jung in relationship (1933–1960)* (pp. 45–69). Asheville, NC: Chiron.

Giegerich, W. (1975). Ontogeny = phylogeny? A fundamental critique of Erich Neumann's analytical psychology. *Spring: An Annual of Archetypal and Jungian Thought*, 110–29.

Gilligan, C. (1982). *In a different voice*. Cambridge, MA: Harvard University Press.

Graves, R. (1992). *The Greek myths: Complete edition*. London, England: Penguin.

Grossman, J. (July 24, 2017). *Why didn't Jacob climb up the ladder?* (in Hebrew). Herzog Institute. Retrieved from https://www.youtube.com/watch?v=WNpC1oWJ5Vk

Grossman, J. (July 17, 2018). *Jacob's struggle with the angel*. (in Hebrew), Herzog Institute. Retrieved from https://www.youtube.com/watch?v=j54q7LgRXjk

Jacobi, J. (1974). *Complex/archetype/symbol in the psychology of C. G. Jung* (R. Manheim, Trans.). New York, NY: Princeton University Press. (Original work published 1959)

Jorgensen, G. (2006a). Kohlberg and Gilligan: Duet or duel? *Journal of Moral Education, 35*(2), 179–196.

Jorgensen, G. (2006b). Stage 7 Convergence of Cross-Paradigmatic issues. Paper presented at the Association for Moral Education Conference, Fribourg, Switzerland.

Jung, C. G. (1934). *Wirklichkeit der seele: Anwendungen und Fortschritte der neueren Psychologie* [Reality of the soul: Applications and advances in modern psychology]. Zurich, Switzerland: Rascher.

Jung, C. G. (1957–1983). *The collected works of C. G. Jung* (H. Read, M. Fordham, G. Adler,& W. McGuire, Eds.; R. F. C. Hull, Trans.). Bollingen Series XX. New York, NY: Bollingen Foundation/Princeton University Press.

Jung, C. G. (1965). *Modern man in search of a soul* (W. S. Dell & C. F. Baynes, Trans.). New York, NY: Harcourt. (Original work published 1933)

Jung, C. G. (1969a). Transformation symbolism in the Mass (R. F. C. Hull, Trans.). In H. Read, M. Fordham, G. Adler, & W. McGuire (Eds.), *The collected works of C. G. Jung* (2nd ed.): *Vol. 11. Psychology and religion: West and east* (pp. 201–296). Princeton, NJ: Princeton University Press. (Original work published 1954)

Jung, C. G. (1969b). Psychological commentary on *The Tibetan Book of the Great Liberation. In H. Read, M. Fordham, G. Adler, & W. McGuire. (Eds.),* The collected works of C. G. Jung (2nd ed): Vol. 11. Psychology and religion: West and east (pp. 475–508). Princeton NJ: Princeton University Press. (Original work published 1954)

Jung, C. G. (1970). Appendix: Editorial (R. F. C. Hull, Trans.). In H. Read, M. Fordham, G. Adler, & W. McGuier. (Eds.), The collected works of C. G. Jung (2nd ed.): Vol. 10. Civilization in transsition (pp. 533-567). Princeton , NJ: Princeton University Press. (Original work published 1933)

Jung, C. G. (1970). The state of psychotherapy today (R. F. C. Hull, Trans.). In *H. Read, M. Fordham, G. Adler, & W. McGuire. (Eds.)*, The collected works of C. G. Jung (2nd ed.): Vol. 10. Civilization in transition (pp. 157–173). Princeton, NJ: Princeto University Press. (Original work published 1934)

Jung, C. G. (1970). Epilogue to "Essay on Contemporary Events" (R. F. C. Hull, Trans.). In *H. Read, M. Fordham, G. Adler, & W. McGuire. (Eds.), The collected works of C. G. Jung* (2nd ed.): *Vol. 10. Civilization in transition* (pp. 227–243). Princeton, NJ: Princeto University Press. (Original work published 1946)

Jung, C. G. (1970). The undiscovered self (R. F. C. Hull, Trans.). In *H. Read, M. Fordham, G. Adler, & W. McGuire. (Eds.) The collected works of C. G. Jung* (2nd ed.): *Vol. 10. Civilization in transition* (pp. 245–305). Princeton, NJ: Princeton University Press. (Original work published 1957)

Jung, C. G. (1972a). On psychic energy. (R. F. C. Hull, Trans.). In H. Read, M. Fordham, G. Adler, & W. McGuire (Eds.), *The collected works of C. G. Jung*: (2nd ed.): *Vol. 8. Structure & dynamics of the psyche* (pp. 3–66). Routledge & Kegan Paul. (Original work published 1928)

Jung, C. G. (1972b). The relation between the ego and the unconscious (R. F. C. Hull, Trans.). In H. Read, M. Fordham, G. Adler, & W. McGuire (Eds.), *The collected works of C. G. Jung* (2nd. ed.,): *Vol. 7. Two essays in analytical psychology* (pp. 121–241). Princeton, NJ: Princeton University Press. (Original work published 1928)

Jung, C. G. (1972). *Two essays in analytical psychology* (R. F. C. Hull, Trans.): *Vol. 7. The collected works of C. G. Jung* (2nd ed.; H. Read, M. Fordham, G. Adler, & W. McGuire Eds.).

Princeton, NJ: Princeton University Press. (Original work published 1928–1943)

Jung, C. G. (1972). Analytical psychology and Weltanschauung (R. F. C. Hull, Trans.). In H. Read, M. Fordham, G. Adler, & W. McGuire. (Eds.), *The collected works of C. G. Jung* (2nd. ed.): *Vol. 8: Structure & dynamics of the psyche* (pp. 358–381). Routledge & Kegan Paul. (Original work published 1931)

Jung, C. G. (1972). A review of complex theory (R. F. C. Hull, Trans.). In H. Read, M. Fordham, G. Adler, & W. McGuire (Eds.), *The collected works of C. G. Jung* (2nd ed.): *Vol. 8. Structure & dynamics of the psyche* (pp. 92–104). Princeton, N.J.: Princeton University Press. (Original work published 1934)

Jung, C. G. (1972). On the psychology of the unconscious (R. F. C. Hull, Trans.). In H. Read, M. Fordham, G. Adler, & W. McGuire (Eds.), *The collected works of C. G. Jung* (2nd. ed.): *Vol. 7. Two essays in analytical psychology* (pp. 1–119). Princeton, NJ: Princeton University Press. (Original work published 1943)

Jung, C. G. (1972). Synchronicity: An acausal connecting principle. (R. F. C. Hull, Trans.). In H. Read, M. Fordham, G. Adler, & W. McGuire (Eds.), *The collected works of C. G. Jung* (2nd ed.): *Vol. 8. Structure & dynamics of the psyche* (pp. 417–519). Routledge & Kegan Paul. (Original work published 1952)

Jung, C. G. (1972). On the nature of the psyche. (R. F. C. Hull, Trans.). In H. Read, M. Fordham, G. Adler, & W. McGuire (Eds.), *The collected works of C. G. Jung* (2nd ed.): *Vol 8. Structure & dynamics of the psyche* (pp. 159–234). Routledge & Kegan Paul. (Original work published 1954)

Jung, C. G. (1974). Foreword. In J. Jacobi, *Complex/archetype/ symbol in the psychology of C. G. Jung* (R. Manheim, Trans.) (pp. ix–xi). New York, NY: Princeton University Press. (Original work published 1959)

Jung, C. G. (1978). *Aion: Research into the phenomenology of the self* (R. F. C. Hull, Trans.): *Vol. 9, Pt. 2. The collected works of C. G. Jung* (H. Read, M. Fordham, G. Adler, & W. McGuire, Eds.). Princeton, NJ: Princeton University Press. (Original work published 1951)

Jung, C. G. (1983). Commentary on "The secret of the golden flower" (R. F. C. Hull, Trans.). In H. Read, M. Fordham, G. Adler, & W. McGuire (Eds.), *The collected works of C. G. Jung: Vol. 13. Alchemical studies* (pp. 1–56). Princeton, NJ: Princeton University Press. (Original work published 1929)

Jung, C. G. (1987). The "face-to-face" interview with John Freeman, BBC Television, October 22, 1959. In W. McGuire & R. F. C. Hull (Eds.), *C. G. Jung Speaking,* (pp. 424–439). Princeton, NJ: Princeton University Press.

Jung, C. G. (1988). Introduction. In F. G. Wickes, *The inner world of childhood* (3rd ed., pp. xvii–xxiii). Boston, MA: Sigo Press. (Original work published 1927)

Jung, C. G. (1989). *Memories, dreams, reflections* (Rev. ed.) (A. Jaffe, Ed.; R. Winston & C. Winston, Trans.). New York, NY: Vintage Books. (Original work published 1961)

Jung, C. G. (1990). *Psychological types* (R. F. C. Hull, Trans.): *Vol. 6: The collected works of C. G. Jung* (H. Read, M. Fordham, G. Adler, & W. McGuireEds.). Princeton, NJ: Princeton University Press. (Original work published 1921)

Jung, C. G. (1990). *Symbols of transformation* (R. F. C. Hull, Trans.): *Vol. 5. The collected works of C. G. Jung* (2nd ed.; H. Read, M. Fordham, G. Adler, & W. McGuire Eds.). Princeton, NJ: Princeton University Press. (Original work published 1952)

Jung, C. G. (1990). *The archetypes and the collective unconscious* (R. F. C. Hull, Trans.): *Vol. 9, Pt. 1. The collected works of C. G. Jung* (2nd ed.; H. Read, M. Fordham, G. Adler, & W.

McGuire,Eds.). Princeton, NJ: Princeton University Press. (Original work published 1936–1954)

Jung, C. G. (1990a). Archetypes of the collective unconscious (R. F. C. Hull, Trans.). In H. Read, M. Fordham, G. Adler, & W. McGuire. (Eds.), *The collected works of C. G. Jung* (2nd ed.): *Vol. 9, Pt. 1. Archetypes and the collective unconscious* (pp. 3–41). Princeton, NJ: Princeton University Press. (Original work published 1954)

Jung, C. G. (1990b). Concerning the archetypes, with special reference to the anima concept. (R. F. C. Hull, Trans.). In H. Read, M. Fordham, G. Adler, & W. McGuire (Eds.), *The collected works of C. G. Jung* (2nd ed.): *Vol. 9, Pt. 1. Archetypes and the collective unconscious* (pp. 54–72). Princeton, NJ: Princeton University Press. (Original work published 1954)

Jung, C. G. (1990c). Psychological aspect of the Mother archetype. (R. F. C. Hull, Trans.). In H. Read, M. Fordham, G. Adler, & W. McGuire (Eds.), *The collected works of C. G. Jung* (2nd ed.): *Vol. 9, Pt. 1. Archetypes and the collective unconscious* (pp. 73–110). Princeton, NJ: Princeton University Press. (Original work published 1954)

Jung, C. G. (1991). Analytical psychology and education (R. F. C. Hull, Trans.). In H. Read, M. Fordham, G. Adler, & W. McGuire (Eds.), *The collected works of C. G. Jung: Vol. 17. The development of personality* (pp. 63–132). Princeton, NJ: Princeton University Press. (Original work published 1946)

Jung, C. G. (2013). Depth psychology (R. F. C. Hull, Trans.). In H. Read, M. Fordham, G. Adler, & W. McGuire (Eds.), *The collected works of C. G. Jung: Vol. 18, Pt. 2. The symbolic life* (pp. 477–486). Delhi, India: Facsimile Publisher. (Original work published 1948)

Jung, C. G. (2014). Foreword. In E. Neumann, *The origins and history of consciousness.* (R. F. C. Hull, Trans.) (pp. xiii–xiv).

Princeton, NJ: Princeton University Press. (Original work published 1949)

Jung, C. G., & Neumann, E. (2015). *Analytical psychology in exile: The correspondence of C. G. Jung and Erich Neumann* (M. Liebscher, Ed.; H. McCartney, Trans.). Princeton, NJ: Princeton University Press.

Kalsched, D. E. (2017). Trauma innocence and the core complexof dissociation. *Journal of Analytical Psychology, 62*(4), 474–500.

Kohlberg, L. (1976). Moral stages and moralization: The cognitive developmental approach. In T. Lickona (Ed.), *Moral development and behavior: Theory, research, and social issues* (pp. 31–53). New York, NY: Holt, Rinehart and Winston.

Kohlberg, L. (1986) A current statement on some theoretical issues. In S. Modgil & C. Modgil (Eds.), *Lawrence Kohlberg: consensus and controversy*. Philadelphia, PA: Falmer Press.

Kohlberg, L., & Ryncarz, R. A. (1990). Beyond justice reasoning: Moral development and consideration of a seventh stage. In C. N. Alexander & E. J. Langer (Eds.), *Higher stages of human development: Perspectives on adult growth* (pp. 191–207). New York, NY: Oxford University Press.

Kutzinski, D. (2016). A Brief Comment on Neumann and His Essay "On Mozart's Magic Flute." In E. Shalit E. & M. Stein (Eds.), *Turbulent times, creative minds: Erich Neumann and C. G. Jung in relationship (1933-1960)* (pp. 309–311). Asheville, NC: Chiron.

Kron, T., & Wieler, D. (2013). *Erich Neumann: A Jungian dialogical existentialist.* Lecture presented in the IAAP kongres, Kohpenhagen. The Israeli Institute for Jungian Psychology. Retrieved from http://jung-israel.org/erich-neumann-a-jungian-dialogical-existentialist-tamar-kron-david-wieler

Lahav, R. (2016). Neve Tzeelim--A field of creation and development. In E. Shalit & M. Stein (Eds.), *Turbulent times, creative minds:*

Erich Neumann and C. G. Jung in relationship (1933–1960) (pp. 347–363). Asheville, NC: Chiron.

Lammers, A. (2017, March 23). *Neumann, religion and the numinous* [Webinar]. Asheville Jung Center, Asheville, NC.

Lammers, C. A. (2019a). Introduction. In A. Lammers (Ed.), *The roots of Jewish consciousness: Vol. 1. Revelation and apocalypse* (M. Kyburz, Trans.; pp. xxiii–xli). New York, NY: Routledge.

Lammers, C. A. (2019b). Introduction. In A. Lammers (Ed.), *The roots of Jewish consciousness: Vol. 2. Hasidism* (M. Kyburz, Trans.; pp. xxvi–xxx). New York, NY: Routledge.

Lewis, R. C. (1989). The historical development of the concept of the archetype. *Quadrant, 22*(1), 41–53.

Liebscher, M. (2015a). Introduction. In M. Liebscher (Ed.), *Analytical psychology in exile: The correspondence of C. G. Jung and Erich Neumann* (H. McCartney, Trans.; pp. xi–lviii). Princeton, NJ: Princeton University Press.

Liebscher, M. (2015b). Introduction. In E. Neumann, *The Great Mother* (pp. vii–xi). Princeton, NJ: Princeton University Press.

Liebscher, M. (2016a). The challenges of editorship: A reflection on editing the Jung-Neumann correspondence. *Journal of Analytical Psychology, 61*(2), 155–171.

Liebscher, M. (2016b). Uncertain friends in particular matters: The relationship between C. G. Jung and Erich Neumann. In E. Shalit & M. Stein (Eds.), *Turbulent times, creative minds: Erich Neumann and C. G. Jung in relationship (1933-1960)* (pp. 25–44). Asheville, NC: Chiron.

Liebscher, M. (2017). German émigré psychologists in Tel Aviv (1934–58): Max M. Stern and Margarete Barband-Issac in conflict with Erich Neumann. *History of Human Sciences, 30*(2), 54–68.

Lori, A. (2005, January 28). Jung at heart. *Haaretz.* Retrieved from https://www.haaretz.com/1.4716663

McCurdy, J. C. (1987). Manic-depressive psychosis - A perspective: Binswanger, Jung, Neumann, and the myth of Dionysus. *Journal of Analytical Psychology, 32*(40), 309–324.

Meier-Seethaler, C. (1982). The child: Erich Neumann's contribution to the psychopathology of child development. *Journal of Analytical Psychology, 27*(4), 357–379.

Mitchell, S. A., & Black, M. J. (1995). *Freud and beyond.* New York, NY: Basic Books.

Neumann, E. (1959). The significance of the genetic aspect for analytical psychology. *Journal of Analytical Psychology, 4*(2), 125–137.

Neumann, E. (1966). Narcissism, normal Self-formation and the primary relation to the mother. *Spring,* p. 81–106. (Original work published 1955)

Neumann, E. (1971). *Amor and Psyche: The psychic development of the feminine* (R. Manheim, Trans.). Princeton, NJ: Princeton University Press. (Original work published 1952)

Neumann, E. (1979). Kafka's "The Trial": An interpretation through depth psychology. In *The essays of Erich Neumann: Vol. 2. Creative man* (E. Rolfe, Trans.) (pp. 3–112). Princeton, NJ: Princeton University Press. (Original work writen 1933)

Neumann, E. (1979). C. G. Jung: 1955. In *The essays of Erich Neumann: Vol. 2. Creative man* (E. Rolfe, Trans.) (pp. 246–256). Princeton, NJ: Princeton University Press. (Original work published 1955)

Neumann, E. (1988). The stages of religious experience and the path of depth psychology. *Quadrant, 21*(1), 1–32. (Original work published 1970)

Neumann, E. (1989). Mystical man. In J. Campbell (Ed.), *Papers from the Eranos yearbooks: Vol. 6. The mystic vision* (R. Manheim, Trans.) (pp. 375–415). Princeton, NJ: Princeton University Press. (original work published 1948)

Neumann, E. (1989). The psyche and the transformation of the reality planes: A metapsychological essay. In *The essays of Erich Neumann: Vol. 3. The place of creation* (E. Rolfe, Trans.) (pp. 3–62). Princeton, NY: Princeton University Press. (Original work published 1952)

Neumann, E. (1989). The experience of the unitary reality. In *The essays of Erich Neumann: Vol. 3. The place of creation* (E. Rolfe, Trans.) (pp. 63–130). Princeton, NY: Princeton University Press. (Original work published 1955)

Neumann, E. (1989). The psyche as the place of creation. In *The essays of Erich Neumann: Vol. 3. The place of creation* (E. Rolfe, Trans.) (pp. 320–381). Princeton, NY: Princeton University Press. (Original work published 1960)

Neumann, E. (1990). *Depth psychology and a new ethic* (E. Rolfe, Trans.). Boston, MA: Shambhala. (Original work published 1949)

Neumann, E. (1990). *The child: Structure and dynamics of the nascent personality.* (R. Manheim, Trans.). Boston, USA: Shambala. (Original work published 1963)

Neumann, E. (1991). *The great mother* (R. Manheim, Trans.). Princeton, NJ: Princeton University Press. (Original work published 1955)

Neumann, E. (1994). The psychological stages of women's development. In *The fear of the feminine and other essays on feminine psychology* (B. Matthews, Trans.) (pp. 3–63). Princeton, NJ: Princeton University Press. (Original work published 1951)

Neumann, E. (1994). The meaning of the Earth archetype for modern times. In *The fear of the feminine and other essays on feminine psychology* (E. Rolfe & M. Cullingworth, Trans.) (pp. 165–226). Princeton, NJ: Princeton University Press. (Original work published 1953)

Neumann, E. (1994). *The fear of the feminine and other essays on feminine psychology* (E. Rolfe & M. Cullingworth, Trans.) Princeton, NJ: Princeton University Press. (Original work written 1950—1959)

Neumann, E. (2014). *The origins and history of consciousness.* (R. F. C. Hull, Trans.). Princeton, NJ: Princeton University Press. (Original work published 1949)

Neumann, E. (2015). *Jacob and Esau: On the collective symbolism of the brother motif* (E. Shalit, Ed.; M. Kyburz, Trans.). Asheville, NC: Chiron. (Original work written 1934)

Neumann, E. (2019). *The roots of Jewish consciousness.* (A. C. Lammers, Ed.; M. Kyburz, Trans.). New York, NY: Routledge. (Original work written 1940–1945)

Nietzsche, F. (2019). *Beyond good and evil* (H. Zimmern, Trans.). SDE Classics. (Originaly written 1886)

Owens, L. S. (2018). C. G. Jung and Erich Neumann: The Zaddik, Sopiha, and the Shekhinah. *Psychological Perspectives, 61*(2), 133–151.

Porat, R. (2016). Erich Neumann's concept of distress-ego. In E. Shalit & M. Stein (Eds.), *Turbulent times, creative minds: Erich Neumann and C. G. Jung in relationship (1933–1960)* (pp. 315–346). Asheville, NC: Chiron.

Rosenthal, H. (1934): "Der Typengegensatz in der jüdischen Religionsgeschichte (The type difference in Jewish religious history)," in C. G. Jung, *Wirklichkeit der Seele: Anwendungen und Fortschritte der neueren Psychologie.* Zurich: Rascher, (pp. 355–409).

Samuels, A. (2004). *Jung and the post-Jungians.* New York, NY: Brunner-Routledge.

Shalit, E. (2002). *The complex path of transformation from archetype to ego.* Toronto, Canada: Inner City Books.

Shalit, E. (2015a). Introduction. In *Jacob and Esau: On the collective symbolism of the brother motif* (E. Shalit, Ed.; M. Kyburz, Trans.). Asheville, NC: Chiron.

Shalit, E. (2016, November 26). Jacob and Esau. Lecture at Pacifica Graduate Institute,. Private and authorized recording.

Shalit, E., & Stein, M. (2016). Introduction. In E. Shalit & M. Stein (Eds.), *Turbulent times, creative minds: Erich Neumann and C. G. Jung in relationship (1933–1960)* (pp. ix–xxi). Asheville, NC: Chiron.

Sidoli, M. (1983). De-integration and Re-integration in the first two weeks of life. *Journal of Analytical Psychology, 28*(3), 201–212.

Spohn, W. C. (2000). Conscience and moral development. *Theological Studies, 61*(1), 122–138.

Stewart, L. H. (1990). Foreword. In E. Neumann, *The child: Structure and dynamics of the nascent personality* (R. Manheim, Trans.) (pp. vi–5). Boston, MA: Shambala.

Walsh, C. (2000). The Life and Legacy of Lawrence Kohlberg. *Society, 37*(2), 36–41.

Wickes, F. G. (1988). *The inner world of childhood* (3rd ed.). Boston, MA: Sigo Press. (Original work published 1927)

Winnicott, D. W. (1945). Primitive emotional development. *International Journal of Psychoanalysis, 26*, 137–143.

Winnicott, D. W. (1960). The theory of the parent-infant relationship. *International Journal of Psychoanalysis, 41*, 585–595.

Winnicott, D. W. (1984). Transitional objects and transitional phenomena. In *Through paediatrics to psychoanalysis: Collected papers* (pp. 229–242). London, England: Karnac. (Original work published 1951)

Winnicott, D. W. (1984). Primary maternal preoccupation. In *Through paediatrics to psychoanalysis: Collected papers.* (pp.

300–305). London, England: Karnac Books. (Original work published 1956)

Winnicott, D. W. (1987a). The newborn and his mother. In *Babies and their mothers*. Boston, MA: Addison-Wesley. (Original work published 1964)

Winnicott, D. W. (1987b). *The child, the family, and the outside world*. Boston, MA: DaCapo Press. (Original work published 1964)

Winnicott, D. W. (1987). Communication between infant and mother, and mother and infant, compared and contrasted. In *Babies and their mothers*. Boston, MA: Addison-Wesley. (Original work published 1968)

Winnicott, D. W. (1988). *Human Nature*. London, England: Free Association Books.

Appendix I
Consciousness Levels of
Humanity's Encountering the Shadow

Mythologizing

In *Jacob and Esau* (1934-2015), Neumann referred to the mythologizing stage as the earliest phase of human's conscious ability to hold a mythological comprehension, and he described the development of consciousness leading from mythologizing to the stage to which the midrashim belong. In theorizing about the unconscious psychic layer as the mythologizing stage, Neumann followed Jung (1946/1991), who wrote in the third lecture of Analytical Psychology and Education, published in 1926,

> I have drawn the conclusion that there is a layer of the unconscious which functions in exactly the same way as the archaic psyche that produced the myths . . . the collective unconscious, as I have called this myth-like layer. (p. 119)

Here, Jung established the foundation and validity of Neumann's formulation about the role of mythology for human consciousness development. In another work, Jung (1928/1972a) asserted that, although myth holds an allegoric explanatory function, the "primitives" were not as interested in explanation as they were in "weaving fables," and myth spontaneously forced its "way out of the unconscious" as a mere projection that represented typical psychic phenomena (p. 38).

Neumann (1934/2015) elaborated on Jung's assertions and theorized that the mythologizing stage belongs to a collective unconscious layer, in which humanity was yet in a *participation mystique* with the world and immersed in the "surrounding motherly sea" (p. 52) of the unconscious. Inner and unconscious contents were outwardly and objectively projected and concretized in rituals, which Neumann cleverly exemplified in the Jewish scapegoat ritual (p. 65). When interpreting the Jewish source story, it was natural for him to use the Jewish ritual. Nevertheless, in doing so he was presumably aiming at indicating the development of Jewish consciousness beyond the ritual. Neumann also posited that, at this early stage, myths were the expressions of what was experienced as an "impersonal and suprapersonal event" (p. 54). At the mythological stage, the figures are divine as there was no individuality yet in their faces; thus, myths included gods, deities like the sun and the moon, and also twin brothers. Neumann considered mythological twin brothers as they appear in various cultures. (In addition to the biblical twin brothers, he considered others from the Babylonian [p. 38] and the Egyptian [pp. 40–41] cultures; nevertheless, he differentiated between the twins and the brothers.) He argued that the earlier the myth was created, the more the *participation mystique* was active and world unity ruled and was apparent in the myth. Presumably, and as an elaboration on Owens (2018), Neumann had in mind the Kabbalistic and gnostic perception of the beginning of all beginnings and the primal unity that was then broken into a duality. This is important to mention here, as the traces of these original myths will also be later used in explaining the roots of Neumann's early life theory.

Returning to Neumann's (1934/2015) writing in *Jacob and Esau*, he theorized that at this early stage myth reflected the unity by presenting the twins or deities as the sun and moon in equilibrium (p. 6). He asserted that, for the brothers, one had the advantage of primogeniture and being older whereas the other had the disadvantage of being younger and concluded that "the motif of the twins is the original one" (p. 47). Hence, the biblical story's development of twins in the womb as the situation of unity and complementarity to become hostile brothers as the situation of separation and opposition was anchored by Neumann in the development of human consciousness as manifested in world mythology.

In *Origins*, Neumann (1949/2014) elaborated on this idea when he referred to these myths as creation myths: "The first cycle of myth is the creation myth. Here the mythological projection of psychic material appears in cosmogonic form, as the mythology of creation" (p. 5). In his formulation, he divided the creation myths in such a way that the first and original state is one of perfection and complete wholeness, like identical twins in the womb, which can be described only symbolically as circular (p. 8), or as mostly known in Neumann's theory, the uroboros (p. 11). Following that, the creation myth proceeded to the stage of the "separation of the World Parents" (p. 5). I suggest that here again Neumann referred to (although he did not mention) the Kabbalistic and gnostic primal unity that separates and becomes opposites, as sky and earth, upper and lower, and light and darkness. It is to this stage that the myths of the brothers belong; as opposed to the twins who represent wholeness, the brothers are separated. In *Origins*, Neumann used the example of the twins versus the brothers to indicate the origin of the opposites and to describe their separation as marking the development toward the "consolidation of ego consciousness" (p. 97).

Important for the exploration of his initial analysis in *Jacob and Esau* (1934-2015) and for a better understanding of the significance of twin brother motif, it is relevant to consider his reference to the symbol of the circle in his later work:

> It is also the perfect state in which the opposites are united—the perfect beginning because the opposites have not yet flown apart and the world has not yet begun, the

perfect end because in it the opposites have come together
again in a synthesis and the world is once more at rest.
(Neumann, 1949/2014, p. 8)

Here and retrospectively, Neumann presented his interpretation of
Jacob and Esau as a story of individuation, beginning as equal twins
in Rebekah's womb and going the full circle back to Jacob's return
to psychic unity when he encountered Esau after struggling with the
angel.

A few years later, in a lecture delivered in 1938, Jung
(1954/1990c) presented the same idea of the original unity
separating into the opposites and returning to unity and described
Logos extricating itself from the maternal womb: "the two were one
in the beginning and will be one again at the end" (p. 96). This clear
reference to gnostic myth strengthens the assumption that this was
also what Neumann had in mind and later supported his thinking and
theorizing about early life. This circular movement from initial unity
to concluding synthesis was formulated by Neumann (1948/1989)
in his later article, in which he described three "great" (p. 391)
phases of individual development from birth to death and concluded
his description by saying: "The final phase, that of old age . . .
leads from differentiation to integration . . . from the split between
conscious and unconscious systems to a new synthesis" (p. 392).
It is therefore clear that his interpretation of the story of Jacob and
Esau refers to the final phase, in Jacob's zenith rather than old age.
It is also important to remember that this circular movement that
describes the ego's journey from early infancy to mature fulfilment
is at the center of consciousness development and the individuation
process. Neumann's analysis reached this point of synthesis in both
Jacob and Esau (1934-2015) and *New Ethic* (1949-1990), in which
he described the assimilation of the shadow and the synthesis of the
systems of conscious and unconscious as the highest achievement of
the individual and the goal of the individuation process.

Despite the difference, the two motifs—twin and brothers—are interrelated. Neumann's analysis attempted to indicate that both concern the problem of the shadow, which will emerge later when consciousness develops. In the mythologizing phase, there is yet not enough conscious "light" to cast a shadow; therefore, Neumann believed that the shadow appeared in early myth as the motif of the savior. This is "the motif of salvation, which guides the way out of the cosmic principal of opposites" (Neumann, 1934/2015, pp. 50–51). Salvation, as the Messianic era, is related to the yearning for the never achieved original unity and the perpetuated ritual of the scapegoat, indicating an early developmental stage of consciousness.

One more aspect of the mythologizing stage as theorized by Neumann is important as it points to the origins of his ecological perspective. When analyzing the story of Jacob and Esau, Neumann indicated that the story relates to both an individual process and a collective one. Similarly, the opposition between Jacob and Esau represents both a conflict in the outer world and a conflict within one person's psyche (Neumann, 1934/2015, p. 47). This perception led Neumann to write:

> The dual inner nature of the human person, which becomes apparent in the problem of twins and the shadow, is only one of the many archetypal forms in which we encounter one of the fundamental problems of all human existence: the problem of opposites. This problem which takes the form of good and evil or the ego and the shadow . . . manifests itself as the opposition between mind and nature. (p. 48)

Close reading of the two last sentences indicates that as early as this first manuscript Neumann recognized the shadowed perception of nature as the opposite of the mind and thus the ego. Accordingly, he posited that the body represents the unconscious and thus carries its shadowed projections, and psychological development entails one becoming less subject to the bodily sphere, as a representation of the shadow, instinctual and unconscious (pp. 40–50). Presumably, these concepts on which Neumann wrote so early, can be seen as his initial thoughts on the fundamental connection between psyche and nature and the embodied representation of the shadow. As mentioned previously, twenty years later Neumann (1953/1994) wrote his pivotal eco-psychological essay, "The Meaning of the Earth Archetype for Modern Times," in which these initial ideas became his main theme.

Secondary personalization

While in the mythologizing phase, humanity was still on a purely collective level, and inward psychic contents were outwardly projected; as consciousness developed, some introjection was enabled. In other words, man was able to differentiate between himself and the world outside, and thus mythologizing the deities was replaced by the secondary personalization of folktales.

Psychologically, the fundamental conflict is always that between the conscious and the unconscious, in which the conscious is "only an organ, an exponent, of the unconscious" (Neumann, 1934/2015, p. 51); the tension between the two is a fundamental inherent conflict of man's existence. As an overture to his later monograph *Origins* (Neumann, 1949/2014), Neumann described at length the struggle between the two, when the force of the conscious is pushing upward while the force of the unconscious is pulling downward. This, said Neumann, is the human struggle of the conscious to overcome the unconscious darkness and prevail; hence, a danger awaits when the conscious believes its light can definitively overcome the unconscious's darkness. Significantly, Neumann emphasized that the shadow belongs to the stage in which the conscious has already gained some continuity and therefore its light can cast a shadow. Describing the importance of the shadow for psychological development, Neumann (1934/2015) wrote,

The shadow is the chain that restrains any ascent into the heights. It is the dark adversary and circumciser. It is the eternal memory of limitation and abyss . . . the captivation of consciousness by the dark unconscious and the world. In reality, however, the shadow contains the great treasure of creative life. In contrast to ecstatic life, the creative life arises amid the great oscillation between . . . conscious and the unconscious. (p. 51)

As conscious develops, and with it the awareness of the shadow, it becomes a crucial and decisive element of limitation, preventing inflation, reminding one of an abyss. The struggle between gaining ego strength, and thus consciousness and awareness, and the weakness of fading into the unconscious will never come to an end, as Neumann theorized, since the essence of creative life lies within the oscillation. Whereas ecstatic life becomes a vector outwardly, creative life is a circular movement between conscious and unconscious. The shadow becomes the barrier between the two psychic systems, and the movement is not one of triumph but rather an "engagement" (Neumann, 1934/2015, p. 52).

At this stage, when some consciousness is apparent, the all-inclusive projection becomes selective, and some introjection takes place. What was before a concretization via rituals now becomes an inner dialogue, such as prayer. What was before collective, objective, and projected grows to become more individual, subjective, and introjected: "What happens could be described as the changing of shape and the descent of the gods: from divine events spring humanlike and eventually human events" (Neumann, 1934/2015, p. 55).That is, what was in the mythologizing stage a myth about twin brothers or deities like the sun and the moon becomes in the stage of secondary personalization a folktale about hostile brothers, a family story about Jacob and Esau; thus in this process the impersonal becomes personal.

Personalization and Objectification of the archetype

Neumann (1934/2015) theorized that what follows the secondary personalization is the personalization itself, which entails an objectification of the archetype. In terms of human consciousness development, he asserted that, while in the early stages, all inner contents were projected on the outer world objects; as the conscious develops an introjection takes place, meaning "a taking inward" (p. 53). Neumann described this process as the "formation of the soul" and said that this process explains the transformation of rituals— which are mere projections—into prayers—as a manifestation of the development of interiority (p. 53).

In order to clarify the process of the objectification of the archetype, Neumann explained its essence using the example of a child objectifying the Mother archetype by personalizing his mother to appear as an individual person and as an object (Neumann, 1934/2015, p. 56). Interestingly, Neumann wrote these reflections in 1934, many years prior to theorizing about early life and to the emergence of object relation theories in the psychoanalytical world, and they may indicate that it was for him an intuitive deep understanding of the human psyche. Here, it is important to emphasize that he differentiated between the stage in which inner and outer contents are merged and individuals are perceived via archetypal perception and the more advanced conscious stage, in which the archetypes are objectified "back" into concrete individuals. Indeed, Neumann (1934/2015) wrote:

> This sphere presupposes an ego-consciousness that has gained experience of the world and possesses an awareness of reality. Such experience and awareness are not originally given to the child but must be painstakingly acquired little by little during the development of conscious. (p. 56)

Therefore, in terms of later life development and the individuation process, this stage will correspond to the phase of the dissolution of complexes, in which the shadowed projections are withdrawn and thus the other is perceived more objectively.

In his theorizing, Neumann followed Jung (1943/1972 in terms of psychic energy, explaining this development as a historical phase in which, once the projection was withdrawn, the mythological gods were disposed of and the economy of psychic energy was changed in such way that the freed energy manifests with "uprising of the unconscious destructive forces" (p. 94). Elaborating on Jung, Neumann (1934/2015) theorized a further differentiation of the process; therefore, for him the first stage of introjection of the gods entails the secondary personalization, whereas the further stage is the objectification of the archetype. In terms of personal psychology, Neumann described the process of individuation as the stage in which the withdrawal of projections leads to an "extraordinary transformation of the personality" (p. 57), as the free energy is now directed inward toward the tension between ego-conscious and collective unconscious. This change in the direction of energy extends consciousness and its awareness to the dominating power of the archetypes, and he concluded that "the tension arising between these two systems constitutes the energetic basis of all life and all productivity" (p. 58). Nevertheless, although he described this stage of development theoretically and it is discussed as a theme in the story of Jacob and Esau, Neumann believed that, as a lived experience, it is rather rare to attain (p. 29).

Conclusion

Neumann pointed out that the shadow is a byproduct of consciousness, whose light casts a shadow. Through his developmental lens, he theorized that initially, when humanity was still in its infancy and in a purely collective stage, lack of consciousness led to a mythological perception of the conflict of opposites projected outwardly, and the "not yet shadow" was perceived as the archetype of salvation, allegedly leading to the redemption of the original state of unity. Still in the mythological stage, when human consciousness started to emerge, differentiation was enabled, and the conflict of the opposites ensued. At this stage, the negative side was projected and concretized via rituals, such as the scapegoat. Once human consciousness emerged and became stable enough in the light, the outward projection of the negative was replaced by splitting the inner opposites into ego-conscious and shadow. In this stage, corresponding to modern man's conscious development, the shadow, which is split off the personality, is projected on the "other" as an outside object. This is the departure point for the analysis of the story of the hostile biblical brothers, Jacob and Esau.

www.ingramcontent.com/pod-product-compliance
Lightning Source LLC
Chambersburg PA
CBHW020657270326
41928CB00005B/166